Consideration
Technology and Teachers

THE BEST OF

JRTE

EDITED BY LYNNE SCHRUM

International Society for Technology in Education
EUGENE, OREGON • WASHINGTON, DC

Considerations on Technology and Teachers
The Best of JRTE

EDITED BY LYNNE SCHRUM

Director of Book Publishing: *Courtney Burkholder*
Acquisitions Editor: *Jeff V. Bolkan*
Production Editors: *Lynda Gansel, Tina Wells*
Production Coordinator: *Rachel Williams*
Graphic Designer: *Signe Landin*
Copy Editor: *Kristin Landon*
Proofreader: *Barbara J. Hewick*
Indexer: *Potomac Indexing LLC*
Cover Design: *Signe Landin*
Book Design and Production: *Kathy Sturtevant*

Library of Congress Cataloging-in-Publication Data

Considerations on technology and teachers : the best of JRTE / edited by Lynne Schrum. — 1st ed.
p. cm.
Includes bibliographical references and index.
ISBN 978-1-56484-273-2 (pbk.)
1. Computer-assisted instruction. 2. Educational technology. 3. Internet in education.
4. Distance education. I. Schrum, Lynne. II. Journal of research on technology in education.
LB1028.5.C664 2010
371.33'4—dc22

2010039266

First Edition
ISBN: 978-1-56484-273-2
Printed in the United States of America

About ISTE

The International Society for Technology in Education (ISTE) is the trusted source for professional development, knowledge generation, advocacy, and leadership for innovation. ISTE is the premier membership association for educators and education leaders engaged in improving teaching and learning by advancing the effective use of technology in PK–12 and teacher education.

Home of the National Educational Technology Standards (NETS) and ISTE's annual conference and exposition (formerly known as NECC), ISTE represents more than 100,000 professionals worldwide. We support our members with information, networking opportunities, and guidance as they face the challenge of transforming education. To find out more about these and other ISTE initiatives, visit our website at www.iste.org.

As part of our mission, ISTE Book Publishing works with experienced educators to develop and produce practical resources for classroom teachers, teacher educators, and technology leaders. Every manuscript we select for publication is carefully peer-reviewed and professionally edited. We value your feedback on this book and other ISTE products. E-mail us at books@iste.org.

International Society for Technology in Education

Washington, DC, Office:
    1710 Rhode Island Ave. NW, Suite 900, Washington, DC 20036-3132

Eugene, Oregon, Office:
    180 West 8th Ave., Suite 300, Eugene, OR 97401-2916

Order Desk: 1.800.336.5191
Order Fax: 1.541.302.3778
Customer Service: orders@iste.org
Book Publishing: books@iste.org
Book Sales and Marketing: booksmarketing@iste.org
Web: www.iste.org

About the Editor and Contributors

EDITOR

Lynne Schrum is a professor and coordinator of elementary and secondary education in the College of Education and Human Development at George Mason University. Her research and teaching focus on appropriate uses of information technology, online and distance learning, and preparing teachers for the 21st century. She has written five books and numerous articles on these subjects; the most recent are *Web 2.0 How-To for Educators* and *Leading a 21st-Century School: Harnessing Technology for Engagement and Achievement*. Lynne is currently on AERA's Council, is editor of the *Journal of Research on Technology in Education (JRTE)* (2002–11), and is a past president of the International Society for Technology in Education (ISTE).

CONTRIBUTORS

Damian Bebell is an assistant research professor at Boston College's Lynch School of Education and a research associate at the Technology and Assessment Study Collaborative.

Niki (N. E.) Davis is a professor of e-learning in the University of Canterbury College of Education in Christchurch, New Zealand. At the time of this research Davis was the director of Iowa State University's Center for Technology in Learning and Teaching, a professor of curriculum and instructional technology in learning and teaching, and also a professor of ICT in education in the Institute of Education, University of London, UK. Davis was the principal investigator of the TEGIVS project and the doctoral supervisor of Lily Compton and Amina Charania. Her research focuses on e-learning and professional development for teachers as well as faculty development and organizational change with digital technologies.

Peggy A. Ertmer is a professor of educational technology at Purdue University. Her scholarship focuses on the impact that student-centered instructional approaches and strategies have on learning. She is particularly interested in studying the impact of case-based instruction on higher-order thinking skills; the effectiveness of student-centered, problem-based learning approaches on technology integration; and strategies for facilitating higher-order thinking and self-regulated learning in online learning environments.

Seth Finn is emeritus professor of communications and information systems at Robert Morris University, Pennsylvania. His research interest continues to be the nexus between human information processing and neurophysiological arousal.

Nancy Fordham is an assistant professor at Bowling Green State University, Ohio, in the Division of Teaching and Learning. She teaches courses in literacy and social studies and has an interest in technology use in the university and K–12 classroom.

Judi Harris is a professor and the Pavey Family Chair in Educational Technology in the School of Education at the College of William & Mary. Her research and development focus on curriculum-based educational technology professional development for teachers; telementoring, including professional learning and support for new teachers online; and the curriculum-based development of technological pedagogical content knowledge (TPACK).

John G. Inman is dean of student enrollment services and registrar at Grove City College, Pennsylvania, where digital unity remains a technological objective. All entering students are issued a tablet PC for which technical support and service is available seven days a week.

Matthew Koehler is an associate professor of educational psychology and educational technology in the College of Education at Michigan State University. His research focuses on understanding the affordances and constraints of new technologies; the design of technology-rich, innovative learning environments; and the professional development of teachers. Mishra and Koehler developed the technological pedagogical content knowledge (TPCK/TPACK) framework, first published in 2005.

S. Kim MacGregor is an associate professor of educational research and she coordinates the Applied Research, Measurement and Evaluation graduate program in the College of Education at Louisiana State University. Her research interests focus on student engagement, university–community partnerships, and the role of instructional innovation in facilitating these experiences.

Punya Mishra is a professor of educational psychology and educational technology in the College of Education at Michigan State University. His research focuses on cognitive, aesthetic, and social aspects related to the design and use of computer-based learning environments. Mishra and Koehler developed the technological pedagogical content knowledge (TPCK/TPACK) framework, first published in 2005.

Timothy J. Newby is a professor of educational technology at Purdue University. He currently teaches courses focused on learning theory, instructional design and motivation, instructional strategies, and educational technology and integration. His research involves the impact of various instructional strategies and technology on learning and motivation.

Laura O'Dwyer is an assistant professor in the Lynch School of Education at Boston College. Her research interests include international comparative studies; organizational characteristics related to technology use, experimental design, multilevel power analysis, and hierarchical linear modeling.

Sung Hee Park is an assistant professor at the Graduate School of Education at the Kyungwon University, South Korea. Her research focuses on problem-based learning, technology integration, and effectiveness of e-learning.

M. D. Roblyer, who served as external evaluator for the TEGIVS project, is a professor of learning and leadership at the University of Tennessee at Chattanooga. She has taught, researched, and published extensively in educational technology for over 35 years and has researched virtual schooling student success and evaluated virtual school programs since 1998. Her textbook *Integrating Educational Technology into Teaching* (with Aaron Doering, Pearson Education, 2010) is internationally adopted for undergraduate and graduate instructional technology courses.

Michael Russell is an assistant professor at Boston College's Lynch School of Education. His research focuses on the intersection of educational technology, assessment, and learning.

Neal Strudler is a professor of educational computing and technology in the College of Education at the University of Nevada, Las Vegas. His current research focuses on technology integration in teacher education programs and the role of technology coordinators in K–12 schools.

Rachel A. Vannatta (Rheinhart) is a professor in the College of Education and Human Development at Bowling Green State University. She teaches courses on educational statistics, research, and assessment. Her research interests focus on technology integration in K–12 and teacher education.

Cynthia B. Vavasseur is an assistant professor at Nicholls State University, Louisiana. She serves as chair of the middle school education program, as well as the graduate educational technology program. Her research interests focus on teacher education and professional development, including service learning and non-traditional ways of delivering professional development in regards to the successful integration of technology.

Ling Wang is an assistant professor of computing technology in education at Nova Southeastern University, Florida. Her teaching focuses on learning theories and research design and methodology. Her research interests are educational technology integration, e-learning, and professional development of faculty in higher education.

Keith Wetzel is a professor of educational technology in the College of Teacher Education and Leadership at Arizona State University. His research interests include preservice professional development for technology integration and the improvement of teacher quality.

ACKNOWLEDGMENT

I would like to thank Mary C. English, graduate student extraordinaire, for her efforts and assistance in collecting and organizing the materials in this volume. I also thank the ISTE staff for their idea and support. Additionally, Tam Kidd deserves kudos for her creativity in the JRTE graphical redesign.

DEDICATION

As always, I dedicate this to my daughters and granddaughters for their love and support.

Contents

INTRODUCTION

Revisioning a Proactive Approach to an Educational Technology Research Agenda

Lynne Schrum | George Mason University

In 2005, five educational technology editors and researchers (Bull, Knezek, Roblyer, Schrum, & Thompson) wrote an editorial that was designed both as a call for educational researchers to identify the pressures toward one model of research methodology, and as a call for the joint creation of an agenda that respected the way schools work, the challenges of learning technology, and the impact of pressure to demonstrate academic achievement directly tied to the use of technology. This introduction is designed to revive the conversation, and also to expand the agenda in new ways.

During the past 30 years, technological advances have exceeded even the most optimistic expectations. The steady advance in speed and capacity has produced powerful computers available at modest prices, along with a wide variety of handheld technologies that can accomplish remarkable tasks. This wider accessibility has resulted in wider usage. A recent Pew study found that 93% of teens ages 12–17 now use the Internet, up from 73% in 2000 (Pew Internet & American Life Project, 2007). Additionally, this study found that 69% of online Americans have used "cloud computing" applications (basically Web 2.0 tools) (Jones & Fox, 2009).

Those of us who have committed our professional lives to investigating this educational arena have anticipated that the advances in technological capacity would be matched by parallel enhancements in learning. Recently, we have witnessed a remarkable expansion of Web 2.0 tools and their uses in educational settings. And research on teaching and learning is blending activities inside and beyond the classroom in innovative uses of technology, such as the "Innovative Digital Media and Learning Projects" (The MacArthur Foundation, www.macfound.org/atf/cf/%7Bb0386ce3-8b29-4162-8098-e466fb856794%7D/DMLCOMP2009-PR-090416.PDF).

Technology has had a positive impact on education, even if it has not yet resulted in wholesale educational transformation. However, there are larger issues that have not yet been addressed: for example, disparities in educational outcomes still exist, too many of our youth still drop out of school and do not reach their potential, and students are often disengaged from content and learning. Perhaps our research is unable to answer the questions, or perhaps we are asking the wrong questions. It appears that our conversations are not yet as broad, deep, or inclusive as they will need to be for us to see the type of transformation we desire. An effective return on future investments in educational technology is more likely to be realized to the extent that research captures past impact and provides directions for future use. Best approaches to educational research have been the focus of a major emphasis by the U.S. Department of Education. There is no area in which well-conceived and effectively implemented research could be of greater value than in the area of technological innovation. Our research is about technology; we now must let others see how it is about learners of all ages, teaching, and the future of our democracy.

Challenges for Educational Technology Research

A review of educational technology journals provides an opportunity to survey the landscape of the published research in this area. It raises a concern about our efforts to mentor the next generation of researchers. For example, in 2009 approximately 85% of submissions to the *Journal of Research on Technology in Education* (JRTE) were ultimately rejected for two main reasons. The primary reason was related to quality, methods, and focus. But many were rejected because they did not deepen, expand, or push the envelope on our literature base, nor did they help develop new knowledge that added to what we already know.

Every researcher undertakes a study with the hope of making a substantive contribution to the field. Each of the submissions represents months or years of effort and commitment on the part of one or more authors. A publication process that results in inefficiencies of 80% or more clearly cries out for improvement.

We stand at a crossroads as the U.S. Department of Education is beginning to recognize that not all randomized studies are valuable, and that other types of studies may offer insights and knowledge worth having. At the same time, the funding will still go only to educational researchers who offer strong and worthwhile research designs that are based on sound background literature, theoretical constructs, deep and important research questions, and accepted methods of data collection and analysis.

Some of the reasons for the ongoing challenge, presented when the editorial first was published, are still useful and unfortunately, operational, so they are repeated here:

> ***Unrealistic expectations for technology-based reform.*** Technologies brought about such high-profile reforms in other areas of society that many educators and researchers came to expect similarly widespread impact in education. Other areas of society faced similar challenges. For example, researchers were not able to capture any relationship between investments in technology and increases in productivity throughout the 1980s. Business continued to invest, and eventually the investment in technology was associated with gains in productivity in the 1990s. Education represents an unparalleled set of problems and complexities. In retrospect, it seems apparent that expectations should be based on a more realistic, theory-based appraisal of specific learning problems for which technology applications might be a good solution. Research should have focused on confirming that these applications were instructional strategies of choice and on providing guidelines for conditions under which this was true.
>
> ***Lack of consensus on research questions and methodologies.*** For the first 20 years, educational technology research focused on the question: "Is a technology-based method better than a non-technology-based one?" Eventually, this approach was deemed ill-conceived and unproductive. Yet no more useful paradigm has emerged to take its place. Future research must focus on yet-to-be-articulated research questions.
>
> ***Diminished role of research in school reform.*** Even published studies do not typically result in any change in educational practice. Some educators have argued that this is due in no small part to a "disconnect" between the interests of researchers and the needs of teachers and schools. A more practical, focused research agenda is an essential need, as are strategies for coordinating research efforts and findings across researchers and research centers. (Bull et al., 2005, pp. 218–219)

A New Challenge for Our Design-Based and Collaborative Research

Since this original editorial was written, new Web 2.0 tools, which offer greater potential to increase interactivity and perhaps better address the digital divide, have become commonplace, and almost all use of these tools is voluntary (Alexander, 2008; Solomon & Schrum, 2010). Now we are tasked with investigating their purposeful educational uses and identifying ways these new tools may affect student engagement and academic achievement; the hope is that we have learned about creating a unified research agenda to help guide us.

We are beginning to see research that examines a new type of activity, epistemic games; they are "explicitly based on theory of learning in the digital age and are designed to allow learners to develop domain-specific expertise under realistic constraints" (Rupp et al., 2009, p. 4). The goal is to have learners experience what it is like to really think and act like "journalists, artists, business managers, or engineers by using digital learning technologies to solve realistic complex performance tasks" (p. 4). We might consider this somewhat analogous to an authentic practicum or internship, and these models have been created in a variety of content areas, including history (Johnson & Levine, 2008; Squire, DeVane, & Durga, 2008) with research suggesting powerful and positive results in engaging learners. Research on these tools offers an opportunity to be both formative as well as design based, because reflection on the data leads to modification of the tools. If, as Barab, Thomas, Dodge, Carteaux, and Tuzun suggest, these types of activities sit at the "intersection of education, entertainment, and social commitment" (2005, p. 86), then what are the implications for our research? Annetta (2008) suggests, "These educational games commonly require the use of logic, memory, problem-solving, critical thinking skills, visualization, and discovery" (p. 261). What requirements are placed on researchers to examine the constructs in and out of school? Squire, Giovanetto, DeVane, and Durga (2005) posit, "To date, we actually know relatively little about the consequences of game play on the cognition of those who play them" (p. 35).

More importantly, some research has begun to show that students are really learning in this environment. Hickey, Ingram-Goble, and Jameson (2009), for example, have seen this in their research. In two studies of Quest Atlantis, they found sixth grade students making "larger gains in understanding and achievement" than in classes that used expository text to learn the same concepts and skills (p. 187). In a study of a similar type of project, Ketelhut (2007) found that her results "suggest that embedding science inquiry curricula in novel platforms like a MUVE might act as a catalyst for change in students' self-efficacy and learning processes" (p. 99). Kyza (2009) conducted a multiple-case study looking at middle school students' reasoning in an investigation of data-rich, scientific problems scaffolded by software, the task, and the teacher. Although she found statistically significant growth in learning and that the scaffolding contributed to the inquiry, she also found that they required "epistemologically targeted discourse alongside guided inquiry experiences" to be able to really understand alternative hypotheses and to support their scientific reasoning processes (p. 377).

We hear a great deal about the preparation of teachers these days, and how many still are not changing their teaching to take advantage of technology. Recently some researchers have begun to reexamine the preparation and role of school leaders and their need for specific types of preparation to lead our 21st-century schools (Schrum, Galizio, & Ledesma, in press; Schrum & Levin, 2009). The reality is that without support, leadership, and commitment from all stakeholders in a school system, the type of learning we have often dreamed of may not be realized. The need then is for a comprehensive plan with complementary comprehensive research to document what we find.

Are these studies and efforts the beginning of a new research agenda? Are they perhaps the beginning of a new effort to demonstrate that in certain circumstances, under particular conditions, technology may assist in enhancing learning outcomes? Or will we again see that real systemic changes happen only with funding, and that well-designed projects are not scalable or applicable in other situations?

A Renewed Proposal for a Proactive Research Agenda

One editorial function is to serve as a nexus for quality control. However, being an editor also offers an opportunity to provide leadership, either implicitly by what is published, or explicitly by purposefully seeking important and thoughtful additions to our literature base. Discussions regarding the potential value of a proactive approach to research continue within this context. After many years as editor of JRTE, I consider it important to explicate the importance of what needs to be published, to explore ways to influence the conversation, and to encourage new scholars to join us; such discussion also allows us to courageously draw a deep line in the sand to only approve and accept rigorous and valuable research.

An effective conversation must include discourse among leading educational technology researchers. However, to be successful, it will be equally important to involve other stakeholders to ensure strong linkages between applied research and explicit connections and value to schools. It is also important to include input from corporate partners, the K–12 school community, developers, and policy makers in the questions we ask, in the research we conduct, and in the interpretations and policy that ensue.

Two further outcomes may emerge from this dialogue. The process of preparing doctoral students to design, conduct, and analyze good research is a nontrivial task, and yet we continue to see less funding, fewer full-time positions, and thus less time for faculty to devote to this important goal. If educational technology researchers and journal editors can proactively work toward a measure of consensus on productive directions for future research, it may be possible to increase the positive outcomes for our future colleagues.

Second, as previously addressed, the introduction of technology into our schools has not resulted in the expected educational reform. One reason for that may be the missing relationship between educators and their burning questions and the questions educational researchers choose to investigate. If we can assist in creating a dialogue, stronger collaboration, and recursive conversation between these two groups, that too would be an excellent outcome. After all, teaching and learning require support from the teacher in designing an educational environment, and technology must be embedded in thoughtfully planned ongoing instruction to be effective in supporting student outcomes. Educators and researchers have common goals, and synergy between them would benefit all.

Conclusions

The purpose of this compilation of research articles from JRTE is to provide a context and trail of where we have been and what our research base has established thus far. At present the technological capacity available to schools exceeds our ability to use it effectively to enhance learning. A proactive approach to establishing a research agenda can potentially provide guidance to future investigators. The substantial continuing cost of technology in schools makes it important to ensure that research produced is relevant. Providing researchers with context and guidelines will increase the likelihood that efforts are productively directed. Barab, Dodge, Thomas, Jackson, and Tuzun (2007) suggest that a larger purpose may result from the community of educational researchers, if they decide to work together to build true transformative materials and move theory into directions that take advantage of our collective knowledge. They state that a collective effort would be

> significantly heightened if we as a community embrace the critical agendas that are central to so many discussions in anthropology, philosophy, or even curriculum development more generally. Instead of simply building an artifact to help individuals accomplish a particular task, or to meet a specific standard, the focus of critical design work is to develop sociotechnical structures that facilitate individuals in critiquing and improving themselves and the societies in which they function, and then we use our understanding of participation with these structures to advance theory. (p. 264)

A consensus on every point will not be reached, nor is that the intent. There will always be diverse perspectives within an academic community. However, the dialogue will encourage more sharply articulated research objectives and guidelines. The result should facilitate much needed research in this area.

References

Alexander, B. (2008). Web 2.0 and emergent multiliteracies. *Theory into Practice, 47*(2), 150–160.

Annetta, L. A. (2008). Video games in education: Why they should be used and how they are being used. *Theory into Practice, 47*(3), 229–239.

Barab, S., Thomas, M., Dodge, T., Carteaux, R., & Tuzun, H. (2005). Making learning fun: Quest Atlantis, a game without guns. *Educational Technology Research and Development, 53*(1), 86–107.

Barab, S., Dodge, T., Thomas, M. K., Jackson, C., & Tuzun, H. (2007). Our designs and the social agendas they carry. *Journal of the Learning Sciences, 16*(2), 263–305.

Bull, G., Knezek, G., Roblyer, M. D., Schrum, L., & Thompson, A. (2005). A proactive approach to a research agenda for educational technology. *Journal of Research on Technology in Education, 37*(3), 217–220.

Digital Learning Environments. (2009). *Technology's Impact on Learning.* Retrieved August 14, 2009, from www.guide2digitallearning.com

Dodge, T., Barab, S., & Stuckey, B. (2008). Children's sense of self: Learning and meaning in the digital age. *Journal of Interactive Learning Research, 19*(2), 225–249.

Hickey, D. T., Ingram-Goble, A. A., & Jameson, E. M. (2009). Designing assessments and assessing designs in virtual educational environments. *Journal of Science Education and Technology, 18,* 187–208.

Johnson, L. F., & Levine, A. H. (2008). Virtual worlds: Inherently immersive, highly social learning spaces. *Theory into Practice, 47*(2), 161–170.

Jones, S., & Fox, S. (2009). Generations online in 2009. *Pew Internet and American Life Project.* Retrieved on October 25, 2009, from www.pewInternet.org/~/media//Files/Reports/2009/PIP_Generations_2009.pdf

Ketelhut, D. J. (2007). The impact of student self-efficacy on scientific inquiry skills: An exploratory investigation of River City, a multi-user virtual environment. *Journal of Science Education and Technology, 16*(1), 99–111.

Kyza, E. A. (2009). Middle-school students' reasoning about alternative hypotheses in a scaffolded, software-based inquiry investigation. *Cognition and Instruction, 27*(4), 277–311.

Pew Internet & American Life Project. (2007). *Teens and social media.* Retrieved March 15, 2009, from http://pewInternet.org/PPF/r/230/report_display.asp

Rupp, A., Choi, Y., Gushta, M., Mislevy, R., Thies, M. C., Bagley, E., et al. (2009). *Modeling learning progressions in epistemic games with epistemic network analysis: Principles for data analysis and generation.* Paper presented at the Learning Progressions in Science conference (LeaPS), Iowa City, IA, USA. Retrieved August 1, 2009, from http://epistemicgames.org/eg/wp-content/uploads/leaps-learning-progressions-paper-rupp-et-al-2009-leaps-format1.pdf

Schrum, L., Galizio, L. M., & Ledesma, P. (in press). Educational leadership and technology integration: An investigation into preparation, experiences, and roles. *Journal of School Leadership.*

Schrum, L., & Levin, B. (2009). *Leading a 21st century school: Harnessing technology for engagement and achievement.* Thousand Oaks, CA: Corwin.

Solomon, G. & Schrum, L. (2010). *Web 2.0 How-To for Educators.* Eugene, OR: International Society for Technology in Education.

Squire, K. D., DeVane, B., & Durga, S. (2008). Designing centers of expertise for academic learning through video games. *Theory into Practice, 47*(3), 240–251.

Squire, K. D., Giovanetto, L., DeVane, B., & Durga, S. (2005). From users to designers: Building a self-organizing game-based learning environment. *TechTrends, 49*(5), 34–42, 74.

CHAPTER

1

Digital Unity and Digital Divide: Surveying Alumni to Study Effects of a Campus Laptop Initiative

Seth Finn | Robert Morris University

John G. Inman | Grove City College

This research study assessed the effects of an information technology initiative on undergraduates at a Western Pennsylvania college. A random sample of alumni from the classes of 1997, 1998, and 2000 were surveyed to gauge their attitudes about a technology program instituted in 1994, which provided laptop computers to all incoming freshmen. The results indicated that not only was there a positive change in attitudes after the program was initiated, but digital divides based on sex and field of study were diminished during the students' time on campus. Interestingly, parts of the divide reappear after graduation, by field of study.

Assessing the Effects of a Campus Laptop Initiative

According to a recent survey of college students published by the Pew Internet research project, 85% of college students between the ages of 18 and 24 own their own computer, and 86% of them have gone online, whereas only 59% of the general population have done so (Jones, 2002). Much of this disparity between college students and the general population is attributed to college students' early exposure to computers at home or at school, but it is also explained as a naturally occurring diffusion of Internet access from college faculty to the college community as a whole. Even before the creation of the World Wide Web, however, college administrators wrestled with two primary options in the diffusion of computer technology on campus. One was to network the campus, making technology universally available in classrooms, laboratories, offices, and residence halls. However, a small number of campuses took an even more comprehensive approach. They began distributing laptop computers to every entering first-year student. As this practice gained momentum, some of its advocates adopted the name *ubiquitous computing* to characterize its primary objective of universal access.

We think, however, that the reasons for creating such an environment by implementing a laptop distribution program are better characterized by the term *digital unity*, because such preemptive academic initiatives have often been motivated by vague concerns that either the institution or its students might otherwise find themselves on the wrong side of a *digital divide*. In addition, we see a further benefit in addressing the effects of campus laptop initiatives as an issue of digital unity versus digital divide. By framing research questions within this larger context, observations about the implementation of a digital unity (comprehensive computing) plan within a college community may be generalizable not only to populations situated in other educational environments (Attewell, 2001) but also to populations that are split by social (Light, 2001) and geographical (Hindman, 2000) differences.

To make this claim more coherent, the convergence of these terms—ubiquitous computing, digital divide, and digital unity—requires some historical explication. The term ubiquitous computing has been attributed to Marc Weiser, a researcher at Xerox PARC near Stanford University (MacDonald, 1997). Weiser (1998), in fact, has written about three waves of computing on campus, the first being mainframes, the second being networked PCs, and a third, yet to come, in which digital technology is so integrated into campus activities that it would be nearly invisible. Students would pull credit card interfaces out of their wallets to exploit the applications they needed. Brown, Burg, and Dominick (1998) apparently adopted the term to characterize the goal of the laptop initiative at Wake Forest University and to name a national movement that included other campuswide efforts that can be traced back as far as a faculty decision at Drew University in 1983 (Candiotti & Clarke, 1998; Candiotti, 2003). The term digital divide, by contrast, arose in the domain of public policy. The term was popularized by the U.S.

National Telecommunications and Information Administration in the mid-1990s to reflect the increasing concern of policy leaders and social scientists that socioeconomic differences could be exacerbated if the diffusion of digital technology was dependent on an individual's means to acquire it (Warschauer, 2003).

What we find analogous between the two movements is the insistence on universal access. Both movements, though operating in different spheres, chose as their catchwords terms that convey a sense that no community should be divided between *haves* and *have-nots*. Proponents of ubiquitous computing argue for universal access, among other reasons, (a) to prepare students to move into the workforce, (b) to make sure their institutions are competitive, and (c) to ensure that all students within an institution have equal tools with which to learn (Brown, 2003). All these concerns constitute potential digital divides between learning and work, between one institution and another, and between one student and another. The problem with the term *ubiquitous computing*, however, as Brown and Petitto (2003) have noted, is that with "at least half of all colleges and universities 'practicing ubiquity'… the tight definition of *ubiquitous computing* no longer prevails because the concept itself has become ubiquitous" (p. 24).

For the purposes of this study, however, we have chosen to perpetuate that tight definition of ubiquitous computing with the term *digital unity*. There are by current estimates from as few as 36 confirmed notebook universities (Confirmed, 2003) to as many as 100 campuses with universal laptop programs and another 50 where individual schools or other campus units have adopted laptop initiatives (Brown & Petitto, 2003). In addition to the obvious portability advantages of a laptop computer, Brown (2003) lists multiple advantages for campus standardization of hardware and software, ranging from enhanced reliability because of system redundancy to facilitated problem solving, because using similar equipment makes every member of the campus community a potential volunteer helper. Metaphorically speaking, campus laptop initiatives impose the same digital unity among computer users that government-regulated monopolies once imposed on telephone service. When telephone service was a regulated monopoly, every subscriber was issued the same black telephone manufactured by Western Electric. The telephone became an icon of universal service. We think it important to highlight this point, however, to illustrate that the metaphor may not be fully applicable. The current rate of innovation in digital technology precludes the degree of uniformity that was once achievable with phone systems. This disparity in the environment has always been a weakness in the digital unity concept and points up the importance of systematic research to determine if laptop programs remain justifiable now that college student ownership of computers has reached 85% (Jones, 2002).

Anecdotal and Systematic Research into Ubiquitous Computing

The literature on campuswide laptop initiatives can be divided into two branches. One branch is devoted to anecdotal reports designed to provide guidance and encouragement at every level of the process from campuswide implementation (Brown, Burg, & Dominick, 1998; Brown & Petitto, 2003; Candiotti & Clarke, 1998; LeBlanc & Teal, 1998) to how curriculum and courses might be transformed (Brown, 2003; Kiaer, Mutchler, & Froyd, 1998). The other branch is composed of systematic studies documenting the effects of mandatory computing programs on student attitudes and learning as well as modes of teaching. Despite the dozens of campuses that have instituted laptop programs, the literature is limited to a handful of studies that focus on student experience (Mitra, 1998; Mitra & Steffensmeier, 2000; Platt & Bairnsfather, 2000), faculty experience (Mitra, Steffensmeier, Lenzmeier, & Massoni, 1999) or both (Schrum, Skeele, & Grant, 2002). We can only speculate that programmatic assessments made for institutional use have been too narrowly focused to merit scholarly publication, although summaries of survey data (Holleque, 2002) and verbal journals (McCarty & Robinson, 1999) can be accessed at university websites.

The most widely promoted comprehensive computing program has been the Wake Forest University initiative begun with freshman students matriculating in the fall of 1996 (Brown et al., 1998). In 1995, Wake Forest contracted with IBM to wire classrooms, residence halls, the library, and most offices in preparation for the fall semester of 1996, when all first-year students received IBM Thinkpad laptops. To establish a baseline for student attitudes and frequency of computer use, a detailed survey was undertaken in the fall of 1995 and subsequently readministered at the end of year one of the program in the spring semester of 1997, and again at the end of year two in the spring of 1998 (Mitra & Steffensmeier, 2000).

Summarizing these results both longitudinally and comparatively, Mitra and Steffensmeier (2000) found that the implementation of what they described as a "computer-enriched environment" generated a measurable change in student attitudes about computers. The students who received the laptops expressed more positive feelings about computers in general, their role in teaching and learning, and the opportunity they provided for better communication between faculty and students. The improved communication between faculty and students was strongly acknowledged by the legacy students who arrived at Wake Forest the year before the laptop program began, but who nevertheless benefited from the improved network infrastructure on campus. The improved infrastructure was seen as a plus, of course, but it also highlights one of the ironies of implementing a laptop distribution program. From a methodological perspective it should be noted that in the course of implementing a laptop program, administrators artificially foment a digital divide between legacy students and freshmen, thereby establishing criteria for a quasi-experimental study.

Before this longitudinal study, Mitra alone and with colleagues completed two other studies at Wake Forest that have a bearing on research into the efficacy of a laptop program. In acquiring first-year baseline data on the attitudes and computer use of students (Mitra, 1998) and first- and second-year data on faculty (Mitra et al., 1999), Mitra demonstrated that use and attitudes are multidimensional constructs. Accordingly, a standard was set to incorporate, when possible, questions that take into account varieties of computer use when constructing items for a general survey of users. Further, in evaluating changes in faculty attitudes and use, faculty skill levels differentially affected increased use of various types of computer software, which suggested that administrators must give careful attention to providing sufficient computer training and infrastructural support to maintain positive attitudes about the campuswide initiative.

In a study involving two classes of medical students who were the first participants in a laptop initiative at Louisiana State University, Platt and Bairnsfather (2000) also employed questions that specified a variety of computer uses associated with instruction and learning to assess the impact of a mandatory purchase program. No comparison was made with medical students, who were not participating in the program, but the freshman class of 2000 was subsequently interviewed as sophomores simultaneously with the freshman class of 2001. The researchers reported that students were "very positive" concerning the program and "enthusiastic" about their ability to communicate with faculty, results that, despite the differences in circumstances, are similar to the attitudes measured at Wake Forest. The medical students, however, expressed dissatisfaction in responding to items about computer-based learning. Platt and Bairnsfather (2000) attribute these low ratings to difficulties experienced by faculty in finding appropriate software or developing suitable computer-assisted instruction materials locally.

Schrum, Skeele, and Grant (2002) have reported the results of a two-year study employing both survey and focus-group methods to assess the effects of a grant designed to encourage college of education faculty at a laptop campus to further integrate computer technology into their curriculum and teaching. The analysis suggested that within-school technical support as well as incentives, especially released time, were successful in increasing faculty appreciation, knowledge, and skills for developing computer-assisted instructional materials. Interestingly, although a second-year survey demonstrated impressive progress for faculty in mastering technological skills, students' responses remained the same from year one to year two, owing in part to high self-assessments in the first year of the study, which, although the researchers do not comment on this directly, could be attributed to the university's universal laptop program. From observation and focus-group discussion, it was nevertheless apparent that students were motivated to model the faculty's efforts to incorporate technology into their preservice teaching activities. Further, Schrum et al. (2002) provide a salient example of the students' heightened consciousness about the consequences of an unequal diffusion of computing resources, observing that "during several focus groups the students initiated discussions about the Digital Divide and frequently mentioned the disparity between the suburban and urban schools" (p. 267).

Grove City College Study

From previous research, we recognized the advantage of designing a study that incorporated respondents who had entered as freshmen both before and after the implementation of the universal laptop program, thereby enabling us to analyze the data as a quasi-experimental study. In our case, however, this strategy provided a second major advantage over previous studies. Grove City's Information Technology Initiative (ITI) had been in operation long enough that we could survey alumni rather than students and benefit from their long-term perspective. The ITI had been implemented in conjunction with Compaq Computers (now merged with Hewlett-Packard) in 1994, with the distribution of laptops to all full-time faculty in the spring and to all full-time freshmen in the fall. Thus, three classes that had received laptop computers as entering first-year students had already graduated in 1998, 1999, and 2000 when this study was in its planning stage. College alumni had already entered the workforce or graduate school, and although they could not answer specific questions about the laptop program in its current configuration, they were uniquely qualified to comment on how they had fared in transcending the digital divide between college and the workplace, and to some extent indicate whether a digital divide existed between Grove City and other colleges with their ratings of the program's contribution to their professional achievements. Therefore, for this study, we surveyed alumni from the class of 1997, who were the last students required to bring their own computers to campus, along with the alumni from the classes of 1998 and 2000, who represented, respectively, the first class to receive laptops and the most recent class to receive them who could be expected to be settled at work or in graduate school at the time of the survey.

The survey was supported by the college, and thus had an immediate administrative objective. More than seven years after the Information Technology Initiative's implementation, administrators were eager to assess how well the stated goals of the college's plan had been met. Those goals included providing an acceptable level of convenience for students, integrating computer technology into courses, and preparing students for their professions. This third goal, focused on the long-term effects of the laptop program, led to a set of more expansive research questions. First, how did the level of computing activity during the students' four years on campus compare with their subsequent experience as working professionals as well as their previous experience as high school students? In this regard, we were cognizant of how various types of computer use should be included in the survey

(Mitra, 1998) and that gender may be a critical variable because of differential experiences in school and at home (Chen, 1986, 1987). Recent data have suggested, in fact, that gender differences lie more often in type of use than frequency of use (Ono & Zavodny, 2003).

Second, was there an indicator of cognitive style or intellectual disposition associated with the types and frequency of an individual's computer use? After nearly a decade of debate over the merits of universal access to the Internet, researchers have begun to focus on the fit between technology and "context into which that hardware would be put" (Warschauer, 2003). Although it is understandable that early assessments of laptop computing programs would focus on institutional objectives of encouraging usage and integration of technology, we thought it odd that such measures would be gathered with little consideration for the mechanisms of learning. As a first step, we decided to devote a substantial portion of the survey to assessing the respondents' learning styles to provide a context for their use of computer technology.

In this domain, we made a comprehensive review of the learning style literature, ultimately incorporating the most widely cited instrument, Kolb's *Learning Style Inventory (LSI)*, into our questionnaire. Kolb's (1984, 1993) instrument is based on a model of learning composed of four primary modes: concrete experience (CE), reflective observation (RO), abstract conceptualization (AC), and active experience (AE). Kolb contends that learners have preferred modes of acquiring information that "result from individuals' preferred ways for adapting to the world" (Kolb, Boyatzis, & Mainemelis, 2001, p. 227). Although Kolb's experiential learning model (ELM) is well established (Loo, 1997) and the *LSI* is recognized for its popularity and high face validity (Atkinson, 1991), we opted for this measure despite an intense debate about the stability of Kolb's measure and the limitations of his theory (Atkinson, 1991; Caño-Garcia & Hughes, 2000; Garner, 2000; Geiger, Boyle, & Pinto, 1992; Loo, 1997) because, unlike most other learning style measures, the extensive literature provided a basis for alternative methods of interpreting results.

Methodology

DATA COLLECTION

A total of 600 surveys, color coded by class—1997, 1998, and 2000—were mailed out anonymously to a random sample of Grove City College alumni on October 31, 2001. The 1997 and 1998 alumni were selected because their classes bridged the initiation of the comprehensive computing program at Grove City. The class of 1998 alumni were the first to receive laptop computers when they arrived on campus in the fall of 1994; the class of 1997 alumni were the last students who were expected to purchase their own machines.

The class of 2000 alumni were included in the survey to provide additional validation of the effects of the program and reveal further trends. The sample of 600 represented just over 41% of the alumni for the three classes surveyed. Because the survey was completed anonymously, follow-up was limited to a postcard mailed to the entire sample on November 20, 2001, thanking those who had sent in their questionnaires for their participation and urging all others to submit them.

A total of 212 questionnaires were ultimately returned, representing an equal response rate of 37.5% for the classes of 1997 and 1998 and a lower rate of 31.0% for the class of 2000. Because the response rate was less than 50%, a number of analyses were completed to determine the representativeness of the sample obtained. A comparison of responses to demographic items with known parameters for the three classes indicated that female students, representing 56.1% of the sample, were overrepresented by 7.0%. However, the general distribution of majors in the sample—liberal arts (27.4%), education (15.6%), business (27.4%), math and science (17.9%), and engineering (11.8%)—deviated only 0.5 to 3.5% from the population parameters for the three classes.

To evaluate the relative geographic distribution of respondents, the zip codes from the survey sample addresses were compared with the postmarked zip codes on the envelopes containing completed questionnaires. The analysis showed that 49.6% of the questionnaires had been mailed to Pennsylvania zip codes, whereas 42.9% of the returned questionnaires were postmarked in Pennsylvania, a deviation of less than 7%. Zip code comparisons for the next five states with substantial alumni sample addresses—Ohio (11.5% mailed versus 12.3% returned), Maryland (5.1% versus 6.1%), Virginia (4.7% versus 3.3%), New York (4.7% versus 3.8%), and New Jersey (2.5% versus 2.8%)—revealed no deviation greater than 1.5%.

Finally, to check the internal representativeness of the returned surveys, they were grouped according to date of receipt. Reponses from the first 106 questionnaires received were compared item by item with the responses of the second 106 questionnaires. Only a handful of items revealed statistically significant differences, suggesting that there was no systematic difference between early and late respondents and by inference that nonrespondents would not be expected to provide systematically different answers either. Accordingly, no further efforts, such as sending new copies of the questionnaire to the entire sample to increase the response rate, were made.

VARIABLES

Opinion Measures. The three original stated goals of the Information Technology Initiative (ITI) at Grove City College were (a) to make computer technology convenient for students to use, (b) to integrate computer technology into courses, and (c) to prepare students better for their professions. Two components of the survey addressed these questions directly. A set of eight statements focused on practical matters of convenience and support afforded by the ITI, including how the initiative facilitated completing assignments, using computers in classrooms and dormitories, obtaining repairs, securing help with problems, and generating favorable attitudes toward the college. Using a 5-point scale, ranging from 1—strongly disagree to 5—strongly agree, alumni were asked to circle an *SD, D, N, A,* or *SA*. The same format was used to rate a set of ten additional statements asking alumni to assess how well computer technology was integrated into courses, enhanced their learning, and contributed to their professional development, and whether the laptop initiative was worth continuing.

Computer Use Measures. These two opinion sections of the questionnaire were separated by a section devoted to the type and frequency of computer technology used during high school, college, and the present day. The alumni were asked about six generic applications—word processing, spreadsheets, presentation software, Internet use, e-mail, and computer games—indicating the frequency of use with a scale adapted from the Pew Internet Project (www.pewInternet.org). The ordinal scale included five levels with scores ascending from 1 to 5 as recalled frequency of use increased: (1) Never, (2) Once a week or less, (3) Once every few days, (4) About once a day, and (5) Several times per day.

Learning Styles. Permission was obtained from the publisher, McBer & Company, to include the *Learning Style Inventory* (Kolb, 1993) to generate primary learning style scores for each participant. The inventory includes 12 introductory statements, all indicating the same theme—"I learn best when…"—that are followed by four choices describing different modes of learning. The participants are asked to rank these four choices according to how well they think each one fits the way they would go about learning something. The first item in the *LSI*, for example, asks the respondent, in response to the statement "When I learn," to rank the following four possibilities—(a) "I like to deal with my feelings," (b) "I like to think about ideas," (c) "I like to be doing things," or (d) "I like to watch and listen." Each item must be uniquely ranked, giving four points to the item "*most like you*," three points to the item "*second most* like you," two points to the "*third most*" item, and one point to the "*least* like you" item.

These four "like" items reflect the four dimensions—feeling, thinking, doing, and watching—of Kolb's theory of experiential learning. The set of choices for each statement about learning always reflects these four dimensions, although the item order is staggered for each of the 12 questions. It is Kolb's practice to assign each respondent to one of four categories of learning styles by combining the scores from two adjacent learning dimensions. The validity of this categorization process is strongly disputed by critics (Cornwell & Manfredo, 1994; DeCiantis & Kirton, 1996). Accordingly, after classifying the students according to Kolb's procedures, we retained the total scores for each of the four dimensions and used each participant's highest score as the measure of his or her primary learning style (Cornwell & Manfredo, 1994).

ANALYSIS

The analysis naturally evolved from the quasi-experimental design of the survey. Alumni who graduated in 1998 and 2000 were considered a treatment group because they had received laptops when they arrived on campus as freshmen. By contrast, alumni who graduated in 1997, who comprised the last freshman class whose members were expected to bring personal computers to campus, were the control group. Analysis of variance (ANOVA) procedures were used to determine whether the mean scores of the 1998 and 2000 alumni's responses differed significantly from the mean scores of the 1997 alumni, thereby indicating that implementation of the laptop initiative had had an effect. In addition, because the laptop program itself was continually evolving in this period (e.g., specifications for the laptops improved each year), there was a possibility that there would be differences in the responses between the classes of 1998 and 2000 as well, although certainly not as dramatic.

Once this initial analysis, which focused solely on survey items that reflected ITI goals, was completed, a second exploratory analysis was undertaken, which focused on the alumni's computer usage, not only as college students, but currently as professionals, and retrospectively as high school students. This analysis also evaluated differences in mean scores, but the dependent measure was frequency of use of various computer applications, whereas the independent variables included—in addition to graduation year—gender, time period, and field of study. The use of multiple independent variables required the use of multivariate analysis of variance (MANOVA) procedures in which frequency of use means between various subgroups were compared.

Results and Discussion

The three primary goals of the Information Technology Initiative were (a) to make computer technology convenient for students to use, (b) to integrate computer technology into courses, and (c) to prepare students better for their professions. Two components of the survey, composed of 8 and 10 items each, addressed these questions directly.

TECHNOLOGICAL CONVENIENCE AND SUPPORT

The responses of the alumni to the convenience and support items (see Table 1.1) demonstrate that the 1998 and 2000 alumni who received laptops were for the most part more positive about the state of technology on campus than the 1997 alumni who had had to bring their own computers to campus or depend solely on public computer labs. In particular, the 1998 and 2000 alumni had statistically significant higher mean scores when it came to agreeing that the technology made it convenient to do assignments ($F(2, 207) = 40.02$, $p < .001$), and they had statistically significant lower mean scores than the 1997 alumni, showing that they would have found it inconvenient to bring their own computers ($F(2, 205) = 40.58, p < .001$) to campus. In addition, after their four-year experience their mean scores showed them to be more satisfied with the college's computer repair service than their 1997 classmates ($F(2, 199) = 24.82, p < .001$). In fact, based on the difference in means scores, they were even more likely than the 1997 alumni to express the opinion that the technology available to them was better than at other colleges ($F(2, 205) = 14.57, p < .001$). For these four items the statistically significant differences in mean scores between the 1997 alumni control group and the 1998 and 2000 alumni experimental group were confirmed using a post-hoc Scheffé's test.

Table 1.1 One-Way ANOVA: Technology Convenience and Support by Graduation Year

	Mean			One-Way ANOVA		
Convenience Items	1997^{a}	1998^{b}	2000^{c}	*F*-Ratio	*df*	*signif.*
1. Computer technology provided by Grove City College made it convenient for me to complete assignments.	$3.12^{b,c}$	4.12^{a}	4.40^{a}	40.02	2,207	$p < .001$
2. The College's classrooms were well equipped to support the use of computer technology during class time.	1.95^{c}	2.27	2.34^{a}	4.28	2,207	$p < .02$
3. The College's dormitory rooms were well equipped to support the use of computer technology.	2.40^{c}	2.78^{c}	$3.95^{a,b}$	34.54	2,203	$p < .001$
4. While I was a student, I believed the computer technology available on campus was better than what was available at other similar colleges.	$2.62^{b,c}$	3.38^{a}	3.57^{a}	14.57	2,205	$p < .001$
5. I found it more convenient to bring my own personal computer than to use the College's equipment.	$3.77^{b,c}$	2.26^{a}	2.27^{a}	40.58	2,205	$p < .001$
6. I was satisfied with the service provided by the College's computer repair shop.	$2.83^{b,c}$	3.77^{a}	3.60^{a}	24.82	2,199	$p < .001$
7. I was satisfied with the service provided by the College's computer help desk.	3.13	3.47	3.31	2.42	2,205	$p < .10$
8. When I had problems using computer technology, friends and classmates most often provided the help I needed.	4.09	3.97	4.02	0.47	2,207	*n.s.*

Note: Superscripts a, b, and c are used to designate the three graduation years 1997, 1998, and 2000, respectively. Scheffé's test, a post-hoc multiple comparison statistic, was used to determine whether differences between mean scores were statistically different for any particular item. When a mean score is superscripted with a letter, then that score is statistically different from the mean score for the graduation year denoted by the letter.

Table 1.2 One-Way ANOVA: Career Preparation Ratings by Graduation Year

Career Preparation Items	Mean			One-Way ANOVA		
	1997[a]	1998[b]	2000[c]	*F*-Ratio	*df*	*signif.*
1. Computer technology was an essential tool that I used during my career at Grove City College.	3.58[b,c]	3.99[a]	4.02[a]	4.65	2,207	$p < .01$
2. Student use of computer technology to complete assignments enhanced student learning.	3.53	3.88	3.79	3.33	2,207	$p < .05$
3. Use of computer technology in college frequently increased my understanding of course content.	2.81	3.01	3.03	1.28	2,207	*n.s.*
4. My professors frequently provided assignments that required the use of computer technology.	3.27	3.27	3.66	2.34	2,206	$p < .10$
5. The College's administration supported and encouraged faculty to develop technology-integrated courses.	3.04	3.08	3.29	1.33	2,206	*n.s.*
6. It was beneficial to have a portable laptop computer during my College career. (Answer if applicable.)	3.80[b,c]	4.49[a]	4.53[a]	6.81	2,152	$p < .001$
7. As a student, a desktop computer would have been more beneficial to own and use than a portable laptop computer.	2.69[b,c]	2.19[a]	2.24[a]	5.52	2,198	$p < .005$
8. The computer technology I used at Grove City College helped to prepare me for my chosen profession.	3.16[b]	3.73[a]	3.53	7.28	2,207	$p < .001$
9. Using computer technology in college was essential for my later professional success.	3.63	3.76	3.71	0.28	2,207	*n.s.*
10. I believe the Grove City College laptop computer program is important to continue for future students.	4.19[c]	4.45	4.56[a]	4.70	2,207	$p < .01$

Note: Superscripts a, b, and c are used to designate the three graduation years 1997, 1998, and 2000, respectively. Scheffé's test, a post hoc multiple comparison statistic, was used to determine whether differences between mean scores were statistically different for any particular item. When a mean score is superscripted with a letter, then that score is statistically different from the mean score for the graduation year denoted by the letter.

The evaluations, despite their generally positive character, were nevertheless surprisingly discriminating. In response to an item about dormitory rooms being well-equipped for technology, a post-hoc Scheffé analysis demonstrated that, when warranted, the 1998 alumni held opinions more in line with the laptop-deprived 1997 alumni. College dormitories had not been fully wired when the laptop initiative had begun. Accordingly, only the members of the class of 2000, who arrived on campus two years later, agreed that dormitories were technologically well equipped ($F(2, 203) = 34.54$, $p < .001$). A similar disparity occurred in regard to classroom facilities. Essentially, all three alumni groups registered means below 3.0, which means they disagreed with the proposition that classrooms were well equipped to support computer technology. However, the mean response for the 2000 alumni was sufficiently higher than that of the 1997 alumni to infer that the later laptop class, who arrived on campus as freshmen the year the 1997 class graduated, found classroom conditions significantly better but not satisfactory. The 1998 alumni, though their mean score on this item is closer to that of the 2000 alumni, cannot be statistically differentiated from either group, which means there was considerable variation in the responses provided by the class, resulting in a statistically significant but lower F-ratio ($F(2, 207) = 4.28$, $p < .02$).

Finally, the survey results provided a dose of reality about the contribution made by computer help desks. Whether they were part of the laptop program or not, alumni in all three classes exhibited remarkable agreement about the role of friends and classmates in providing computer help ($F(2, 207) = 0.47$, *n.s.*), which may not be a programmatic failure to the extent that digital unity enables every user to become a potential helper (Brown, 2003). In that regard, it is interesting to note how the mean rating of the help desk is highest for the 1998 alumni, who were the first to get laptops, but falls for the 2000 alumni, who by the time of their arrival may have had less interaction with the help desk because after their freshman year everyone on campus had a laptop, thereby establishing digital unity ($F(2, 205) = 2.42$, $p < .10$).

EFFECTS ON COURSES AND PREPARING FOR A CAREER

The Information Technology Initiative was not limited, of course, to just technical improvements in infrastructure. The new information technology was expected to have a substantial effect on how courses were taught, thereby creating an environment that was also substantially more attuned to the work environment that students would face after graduation. Alumni assessments of these dimensions of the technology initiative are, on the whole, positive, but their opinions also reveal gaps in the laptop program (see Table 1.2). In their responses, the 1998 and 2000 alumni clearly registered higher mean scores than the 1997 alumni, demonstrating more enthusiasm for computer technology as an essential tool at college ($F(2, 207) = 4.65$, $p < .01$) and the benefits of having a laptop computer at college ($F(2, 152) = 6.81$, $p < .001$), specifically preferring it to a desktop computer ($F(2, 198) = 5.52$, $p < .005$).

However, only the 1998 alumni members were demonstrably more positive than the 1997 alumni in agreeing with the statement that technology helped prepare them for their profession ($F(2, 207) = 7.28$, $p < .001$). The members of the class of 2000, perhaps because they are not as far along in their professional development, were not as sure. Further, the mean scores for the three alumni classes were virtually indistinguishable in response to the idea that using technology in college is essential for later success ($F(2, 207) = 0.28$, *n.s.*).

Responses to the remaining items in this section of the questionnaire suggest, in fact, that the anticipated curricular revolution was lagging behind the technological innovations that occurred while these alumni were on campus. There is no evidence in the data to support the notion that the technology initiative automatically led to better learning. Mean scores were neutral (2.81 M3.03) when it came to technology increasing the understanding of course content ($F(2, 207) = 1.28$, *n.s.*) and barely higher (3.04 M3.29) in regard to perceptions about faculty being encouraged to integrate technology in courses ($F(2, 206) = 1.33$, *n.s.*) with no significant differences between classes. Nevertheless, the 2000 alumni ranged from *agreement* to *strong agreement* ($M = 4.56$) when asked if it were important for the laptop program to continue. Their attitude was significantly more favorable than the 1997 alumni ($F(2, 207) = 4.70$, $p < .01$), who despite having missed the laptop program by a year, nevertheless agreed ($M = 4.19$) that the program should be continued for incoming undergraduates.

In sum, then, the responses to this section of the questionnaire may be interpreted as a vote of confidence in the Grove City Information Technology Initiative, although the responses also have hallmarks of other student surveys at laptop institutions that reveal skepticism or impatience with the pace of integrating technology into the curriculum (Platt & Bairnsfather, 1999; Mitra & Steffensmeier, 2000). As far as encouragement to faculty is concerned, Schrum et al.'s (2002) analysis of the effects of a faculty development grant awarded at a laptop university indicated that incentives are useful for motivating faculty participation. Their study also demonstrated the efficacy of using qualitative methods—rather than surveys—to understand faculty attitudes and behavior.

ASSESSING THE EFFECTS OF DIGITAL UNITY ON FREQUENCY OF COMPUTER USE

To answer the research question about how the laptop initiative may have affected computer use, it may be useful to hypothesize first what would constitute a positive result. A major section of the questionnaire included questions to gauge how frequently the participants used (1) word processing, (2) spreadsheet, and (3) presentation software or accessed the (4) Internet, (5) e-mail, and (6) computer games, measured on a 5-point scale from 1—never to 5—several times a day. Further, participants provided estimates for each activity during three different periods in their lives—high school, college, and current work—that were interpreted as repeated measures over time.

The question reduces to how these data would be arrayed if the laptop initiative were having an optimal effect. In our analysis, we have used both alumni graduation year (which alumni class) and sex as surrogates for preexisting digital divides. Many studies have demonstrated that males in high school use computers more than females, so we can expect a digital divide in our data during the high school time period (Young, 2000). At the same time, however, if digital unity is an antidote to preexisting digital divides, then the discrepancy between males' and females' frequency of computer use should have diminished while the 1998 and 2000 alumni were on campus, and, in an ideal case, should not reappear when the same men and women enter the workforce or continue in graduate school. On the other hand, the implementation of the laptop initiative artificially created a digital divide between 1997 alumni who were sophomores, when 1998 alumni arrived as freshmen and received the first set of laptops and were seniors when the class of 2000 alumni arrived as freshmen and received even better laptops. Their technology ratings were generally lower than those of the 1998 and 2000 alumni. Their frequency of use might be expected to be lower as well.

Table 1.3 presents mean frequency-of-use scores for six generic applications, sorted according to life period, sex, and graduation year. The frequency-of-use responses for three time periods in the respondents' lives (high school, college, and current work) were submitted as repeated measures using the General Linear Model function on SPSS 10.0. At the most inclusive level, the gender divide can be evaluated by looking at the most right-hand column of Table 1.3, which lists the statistical probabilities of the between-subjects effects of sex, graduation year, and their joint interaction on each type of computer use. Gender differences are apparent in the frequencies reported of using spreadsheets (males use them more often, especially as undergraduates), presentation software (males use them more at their current work), the Internet (males access it more often during all life periods), and computer games (males are overwhelmingly more active, especially in high school). Within these four domains, at least, the digital divide appears to be unabated by the existence of Grove City's technology initiative.

Table 1.3. Mean Frequency of Use Scores by Time Period, Sex, and Graduation Year

		High School		Undergraduate		Current Work		Between Subjects	
		Male	Female	Male	Female	Male	Female	Between Subjects	
	Grad Year	*n* = 90	*n* = 116	*n* = 90	*n* = 116	*n* = 90	*n* = 116	Effects	*p*-values
Word Processing	1997	2.30	2.49	3.43	3.51	4.30	3.88	Sex	*n.s.*
	1998	2.45	2.37	3.81	3.29	4.23	3.80	Grad Year	*n.s.*
	2000	2.66	2.62	3.72	3.81	3.83	3.84	S x Y	*n.s.*
	Average	2.47	2.48	3.66	3.52	4.12	3.84		
Spreadsheet	1997	1.30	1.42	2.40	2.09	3.70	3.12	Sex	*p* = .004
	1998	1.56	1.44	2.66	2.22	3.47	2.98	Grad Year	*n.s.*
	2000	1.66	1.47	2.72	2.28	3.21	2.81	S x Y	*n.s.*
	Average	1.51	1.44	2.59	2.19	3.46	2.98		
Presentation Software	1997	1.03	1.05	1.79	1.60	2.41	1.95	Sex	*p* = .041
	1998	1.09	1.07	1.63	1.76	2.44	2.15	Grad Year	*n.s.*
	2000	1.31	1.18	2.03	1.79	1.97	1.76	S x Y	*n.s.*
	Average	1.14	1.09	1.81	1.71	2.28	1.97		
Internet	1997	1.17	1.21	2.87	2.64	4.70	4.43	Sex	*p* = .001
	1998	1.47	1.17	3.31	3.34	4.72	4.41	Grad Year	*p* = .000
	2000[7,8]	2.21	1.76	4.48	3.85	4.52	4.03	S x Y	*n.s.*
	Average	1.60	1.35	3.54	3.23	4.65	4.31		
E-mail	1997[8,0]	1.07	1.19	2.83	3.42	4.77	4.56	Sex	*n.s.*
	1998[7,0]	1.52	1.12	3.61	4.02	4.77	4.54	Grad Year	*p* = .000
	2000[7,8]	1.97	1.52	4.59	4.27	4.55	4.24	S x Y	*p* = .031
	Average	1.51	1.26	3.67	3.87	4.70	4.46		
Computer Games	1997	2.30	1.69	2.70	1.74	2.17	1.64	Sex	*p* = .000
	1998	**2.65**	**1.76**	2.77	2.49	2.16	1.59	Grad Year	*n.s.*
	2000	**2.76**	**1.79**	2.83	1.88	1.79	1.52	S x Y	*n.s.*
	Average	2.57	1.74	2.77	2.04	2.04	1.59		

Note: Numeral superscripts in Grad Year column indicate statistically significant differences in means between the 1997, 1998, and 2000 alumni with superscript numerals corresponding to last numeral of differentiated Grad Years; statistically significant differences in mean scores in a time period between males and females who are alumni in the same Grad Year class are indicated with **bold** (p < .001) *or underlined* (p < .05) *figures; Between Subjects Effects p-values designate differences in means for Sex regardless of Time Period or Grad Year and for Grad Year regardless of Sex or Time Period as well as interactions between Sex and Grad Year without regard for Time Period.*

However, there are notable exceptions. Within the word-processing domain, the difference in only one pair of means is noted as statistically significant. Thus, the realm of word processing appears gender-neutral. The other exception is e-mail, where the 1998 and 2000 alumni remember accessing it more frequently than the alumnae do during high school, but once at Grove City the difference in mean frequency diminishes to the point that it is no longer statistically significant. Interestingly, there is a statistically significant difference between the sexes for the 1997 alumni, but in this case the frequency of use is higher among the alumnae. This mixed result is ultimately reflected in the weak "sex by graduation year" interaction effect for e-mail. What is equally noteworthy about both e-mail and Internet use are the real differences in means between the three classes (confirmed using a post-hoc multiple comparison test and noted with superscripts on Table 1.3). Although some of the between-group difference may be attributed to the technology initiative, the parallel increases in the frequency of Internet and e-mail use in high school suggest that simple diffusion of the technologies also contributes to the annual increases. This is especially apparent in the jump in the frequency of Internet use, which statistically differentiates the 2000 alumni from 1998 alumni even though they are both participants in the laptop program.

ASSESSING THE EFFECTS OF COGNITIVE STYLE ON COMPUTER USE

The final research question—searching for a measure of cognitive style that is associated with computer use—turned out to be the most vexing problem. When developing the questionnaire, we devoted a major portion (one and a half pages) to the inclusion of Kolb's (1993) *Learning Style Inventory*. In a quandary about its validity (Cornwell & Manfredo, 1994; De Ciantis & Kirton, 1996), we used it because no other instrument had been so widely cited or discussed in the educational research literature. In the end, we found, however, that Kolb's idiosyncratic scoring system was not as coherent as the four basic scales—concrete experience, reflective observation, active experimentation, and abstract conceptualization—that are comprised in his measurement tool. Assigning respondents to one of those four dimensions, based on their highest score, was one reasonable alternative to using Kolb's own scoring system (Cornwell & Manfredo, 1994). Cohen's (2001) finding that exposure to a technology-rich environment can change learning style added yet another dimension to our quandary.

A reasonable solution to this dilemma became apparent when we found that the four primary learning styles were significantly associated with the alumni's major field of study—liberal arts, education, math and science, business, and engineering ($X^2 = 23.72$, $df = 12$, $p = .02$). By contrast, Kolb's scoring procedure resulted in categories that failed to exhibit any connection with the alumni's major fields of study, or for that matter, virtually any other measure of technology use or attitudes gathered during the course of the survey. Justification for using field of study as a surrogate for learning style is provided by Jones, Reichard, and Mokhtari (2003), who have demonstrated that primary learning styles of community college students were discipline-specific with regard to English, mathematics, science, and social studies, and by Loo (2002), who has found that primary learning styles distinguish the orientation of undergraduate business students toward choosing hard (accounting, finance, and MIS) or soft (marketing and general management) majors. We finally reasoned that an improvised measure based on Kolb's instrument would surely complicate the explication of results, and therefore it was better to use field of study as an indicator of cognitive style, because its meaning was empirically derived.

The results are presented in Table 1.4, whose format is essentially the same as Table 1.3 except that the respondents' fields of study, rather than sex, comprise the independent variable. Because there are five fields of study, the table includes 360 mean scores. Thus, it can be best comprehended by looking at the patterns generated by bold and underlined results. For each class, for each type of computer use, in each life period, we have compared the means to determine if there is a statistically significant difference between them. When the one-way ANOVA was significant at the .001 level, we listed the set of five means in bold print. When the statistic was significant at the .05 level or less, we underlined the five means. Thus, the most efficient way to look at Table 1.4 is to think of it as a two-way table with six rows, depicting computer use, and three columns, depicting life periods (high school, college, and current work). The points of interest are wherever the numerals are in bold or underlined.

Given these criteria, the most important section of the table is the second row, which depicts the means for the frequency of spreadsheet use. Only 1 set of mean scores out of 12 is not statistically significant. In fact, 10 of 12 are statistically significant at the .001 level. Quite simply, the frequency of the use of spreadsheets during college and currently at work, and even more remarkably during the high school years, appears to differentiate business and engineering majors from education majors.

Using this criterion, two other cells are of particular interest. During their college years, the frequency of use of presentation software consistently distinguishes the business and engineering students once again from education majors, although the degree of difference is not as great for the 1998 or 2000 alumni as it is for the 1997 alumni—perhaps an outcome of the technology initiative leveling the cognitive playing field. Another interesting point is that for the 1998 and 2000 alumni, the frequency of word processing use reported at work distinguishes business and engineering students from math and science majors.

Table 1.4 Mean Scores of Six Types of Computer Use by Life Period, Field of Study, and Graduation Year

		Frequency of Use in High School					Frequency of Use as Undergraduate					Frequency of Use at Current Work				
		Lib Art	Educ	M/Sci	Busi	Engn	Lib Art	Educ	M/Sci	Busi	Engn	Lib Art	Educ	M/Sci	Busi	Engn
	Grad Year	*n*=50	*n*=32	*n*=47	*n*=54	*n*=24	*n*=50	*n*=33	*n*=47	*n*=55	*n*=24	*n*=50	*n*=33	*n*=47	*n*=55	*n*=24
Word Processing	1997	2.23	2.36	2.44	2.47	2.55	3.38	3.50	3.56	3.42	3.55	<u>4.46</u>	<u>3.43</u>	<u>3.69</u>	<u>4.58</u>	<u>3.92</u>
	1998	2.33	2.00	2.38	2.62	2.50	3.57	3.78	3.31	3.64	3.17	<u>4.05</u>	<u>3.89</u>	<u>3.25</u>	<u>4.41</u>	<u>4.33</u>
	2000	2.81	2.70	2.53	2.64	2.43	3.88	4.10	3.50	3.57	4.00	<u>3.38</u>	<u>4.10</u>	<u>3.36</u>	<u>4.43</u>	<u>4.29</u>
	Average	2.46	2.38	2.45	2.57	2.50	3.62	3.76	3.46	3.55	3.58	**3.94**	**3.76**	**3.43**	**4.47**	**4.12**
Spreadsheet	1997	1.23	1.07	1.38	1.58	1.55	**1.38**	**1.71**	**2.13**	**2.53**	**3.45**	**3.00**	**2.43**	**2.94**	**4.32**	**3.83**
	1998	<u>1.43</u>	<u>1.00</u>	<u>1.38</u>	<u>1.68</u>	<u>2.00</u>	**1.16**	**2.22**	**2.63**	**2.73**	**3.17**	**2.62**	**3.00**	**2.13**	**4.27**	**4.17**
	2000	**1.25**	**1.20**	**1.53**	**1.93**	**2.14**	**1.81**	**2.10**	**2.79**	**2.86**	**3.29**	**2.44**	**2.60**	**2.71**	**3.93**	**3.57**
	Average	**1.32**	**1.09**	**1.43**	**1.71**	**1.83**	**1.68**	**1.97**	**2.50**	**2.69**	**3.33**	**2.66**	**2.64**	**2.59**	**4.20**	**3.84**
Presentation Software	1997	1.00	1.00	1.06	1.05	1.09	**1.46**	**1.14**	**1.50**	**2.11**	**2.27**	2.15	1.50	2.38	2.53	2.00
	1998	1.00	1.00	1.06	1.18	1.00	<u>1.48</u>	<u>1.53</u>	<u>1.56</u>	<u>2.05</u>	<u>1.83</u>	2.00	2.22	1.88	2.73	2.83
	2000	1.19	1.00	1.27	1.50	1.14	<u>1.69</u>	<u>1.40</u>	<u>1.87</u>	<u>2.36</u>	<u>2.29</u>	<u>1.25</u>	<u>2.10</u>	<u>1.67</u>	<u>2.14</u>	<u>2.71</u>
	Average	<u>1.08</u>	<u>1.00</u>	<u>1.13</u>	<u>1.22</u>	<u>1.08</u>	**1.54**	**1.33**	**1.64**	**2.15**	**2.17**	<u>1.80</u>	<u>1.88</u>	<u>1.98</u>	<u>2.51</u>	<u>2.42</u>
Internet	1997	1.31	1.07	1.19	1.22	1.18	2.62	2.86	2.63	2.58	3.18	<u>4.69</u>	<u>4.00</u>	<u>4.44</u>	<u>4.89</u>	<u>4.58</u>
	1998	1.19	1.00	1.25	1.55	1.33	3.24	3.78	3.25	3.45	3.00	4.67	4.11	4.31	4.68	4.83
	2000	1.88	1.20	1.93	2.50	2.29	4.19	3.40	4.40	4.29	4.29	4.06	4.20	4.27	4.50	4.29
	Average	<u>1.44</u>	<u>1.09</u>	<u>1.45</u>	<u>1.69</u>	<u>1.54</u>	3.38	3.27	3.4	3.36	3.46	<u>4.48</u>	<u>4.09</u>	<u>4.34</u>	<u>4.71</u>	<u>4.56</u>
E-mail	1997	1.31	1.00	1.06	1.21	1.09	3.38	3.43	3.00	3.21	2.82	**4.69**	**4.14**	**4.56**	**4.89**	**4.97**
	1998	1.19	1.00	1.16	1.64	1.17	3.76	4.33	3.69	4.00	3.40	4.67	4.22	4.50	4.82	4.80
	2000	1.75	1.00	1.80	2.07	1.86	4.44	4.40	4.53	4.29	4.43	4.06	4.70	4.27	4.57	4.57
	Average	<u>1.40</u>	<u>1.00</u>	<u>1.32</u>	<u>1.60</u>	<u>1.33</u>	3.88	3.97	3.72	3.8	3.43	<u>4.48</u>	<u>4.33</u>	<u>4.45</u>	<u>4.78</u>	<u>4.79</u>
Computer Games	1997	1.69	1.69	2.13	1.95	2.36	1.92	1.93	2.00	2.32	2.55	1.54	1.62	1.69	2.16	2.17
	1998	1.95	1.75	2.40	2.36	1.83	2.48	2.89	2.75	2.68	2.33	1.71	1.89	1.88	1.91	1.83
	2000	1.88	2.40	2.60	2.21	2.14	1.94	2.00	2.87	2.43	2.29	1.44	1.70	1.80	1.71	1.57
	Average	1.86	1.91	2.37	2.18	2.17	2.16	2.21	2.53	2.49	2.42	1.58	1.72	1.79	1.95	1.92

*Note: **Bold** figures indicate statistically significant* F*-ratios at* $p < .001$ *per field of study and time period; <u>underlined</u> figures indicate* $p < .05$

More speculative, but certainly interesting, are the remaining boldfaced or underlined items in Table 1.4, which appear to repeat the pattern of differentiating former business and engineering students from former education majors. The fact that education majors reported extremely low frequencies of software and e-mail use (often no experience at all) in all areas except word processing and computer games could be cause for alarm. Their considerably higher scores for Internet and e-mail use while at Grove City, however, may be an indication that the Information Technology Initiative played a role in stemming the digital divide that currently afflicts elementary and secondary schools (Levin & Arafeh, 2002). This result is consistent with the outcomes reported by Schrum et al. (2002) in their study of education majors at a laptop university. Some consolation might also be taken by the fact that the digital divide that separates males and females when it comes to computer games is nowhere evident in regard to fields of study, suggesting that it is a matter of personal taste and not individual prowess.

Conclusions

For the administrators and academics at Grove City College, the results of this survey should reassure them that their quest for digital unity on campus had at least one of its desired effects. It generated positive attitudes about the state of technological readiness at Grove City among affected alumni in the classes of 1998 and 2000. There is less consensus, however, about whether the modes of teaching and learning were revolutionized by the distribution of laptops to the full-time faculty and each incoming full-time student.

Beyond such institutional objectives, however, assessing the effects of the Information Technology Initiative has provided a valuable opportunity to investigate what role such programs may play in ameliorating two types of digital divides. Perhaps the most telling aspect about the gender-based usage differences is that they appear to be nonexistent when it comes to conventional office applications. There were no differences in usage for males and females for either word processing or presentation software, and even spreadsheet use in high school and after graduation is roughly equal. Ironically, though, because no difference was exhibited by the 1997 alumni, the implementation of the laptop initiative for the classes of 1998 and 2000 may have effected a four-year digital divide between males and females in the use of spreadsheet programs. Similarly, for the frequency of Internet and e-mail use, only a few statistically significant differences are exhibited, with no discernible pattern. Thus, the most compelling gender divide captured in these data is also the least surprising. Alumni reported more frequent use of computer games than alumnae, a divide between males and females that is universal in high school and seems to continue, somewhat abated, at college and beyond.

The digital divide between male and female alumni in regard to spreadsheet programs takes on even broader implications when we look at differences based on fields of study. In fact, some of the gender differences may only be a result of disproportionately high numbers of males taking business and engineering courses. Nevertheless, one reading of the frequency of usage results for spreadsheet programs is that high school usage may be a precursor of a cognitive divide that is ultimately heightened at college and further during a person's professional career. To some extent, presentation software use shows the same affinity with business and engineering, although the pattern is not discernible in high school. Otherwise, the argument may be made that the laptop initiative may have played a role in diminishing the digital divide. Once college ends, differences occur between alumni based on their fields of study for all applications except computer games, but interestingly, for Internet and e-mail use these differences are not statistically significant for the classes of 1998 and 2000. How much of that modest closing of the digital divide resulted directly from the laptop initiative is difficult to estimate in an era of rapid diffusion of PC technology.

One finding, however, is indisputable. The classes of 1998 and 2000, who fully participated in the laptop computer program, exhibited their highest levels of agreement with two statements in support of digital unity on campus: portable computers were beneficial during their college careers ($4.49 < M < 4.53$) and the laptop program is important to continue for future students ($4.45 < M < 4.56$). This suggests that Weiser's (1998) vision of a third wave of ubiquitous computing—when computer use is fully and seamlessly integrated into student life—would be readily welcomed by these alumni.

Author Update

We are honored by the selection of our research study for publication in this volume. A decade later, however, we find it humbling that the phenomenon we so carefully studied—the effectiveness of a campuswide laptop computer program—is now passé. While we argued that *digital unity* was a more apt term to describe the phenomenon than the more widely adopted one, *ubiquitous computing*, we now find ourselves acknowledging that most institutions of higher learning are on the verge of achieving what Weiser (1998) once identified as the final, third wave of *ubiquitous computing* when students, as we wrote, "would pull credit card interfaces out of their wallets to exploit the applications they needed." Who knew these interfaces would also serve as telephones and video recorders?

Nevertheless, we can now update you on the phenomenon we studied and highlight some aspects of the article that we think have continuing value. On a practical level, the campus described began distributing tablet PCs in 2004—an innovation that has noticeably improved on the PC as a note-taking device in the classroom. Furthermore, maintaining *digital unity* has continued to ensure that students can help other students, that faculty-developed applications are reliable, and that a rural campus can complete repairs locally.

Similarly, some strengths of the study itself have not been seriously diminished over time. Among them, it focused on graduates rather than current students for the purposes of assessment, it paid careful attention to the creation and validation of a representative sample, and it exploited a naturally occurring intervention and a four-year historical perspective to construct a quasi-experimental context for study. But then there's the conundrum. A popular learning styles measure offered no significant insight into the factors that might affect attitudes toward computer use—one of many precursors to the doubts now being expressed about the efficacy of using learning styles to improve education in any respect (Pashler, McDaniel, Rohrer, & Bjork, 2009; Willingham, 2005). Hence, a decade from now, one might hope that research on technology in education will be on the verge of its own third wave—enhanced by theoretical advances in cognitive science and physiological measures that indicate learning (see, for example, Carreiras et al., 2009).

References

Atkinson, G. (1991). Kolb's learning style inventory: A practitioner's perspective. *Measurement & Evaluation in Counseling & Development, 23*(4), 149–161.

Attewell, P. (2001). The first and second digital divides. *Sociology of Education, 74*, 252–259.

Brown, D. G. (2003). *Ubiquitous computing: The universal use of computers on college campuses*. Bolton, MA: Anker Publishing.

Brown, D. G., Burg, J. J., & Dominick, J. L. (1998). A strategic plan for ubiquitous laptop computing. *Communications of the ACM, 41*, 26–35.

Brown, D. G., & Petitto, K. R. (2003). The status of ubiquitous computing. *Educause Review, 38*, 25–33.

Candiotti, A. (2003). Ubiquitous computing at Drew University. In D. G. Brown (Ed.), *Ubiquitous computing* (pp. 155–166). Bolton, MA: Anker Publishing.

Candiotti, A., & Clarke, N. (1998). Combining universal access with faculty development and academic facilities. *Communications of the ACM, 41*, 36–41.

Caño-Garcia, F., & Hughes, E. H. (2000). Learning and thinking styles: An analysis of their interrelationship and influence on academic achievement. *Educational Psychology, 20*, 413–430.

Carreiras, M., Seghier, M. L., Baquero, S., Estévez, A., Lozano, A., Devlin, J. T., et al. (2009). An anatomical signature for literacy. *Nature, 461*, 983–986.

Chen, M. (1986). Gender and computers: The beneficial effects of experience on attitudes. *Journal of Educational Computing, 2*, 265–282.

Chen, M. (1987). Gender differences in adolescents' uses of and attitudes toward computers. In M. L. McLaughlin (Ed.), *Communication yearbook 10* (pp. 200–216). Newbury Park, CA: Sage.

Confirmed notebook universities. (2003). Retrieved December 18, 2003, from Valley City State University Information Technology Center website: http://itc.vcsu.edu/notebookinitiative/notebookcampusmap.htm

Cohen, V. L. (2001). Learning styles and technology in a ninth-grade high school population. *Journal of Research on Computing in Education, 33*(4), 355–366.

Cornwell, J. M., & Manfredo, P. A. (1994). Kolb's learning style theory revisited. *Educational & Psychological Measurement, 54*, 317–327.

De Ciantis, S. M., & Kirton, M. J. (1996). A psychometric reexamination of Kolb's experiential learning cycle construct: A separation of level, style and process. *Educational & Psychological Measurement, 56*, 809–820.

Garner, I. (2000). Problems and inconsistencies with Kolb's learning styles. *Educational Psychology, 20*, 341–348.

Geiger, M. A., Boyle, E. J., & Pinto, J. (1992). A factor analysis of Kolb's revised Learning Style Inventory. *Educational and Psychological Measurement, 52*, 753–759.

Hindman, D. B. (2000). The rural–urban digital divide. *Journalism & Mass Communication Quarterly, 77*, 549–560.

Holleque, K. (2002). Technology and education at Valley City State University—Student survey results. Online document. Available at: http://community.vcsu.edu/facultypages/kathryn.holleque/My_Webpage/Surveys.htm

Jones, C., Reichard, C., & Mokhtari, K. (2003). Are students' learning styles discipline specific? *Community College Journal of Research and Practice, 27*, 363–375.

Jones, S. (2002). The Internet goes to college: How students are living in the future with today's technology. Online document. Available at: www.pewInternet.org/reports

Kiaer, L., Mutchler, D., & Froyd, J. (1998). Laptop computers in an integrated first-year curriculum. *Communications of the ACM, 41,* 45–49.

Kolb, D. A. (1984). *Experiential learning: Experience as the source of learning and development.* Englewood Cliffs, NJ: Prentice Hall.

Kolb, D. A. (1993). *Learning style inventory.* Boston, MA: McBer & Company.

Kolb, D. A., Boyatzis, R. E., & Mainemelis, C. (2001). Experiential learning theory: Previous research and new directions. In L. J. Sternberg and L. F. Zhang (Eds.), *Perspectives in thinking, learning and cognitive styles* (pp. 227–247). Mahwah, NJ: Lawrence Erlbaum.

LeBlanc., R. J., & Teal, S. L. (1998). Hardware and software choices for student computer initiatives. *Communications of the ACM, 41,* 64–69.

Levin, D., & Arafeh, S. (2002). The digital disconnect: The widening gap between Internet-savvy students and their schools. Online document. Available at: www.pewinternet.org/Reports/2002/The-Digital-Disconnect-The-widening-gap-between-Internetsavvy-students-and-their-schools.aspx?r=1

Light, J. S. (2001). Rethinking the digital divide. *Harvard Educational Review, 71,* 709–733.

Loo, R. (1997). Evaluating change and stability in learning style: A methodological concern. *Educational Psychology, 17,* 95–100.

Loo, R. (2002). The distribution of learning styles and types for hard and soft business majors. *Educational Psychology, 22,* 349–360.

MacDonald, L. W. (1997). The impact of developing technology on media communications. *Information Services & Use, 17*(2), 5–22.

McCarty, D. W., & Robinson, G. K. (1999). Chronicles of change (qualitative study)—Summary of results. Unpublished report. Available at: http://adminservices.clayton.edu/provost/aceffect.htm

Mitra, A. (1998). Categories of computer use and their relationship with attitudes toward computers. *Journal of Research on Computing in Education, 30*(3), 281–295.

Mitra, A., & Steffensmeier, T. (2000). Changes in student attitudes and student computer use in a computer-enriched environment. *Journal of Research on Computing in Education, 32*(3), 417–433.

Mitra, A., Steffensmeier, T., Lenzmeier, S., & Massoni, A. (1999). Changes in attitudes toward computers and use of computers by university faculty. *Journal of Research on Computing in Education, 32*(1), 189–202.

Ono, H., & Zavodny, M. (2003). Gender and the Internet. *Social Science Quarterly, 84,* 111–121.

Pashler, H., McDaniel, M., Rohrer, D., & Bjork, R. (2009). Learning styles: Concepts and evidence. *Psychological Science in the Public Interest, 9*(3), 105–119.

Platt, M. W., & Bairnsfather, L. (2000). Compulsory computer purchase in a traditional medical school curriculum. *Teaching and Learning in Medicine, 11*(4), 202–206.

Schrum, L., Skeele, R., & Grant, M. (2002). One college of education's effort to infuse technology: A systemic approach to revisioning teaching and learning. *Journal of Research on Technology in Education, 35*(2), 256–271.

Warschauer, M. (2003). Demystifying the digital divide. *Scientific American, 289*(2), 42–47.

Weiser, M. (1998). The future of ubiquitous computing on campus. *Communications of the ACM, 41,* 41–42.

Willingham, D. T. (2005). Do visual, auditory, and kinesthetic learners need visual, auditory, and kinesthetic instruction? *American Educator, 29*(2), 31–35.

Young, B. J. (2000). Gender differences in student attitudes toward computers. *Journal of Research on Computing in Education, 33*(2), 204–213.

CHAPTER

2

Increasing Preservice Teachers' Self-Efficacy Beliefs for Technology Integration

Ling Wang | Nova Southeastern University

Peggy A. Ertmer | Purdue University

Timothy J. Newby | Purdue University

This study was designed to explore how vicarious learning experiences and goal setting influence preservice teachers' self-efficacy for integrating technology into the classroom. Two hundred and eighty students, enrolled in an introductory educational technology course at a large Midwestern university, participated. Students were divided into eighteen lab sections, which were assigned to one of four conditions (three experimental and one control). Pre- and post-surveys were administered to examine participants' self-efficacy beliefs for technology integration. Results showed significant treatment effects for vicarious experiences and goal setting on participants' judgments of self-efficacy for technology integration. A significantly more powerful effect was found when vicarious learning experiences and goal setting were both present compared to when only one of the two factors was present. Therefore, from the perspective of teacher educators, the use of vicarious learning experiences and the incorporation of specific goals may help preservice teachers develop the confidence they need to become effective technology users within their own classrooms.

Introduction

In an effort to prepare students for the information age, public schools are increasing access to technology tools by installing more hardware and software, connecting classrooms to the Internet, and providing cable and satellite capabilities (Zehr, 1997, 1998). Yet, despite the increased availability and support for classroom computer use, relatively few teachers have fully integrated computers into their teaching (Becker, 2000; Marcinkiewicz, 1996). Teachers' uses of computers are likely to be influenced by multiple factors, including the accessibility of hardware and relevant software, the nature of the curriculum, personal capabilities, and external constraints such as time, equipment, and technical support (Albion, 1999). However, according to Ertmer (1999), "Even if every first-order [external] barrier were removed, teachers would not automatically use technology to achieve the kind of meaningful outcomes advocated" (p. 51).

There is substantial evidence to suggest that teachers' beliefs in their capacity to work effectively with technology—that is, their *self-efficacy* for technology integration—may be a significant factor in determining patterns of classroom computer use (Albion, 1999; Oliver & Shapiro, 1993). For example, according to Eachus and Cassidy (1999), "Self-efficacy has repeatedly been reported as a major factor in understanding the frequency and success with which individuals use computers" (p. 2). Compeau, Higgins, and Huff (1999) conducted a longitudinal study with 394 subscribers to a periodical over a one-year interval to test the influence of computer self-efficacy beliefs, outcome expectations, affect, and anxiety on computer use. Their findings provided strong confirmation that computer self-efficacy beliefs had a significant positive influence on computer use. Another study conducted by Albion (1996) investigated student teachers' dispositions toward computers and their uses of computers in primary school classrooms during a final-year practicum. Results suggested that lack of confidence for teaching with computers was an important factor influencing the levels of computer use by student teachers. Taken together, these studies suggest that teachers' beliefs—and self-efficacy beliefs in particular—are useful indicators of levels of technology integration. Certainly, they provide sufficient reason to undertake further investigations in this area and to consider approaches to teacher education and professional development that might be effective in increasing self-efficacy for teaching with technology.

Bandura (1986) identified four sources of information used to judge self-efficacy: successful performance attainment, observing the performances of others (vicarious learning), verbal persuasion indicating that one possesses certain capabilities, and physiological states by which one judges capability, strength, and vulnerability. Although performance accomplishments are considered to be the most robust source of self-efficacy information, vicarious learning is also a powerful source (Bandura, 1986, 1997). That is, viewing others successfully accomplishing a particular task can increase learners' perceptions of others' efficacy as well as their own efficacy for performing similar tasks (Bandura, 1997).

Vicarious learning experiences have been shown to enhance student teachers' self-efficacy for using computers in their teaching. In 1993, Handler conducted a study with 133 education graduates. Participants responded to a survey regarding their perceptions of the value of preservice computer experiences to their professional preparation. Results showed that observing cooperating teachers using computers during the student teaching experience was one of the three most important factors that influenced feelings of preparedness for the use of computers for instruction in their own classrooms.

Downes (1993) investigated student teachers' uses of computers during practicum sessions to identify relationships among computer uses and specific practicum factors. Results indicated a significant increase in computer use over the three practicum sessions, and this increase was consistent from one practicum group to the next. What is interesting to note, however, is that when examining the factors involved in the practicum environment, only one factor, supervising teachers' uses of computers with children, was significant. No other practicum-related factors, including level taught and technology resources, were significant. The influence of the supervising teachers' uses of computers was so strong that first-year students, whose supervising teachers used computers with children, were more likely to use computers with children than third-year students whose supervising teachers did not. Apparently, observing positive role models (in this case, supervising teachers) favorably influenced the student teachers to perform similarly.

Although novice learners can acquire skills and strategies from social modeling, when performing independently they are likely to over- or underestimate their own capabilities (Schunk, 2001). However, students' judgments of progress, as well as their judgments of self-efficacy, increase in both accuracy and strength when goals are made explicit (Schunk, 2001). Research in education (Schunk, 1990) and organizational management (Lee, Locke, & Latham, 1989) has emphasized the importance of goals directed toward specific performance levels, with concrete, measurable outcomes. Because specific goals help define what constitutes an acceptable level of performance, the explication of these goals can help students make more accurate, as well as more robust, judgments of efficacy. By establishing goals, students typically experience a sense of efficacy for attaining them (Schunk, 2001).

The literature has established independent effects of both vicarious learning experiences and goal setting on learners' judgments of self-efficacy, yet little work has been done to examine how these strategies might be combined to create even more accurate and more robust judgments of efficacy. In 1992, Gist and Mitchell identified three general strategies for enhancing self-efficacy beliefs. Of these three, two related to vicarious learning and goal setting, respectively: providing opportunities to observe experts' practice and providing opportunities to address a specific goal while resolving a particular teaching issue. Gist and Mitchell concluded that these strategies contributed to building teachers' confidence for achieving effective teaching.

According to Neck and Manz (1992), when individuals mentally rehearse a task, they see themselves performing it and thus are exposed to the positive effect of modeling (i.e., they learn through vicarious experiences). Furthermore, the intense cognitive processing that occurs during mental practice can heighten awareness of how to attain specific goals and hence increase goal commitment and task performance. Based on these premises, it was hypothesized that vicarious learning experiences and goal setting could be combined to achieve a significant effect on learners' self-efficacy beliefs and task performance.

Purpose of the Study

This study was designed to examine the impact of vicarious learning experiences and goal setting on preservice teachers' self-efficacy for technology integration. Specifically, this study was guided by the following research question:

> *What are the effects of vicarious experiences and goal setting on preservice teachers' judgments of self-efficacy for technology integration?*

Based on the self-efficacy literature described previously, it was hypothesized that preservice teachers who were exposed to vicarious experiences related to successful technology integration would experience significantly greater increases in judgments of self-efficacy for technology integration than those who were not exposed to these vicarious experiences. Furthermore, it was hypothesized that preservice teachers who were assigned specific goals would experience significantly greater increases in judgments of self-efficacy than those who were not assigned any goals. Finally, it was hypothesized that preservice teachers who were exposed to vicarious experiences *and* assigned specific goals would demonstrate the greatest increases in judgments of self-efficacy compared to students who received either one of these conditions alone.

Methods

RESEARCH DESIGN

A 2 x 2 (Vicarious Experiences x Goal Setting) mixed factorial research design was used to examine how vicarious experiences and goal setting affected preservice teachers' judgments of self-efficacy for technology integration. These independent variables were combined to form four experimental conditions: (a) NVE/NGS: no vicarious experiences and no goal setting (also defined as the control group), (b) NVE/GS: no vicarious experiences but with goal setting, (c) VE/NGS: vicarious experiences with no goal setting, and (d) VE/GS: vicarious learning experiences with goal setting.

PARTICIPANTS

Participation was solicited from the 408 students enrolled in an *Introduction to Educational Technology* course during the spring of 2003. Among these students, 337 agreed to participate in the study, although complete data sets were available from only 280 participants, including 92 males and 188 females. The participants' ages ranged from 18 to 38 years (M = 19.88, SD = 2.69). The majority of the participants were freshmen (n = 153); the rest were sophomores (n = 72), juniors (n = 36), seniors (n = 16), and graduate students (n = 3). Participants were majoring in elementary education (n = 105), secondary education (n = 113) within various content areas, prekindergarten to kindergarten education (n = 13), and others (n = 49). The demographic data collected from the participants also showed that among the 280 participants, 268 students (96%) planned to become teachers after graduating. The majority (n = 221) of the participants had never taken a computer class before. Those participants who had completed previous computer classes reported that the classes were mostly introductory computer literacy courses. Based on a 4-point Likert-style question (1—not confident to 4—very confident), participants' initial confidence levels averaged 2.77 with a standard deviation of 0.82. In general, the participants rated themselves somewhat confident to confident in their ability to use technology to teach.

The participants' pre-course understandings of computer uses and technology integration in teaching were illustrated by their responses to questions about "specific strategies to develop knowledge and skills for teaching with technology" and "important things to consider when planning technology use." Almost every participant emphasized the role of taking a lot of computer classes to improve their computer skills. Participants believed that abundant practice with computers and familiarization with computer programs would sufficiently prepare them for teaching with technology. Only about 20 participants (fewer than 10%) mentioned the role of cooperating with other teachers, and even fewer (n = 4) mentioned things such as experimenting with different software programs to see which worked best for students' learning and to integrate technology into lesson plans where relevant. Based on participants' pre-course responses, little understanding of computer uses and technology integration in teaching was apparent.

INSTRUMENT

A Likert-style survey measuring participants' self-efficacy beliefs for technology integration was developed by the first author and used as pre- and post-survey measures.

The survey (see Appendix 2.A) included 21 items regarding participants' confidence for technology use. The participants were asked to rate their levels of agreement (from 1—strongly disagree to 5—strongly agree) with statements related to their possession of confidence regarding technology use (e.g., "I feel confident that I understand computer capabilities well enough to maximize them in my classroom." "I feel confident I can regularly incorporate technology into my lessons, when appropriate to student learning.").

The survey was reviewed for both content and construct validity. The evidence of content validity is primarily judgmental and therefore was gathered before the actual administration of the instrument. In the process of instrument development, the first author established a panel consisting of six content experts in the area of self-efficacy (five professors and one graduate student). The experts were provided with a bibliography and a summary of the literature review. These served as the content universe. Individually, the experts reviewed the materials and commented on the adequacy of the conceptual definition. The first author also developed a rating sheet so that the experts could rate and make suggestions for each item on the instrument. With the feedback obtained from the experts' ratings, appropriate revisions of the instrument were made. Based on these revisions, it was believed that the content validity of the instrument was convincing.

The evidence of construct validity is primarily empirical. In this study, evidence was gathered after the self-efficacy survey had been administered to the participants. A factor analysis was conducted on both pre-survey data and post-survey data to identify, from the 21 items, subsets of those items that could be clustered together to form constructs (i.e., factors). The factor analysis was exploratory and was conducted to determine if the instrument developed for this study actually measured some meaningful constructs. As suggested by Gable and Wolf (1993), the number of factors and the relationship of items to factors were determined by the analysis rather than by the instrument developer's theoretical predictions.

The factor analysis of the pre-survey data produced a two-factor solution that explained 55.36% of the systematic covariance among the items (see Appendix 2.B). The first factor (eigenvalue = 9.85) accounted for 46.92% of the covariance and consisted of 16 items with loadings ranging from .51 to .84. The items defining this factor represented computer technology capabilities and strategies. The second factor (eigenvalue = 1.77) accounted for 8.4% of the covariance and consisted of five items with loadings ranging from .56 to .77. The five items represented external influences of computer technology uses (e.g., student assessment, restraints, oppositions). Because we were interested in measuring students' abilities to use technology in strategic ways, we decided not to include the items related to this second factor in our analysis. Thus, the final version of the instrument consisted of the 16 items in Factor One. Another factor analysis was then conducted with the 16 items on the post-survey data. A one-factor solution was suggested (see Appendix 2.C). This factor (eigenvalue = 9.58) explained a total of 59.86% of the systematic covariance. Therefore, it was further confirmed that these 16 items formed a valid instrument measuring a single construct.

Cronbach alpha coefficients were calculated for both pre-survey data and post-survey data (on the 16 items) to determine the reliability of the instrument. Alpha coefficients of .94 (for pre-survey) and .96 (for post-survey) indicated that the instrument was highly reliable. Thus, the obtained factor solution and resulting reliability coefficients for the self-efficacy for technology integration scale suggest that the instrument exhibited construct validity and reliability. Thus, it may be concluded that the resulting form of the instrument holds promise for its use in further research.

Procedures

The 18 lab sections of the course were randomly assigned to the four experimental conditions. During the third week of the semester, participants completed the demographic questionnaire, which included 17 questions asking for information about age, gender, major, previous computer classes, self-judgment of confidence for using computers in teaching, and understandings of computer uses and technology integration in teaching. Some questions were in the format of multiple choice, while others were short-answer, open-ended questions. The self-efficacy survey was also administered as a pre-course measure. Both the demographic questionnaire and the pre-survey were administered online, using the existing course management system, WebCT.

During the sixth week of the semester, the researcher (the first author) described the study to the students and solicited participation. Students who agreed to participate in the study signed the informed consent form and spent a regular two-hour lab session completing the assignments for this study, under the direction of the researcher. The participants were offered 5 points toward their course grades for participating. During the experiment, the participants worked actively, following closely the directions they received from the researcher. Almost all participants spent at least one hour viewing either the VisionQuest CD (described later) or the WebQuest website to which they were assigned. During this time, they made notes or wrote responses on the worksheets provided. After the experiment, some participants spoke with the researcher expressing their great interest in the CD and expressed interest in obtaining more information about the content of the software as well as the process by which the software was developed. At the end of the experiment, the participants completed the self-efficacy survey for technology integration as a post-measure, once again accessing the survey online through the course WebCT.

In this study, vicarious experiences for technology integration were presented to the students using VisionQuest, an instructional CD that features the technology practices and beliefs of six K–12 teachers. According to Ertmer et al. (2003), "VisionQuest is designed to provide opportunities for users to explore models of effective technology integration" (p. 100). The various cases highlighted on the CD illustrate that technology integration can be achieved successfully in a variety of contexts despite differences in settings, resources, and student backgrounds.

VisionQuest provides vicarious learning experiences for the users through the use of video segments augmented by electronic artifacts (lesson plans, student products) from teachers' classrooms. Cases are constructed so that users can explore teachers' classrooms either one at a time (case by case) or thematically (i.e., comparing components of technology integration across cases). Each case contains a variety of elements that combine to illustrate how teachers' visions for technology use are translated into practice. Users examine how teachers planned for integration, how they currently implement technology within their classrooms, and how they assess the impact of their efforts.

For the groups that were exposed to vicarious experiences—that is, the VE/GS and VE/NGS groups—participants explored the VisionQuest CD and observed the technology uses and classroom management strategies of the featured teachers. For the groups that were assigned specific goals—the VE/GS and NVE/GS groups—participants were given a number of specific goals. For example, the following goals were assigned to the participants in the VE/GS condition:

> While you are exploring VisionQuest, it helps to keep in mind what you are trying to do. A list of expected outcomes from this activity is shown on this page and can be thought of as goals that you are trying to accomplish. So while you are going through VisionQuest, you should keep in mind the following goals:
>
> For each teacher on VisionQuest, determine:
>
> - his/her beliefs about technology use
> - the roles technology plays
> - the way he/she organizes technology-based class activities
> - the way students are assessed

Students in the NVE/GS condition, who viewed a variety of WebQuests instead of exploring VisionQuest, received the following goals:

> While you are exploring these WebQuests, it helps to keep in mind what you are trying to do. A list of expected outcomes from this activity is shown on this page and can be thought of as goals that you are trying to accomplish. So while you are going through the WebQuests, you should keep in mind the following goals:
>
> For each WebQuest that you view, determine:
>
> - the instructional goal(s)
> - the procedure of how the students might achieve the goal(s)
> - how students' achievement of the goal(s) will be evaluated

For the groups that were not exposed to vicarious learning experiences—the NVE/GS and NVE/NGS groups—participants explored a website containing links to various WebQuests selected for this study. The WebQuests had the content of technology in teaching but did not contain characteristics of vicarious learning. For the groups that were not assigned any goals—the VE/NGS and NVE/NGS groups—participants received only instructions on how to navigate the VisionQuest software or the WebQuest website, but nothing related to what knowledge/information they were expected to gain from the software or the site (i.e., no specific goals were assigned to these participants). In addition, to make sure that the participants would attend to the tasks they were required to accomplish—exploring the information in the software or on the website rather than wasting time on irrelevant tasks—each participant was required to complete a worksheet related to the specific goals or the content of his or her specific tasks, depending on the experimental conditions in which he or she participated.

DATA ANALYSIS STRATEGIES

Demographic data were analyzed to describe the characteristics of the participants in this study. Ranges, frequencies, means, and standard deviations were calculated for descriptive data. Responses to opened-ended questions were analyzed using the standard procedures of pattern seeking that are most commonly adopted by qualitative researchers.

Means and standard deviations were calculated for each experimental group on the pre- and post-surveys of self-efficacy for technology integration. ANOVA results [$F\ (3, 276) = 0.06, p = .9818$] showed that there were no significant differences among the means of the pre-survey scores for the four experimental groups. To see the effects of vicarious learning experiences and goal setting on preservice teachers' self-efficacy for technology integration, two-way ANOVA was used to analyze post-survey data. Furthermore, the ANOVA was also used to determine whether there were statistically significant differences among the means of the four experimental groups.

Results

Table 2.1 presents the mean scores and the standard deviations on the pre- and post-surveys of the four experimental groups. As noted previously, differences among the means and standard deviations from the pre-survey scores were not significant. For the post-survey data, the VE/GS (vicarious experiences with goal setting) group had the highest mean score on ratings of self-efficacy for technology integration. The NVE/NGS (no vicarious experiences with no goal setting) control group had the lowest mean score. The control group had the largest standard deviation, whereas the VE/GS group had the smallest standard deviation.

Table 2.2 presents the results of the two-way ANOVA for the post-survey scores on self-efficacy for technology integration. Significant main effects suggest that vicarious learning experiences [$F(1, 276) = 25.63$, $p < .0001$] and goal setting [$F(1, 276) = 16.59$, $p < .0001$)] significantly increased participants' self-efficacy for technology integration. No significant interaction [$F(1, 276) = 0.38$, $p = .5388$] between the two independent variables was found, suggesting that the effect of vicarious learning experiences on self-efficacy beliefs did not change at the different levels of goal setting, and vice versa. Thus, we can conclude that vicarious learning experiences and goal setting both increased the participants' self-efficacy, but when vicarious learning experiences and goal setting were combined, the increase was the greatest. In addition, the effect size index f was calculated following the method presented by Cohen (1988). It was found that, with $f = .40$, the effect size was large according to Cohen's definition (1988, pp. 284–288), meaning that the systematic variances were largely explained by the specific conditions to which the participants in this study were assigned.

Table 2.1 Means and Standard Deviations for the Pre- and Post-Survey Scores on Self-Efficacy for Technology Integration

		Mean		Standard Deviation	
Experimental Group	N	Pre-Survey	Post-Survey	Pre-Survey	Post-Survey
VE-GS	71	3.79	4.35	0.58	0.46
VE-NGS	70	3.82	4.06	0.62	0.52
NVE-GS	71	3.82	4.00	0.55	0.47
NVE-NGS	68	3.82	3.79	0.54	0.59

Table 2.2 Two-way ANOVA for the Post-Survey Scores on Self-Efficacy for Technology Integration

Source	*df*	Type III SS	Mean Square	*F*	*p*	ES Index *f*
VE-NVE	1	6.7601	6.7601	25.63	< .0001	.40
GS-NGS	1	4.3770	4.3770	16.59	< .0001	
VE-NVE*GS-NGS	1	0.0999	0.0999	0.38	.5388	

The ANOVA results also demonstrate the pairwise differences among the four experimental groups: The mean score of the group in which both vicarious learning experiences and goal setting were present was significantly higher than the mean score of the control group ($p < .0001$). In addition, the mean score of the group in which both vicarious learning experiences and goal setting were present was significantly higher than the mean scores of the groups where only vicarious learning experiences ($p = .0010$) or goal setting ($p < .0001$) was present. The mean score of the group where only vicarious learning experiences was present was significantly higher than the mean score of the control group ($p = .0020$), and the mean score of the group where only goal setting was present was also significantly higher than the mean score of the control group ($p = .0155$). Figure 2.1 visually presents the mean score differences.

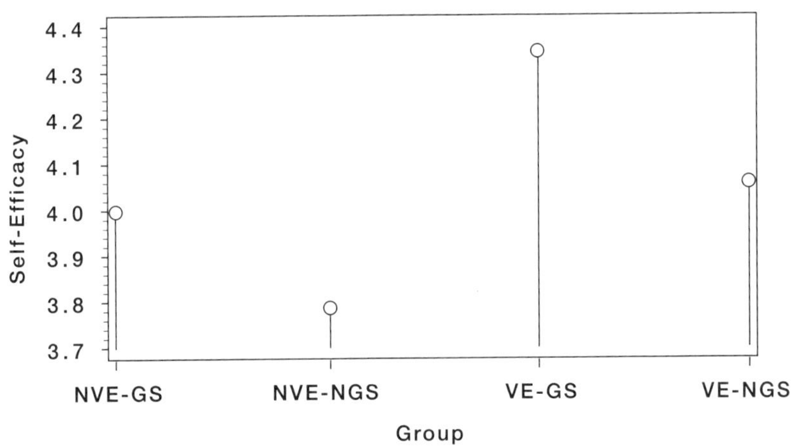

Figure 2.1 Mean score differences of the four experimental groups for the post-survey

Discussion

The results of this study indicated that preservice teachers who were exposed to vicarious experiences that were related to successful technology integration (with and without goal setting) experienced significantly greater increases in judgments of self-efficacy for technology integration than those who were not exposed to these vicarious experiences. These results support previous research regarding the benefits of vicarious learning on judgments of self-efficacy (Albion, 1996; Downes, 1993; Ertmer et al., 2003; Handler, 1993) and highlight the potential benefit to providing preservice teachers with opportunities for observing exemplary technology-using teachers as one way to increase their self-efficacy for effectively using technology in their own classrooms. Specifically, in this study, vicarious learning experiences were provided through an electronic instructional tool, the VisionQuest CD. This type of modeling helps eliminate logistical problems that might be associated with direct classroom observations and can be easily incorporated into a teacher education program as either a self-paced reflection tool or an instructor-led class activity. Other forms of electronic vicarious learning experiences, such as those provided by videos and web pages, may also bring about similar effects on self-efficacy beliefs for technology integration.

The results of this study also indicated that preservice teachers who used specific goals, with and without vicarious experiences, experienced significantly greater increases in judgments of self-efficacy for technology integration than those who were not assigned any goals. These results also support previous research regarding the benefits of goal setting on self-efficacy beliefs (Bandura, 1997; Schunk, 2001; Schunk & Ertmer, 1999). Thus, providing preservice teachers with goals seems to be an effective way to enhance efficacy levels for technology integration, which can be easily achieved by making the link between class objectives and learning goals explicit.

More important, the results of this study showed that preservice teachers who were exposed to vicarious learning experiences and who were assigned specific goals experienced significantly greater increases in judgments of computer self-efficacy than those who received only one of these two conditions. These results support the suggestion made by others (Gist & Mitchell, 1992; Neck & Manz, 1992) regarding effective strategies for increasing self-efficacy as well as the possible benefit to be gained by combining strategies. Thus, teacher educators might consider using both strategies when helping preservice teachers learn about technology integration. For example, instructors might anticipate increases in students' self-efficacy for technology integration when exemplary uses of technology in K–12 classrooms are presented and students explore these uses according to specific goals. What makes this practice more desirable is that both the exemplary uses and goals can be easily incorporated into software packages or other forms of electronic delivery.

Limitations and Suggestions for Future Work

The characteristics of the participants in this study may limit generalizability to participants with different characteristics. For example, the participants in this study were primarily female residential undergraduate students at the beginning of their teacher education programs (i.e., 67% female with an average age of less than 20, with over half being freshmen). In addition, participants did not demonstrate much initial understanding of computer uses and technology integration in teaching. These characteristics of the participants would make it difficult to generalize the results of this study to preservice teachers in other programs who might have different characteristics, although careful descriptions of the participants' characteristics may help increase the generalizability of the findings of this study.

Another unique feature of this study was that the experiment was administered to the participants during a regular two-hour lab session of the course, which would be considered a relatively short treatment time. Therefore, there would be no indication of long-term, lasting effects of the treatment from the results of this study.

In addition, the goals used in this study were structured in such a way that they may have been used by the students as a form of advance organizer. Therefore, it is arguable that the effect observed on self-efficacy beliefs might be, at least in part, due to the role of cognitive scaffolding these goals played in affecting participants' self-efficacy. It should be advisable that the cognitive scaffolding features of these goals be removed to determine whether the findings of this study are replicable.

Therefore, for future research work, considerations might be made to administer the experiment over a longer period of time to investigate the long-term effects of vicarious learning experiences and goal setting. If any differences or interesting patterns were found in preservice teachers' self-efficacy beliefs compared with the one-time brief exposure to vicarious learning experiences and goal setting, meaningful implications might be made to the benefit of teacher education programs. The results of this study should also be further qualified by using the same research design and experiment with preservice teachers in different types of teacher education programs, where students' characteristics vary from one to another. Last, it would be important to examine the actual technology use by the students who have achieved high levels of computer self-efficacy, to further verify the hypothesized relationship between high efficacy and actual classroom use.

Conclusions

The findings of this study contribute to the existing body of literature in two significant ways: (1) This study confirmed the findings from previous research that demonstrated how preservice teachers benefit from observing teacher models presented through vicarious learning experiences, such as those provided by VisionQuest (Ertmer et al., 2003), and from using specific goals for mastering computer-related tasks (Schunk & Ertmer, 1999), and (2) this study provided support for the hypothesized combined effect of vicarious learning experiences and goal setting on increasing preservice teachers' self-efficacy for technology integration. Though enhanced self-efficacy beliefs do not automatically slate into the actual use of technology among teachers, they are a necessary condition for technology integration. Teachers' self-efficacy beliefs have been found to be useful indicators of likely success at technology integration (Oliver & Shapiro, 1993). Furthermore, increased performance with computer-related teaching practices has also been found to be significantly related to higher levels of computer self-efficacy (Harrison, Rainer, Hochwarter, & Thompson, 1997).

Therefore, from the perspective of teacher educators, the use of electronic vicarious learning experiences and the incorporation of specific goals may help preservice teachers develop the confidence they need to become effective technology users within their own classrooms. Thus, as our future teachers achieve high confidence levels for technology integration and develop powerful strategies for technology implementation, meaningful technology use can come closer to being the norm, rather than the exception, in our K–12 classrooms.

Author Update

When making decisions about if and how to use technology in the classroom, teachers' self-efficacy beliefs play an extremely important role. Even if teachers *know* how to use technology, if they don't *believe* they can use it successfully in the classroom, they will not even attempt it. In fact, current research (Piper, 2003) suggests that confidence may be *even more important* than skills. In the research reported in this article, we examined two methods for increasing self-efficacy for technology integration among preservice teachers: using video-based models (vicarious experiences) and goal setting. Although both interventions led to significantly higher levels of self-efficacy in the students, combining these factors produced an even more powerful effect.

Both researchers and educators in the field today recognize the potential impact of vicarious experiences, and numerous projects have been developed that allow students to view video- and text-based examples of exemplary technology-using teachers (Bulgar, 2007; Dreon & Dietrich, 2009; KITE, 2001). Employing a related approach, projects have also been developed that enable students to reflect on their own practice using video recordings (Bryan & Recesso, 2006; Calandra & Brantley-Dias, in press). All of these projects are designed to help build students' confidence and knowledge for classroom teaching, in general, and technology integration, more specifically.

In contrast we have seen very little work that has incorporated goal setting as a strategy for building self-efficacy, specifically related to technology integration. Given the relative ease with which this can be implemented, additional efforts in this area may be warranted. For example, future research might consider whether goal setting has an equally powerful effect on changing other beliefs (e.g., pedagogical). Finally, future research should include longitudinal studies that examine how changes in beliefs during students' preservice years translate into practice in their future classrooms.

References

Albion, P. R. (1996). Student teachers' use of computers during teaching practice in primary classrooms. *Asia-Pacific Journal of Teacher Education, 24,* 63–73.

Albion, P. R. (1999). *Self-efficacy beliefs as an indicator of teachers' preparedness for teaching with technology.* Retrieved July 25, 2002, from www.usq.edu.au/users/albion/papers/site99/1345.html

Bandura, A. (1986). *Social foundations of thought and action: A social cognitive theory.* Englewood Cliffs, NJ: Prentice-Hall.

Bandura, A. (1997). *Self-efficacy: The exercise of control.* New York, NY: Freeman.

Becker, H. J. (2000). Access to classroom computers. *Communications of the ACM, 43(6)*, 24–25.

Bryan, L., & Recesso, A. (2006). Promoting reflection among science student teachers using a web-based video analysis tool. *Journal of Computing in Teacher Education, 23,* 31–39.

Bulgar, S. (2007). Using supported video exemplars for the professional development of preservice elementary school teachers. *Contemporary Issues in Technology and Teacher Education, 7*(2), 28–41.

Calandra, B., & Brantley-Dias, L. (in press). Using digital video editing to shape novice teachers: A generative process for nurturing professional growth. *Educational Technology.*

Cohen, J. (1988). *Statistical power analysis for the behavioral sciences* (2nd ed.). Hillsdale, NJ: Lawrence Erlbaum.

Compeau, D., Higgins, C. A., & Huff, S. (1999). Social cognitive theory and individual reactions to computing technology: A longitudinal study. *MIS Quarterly, 23,* 145–158.

Downes, T. (1993). Student-teachers' experiences in using computers during teaching practice. *Journal of Computer Assisted Learning, 9,* 17–33.

Dreon, O., Jr., & Dietrich, N. I. (2009). Turning lemons into lemonade: Teaching assistive technology through Wikis and embedded video. *TechTrends, 53*(1), 78–80.

Eachus, P., & Cassidy, S. (1999). *Developing the computer self-efficacy (CSE) scale: Investigating the relationship between CSE, gender and experience with computers.* University of Salford, UK. Retrieved November 12, 2002, from www.salford.ac.uk/healthSci/selfeff/ selfeff.htm

Ertmer, P. A. (1999). Addressing first- and second-order barriers to change: Strategies for technology integration. *Educational Technology Research and Development, 47*(4), 47–61.

Ertmer, P. A., Conklin, D., Lewandowski, J., Osika, E., Selo, M., & Wignall, E. (2003). Increasing preservice teachers' capacity for technology integration through use of electronic models. *Teacher Education Quarterly, 30*(1), 95–112.

Gable, R. K., & Wolf, M. B. (1993). *Instrument development in the affective domain: measuring attitudes and values in corporate and school settings* (2nd ed.). Norwell, MA: Kluwer Academic.

Gist, M. E., & Mitchell, T. R. (1992). Self-efficacy: A theoretical analysis of its determinants and malleability. *Academy of Management Review, 17,* 183–211.

Handler, M. G. (1993). Preparing new teachers to use computer technology: Perceptions and suggestions for teacher educators. *Computers and Education, 20,* 147–156.

Harrison, A. W., Rainer, R. K., Jr., Hochwarter, W. A., & Thompson, K. R. (1997). Testing the self-efficacy-performance linkage of social-cognitive theory. *Journal of Social Psychology, 137,* 79–87.

Knowledge Innovation for Technology in Education (KITE) (2001). Retrieved December 10, 2009, from http://kite.missouri.edu/index.html

Lee, Y. E., Locke, E. A., & Latham, G. P. (1989). Goal setting theory and job performance. In L. A. Pervin (Ed.), *Goal concepts in personality and social psychology* (pp. 291–326). Hillsdale, NJ: Erlbaum.

Marcinkiewicz, H. R. (1996). *Motivation and teachers' computer use.* (Eric Document Reproduction Service No. ED 397 818)

Neck, C. P., & Manz, C. C. (1992). Thought self-leadership: The influence of self-talk and mental imagery on performance. *Journal of Organizational Behavior, 13*, 681–699.

Oliver, T. A., & Shapiro, F. (1993). Self-efficacy and computers. *Journal of Computer-Based Instruction, 20*, 81–85.

Piper, D. (2003). The relationship between leadership, self-efficacy, computer experience, attitudes, and teachers' implementation of computers in the classroom. In C. Crawford, D. Willis, R. Carlsen, I. Gibson, K. McFerrin, J. Price, et al. (Eds.), *Proceedings of the Society for Information Technology in Teacher Education* (pp. 1057–1060). Chesapeake, VA: AACE.

Schunk, D. H. (1990). Goal setting and self-efficacy during self-regulated learning. *Educational Psychologist, 25*, 71–86.

Schunk, D. H. (2001). Social cognitive theory and self-regulated learning. In B. J. Zimmerman & D. H. Schunk (Eds.), *Self-regulated learning and academic achievement: Theoretical perspectives*, 2nd ed. (pp. 125–151). Mahwah, NJ: Lawrence Erlbaum.

Schunk, D. H., & Ertmer, P. A. (1999). Self-regulatory processes during computer skill acquisition: Goal and self-evaluative influences. *Journal of Educational Psychology, 91*, 251–260.

Zehr, M. A. (1997). Teaching the teachers. *Education Week: Technology Counts, 17*(11), 26–29.

Zehr, M. A. (1998). The state of the states: Many still haven't dealt with the most difficult policy issues. *Education Week: Technology Counts, 18*(5), 69–71.

APPENDIX

2.A

Computer Technology Integration Survey

DIRECTION

The purpose of this survey is to determine how you feel about integrating technology into classroom teaching. For each statement below, indicate the strength of your agreement or disagreement by circling one of the five scales. Below is a definition of technology integration with accompanying examples:

TECHNOLOGY INTEGRATION

Using computers to support students as they construct their own knowledge through the completion of authentic, meaningful tasks.

Examples:

- Students working on research projects, obtaining information from the Internet.
- Students constructing web pages to show their projects to others.
- Students using application software to create student products (such as composing music, developing PowerPoint presentations, developing HyperStudio stacks).

Using the above as a baseline, please circle one response for each of the statements in the table:

	SD = Strongly Disagree D = Disagree NA/ND = Neither Agree nor Disagree	A = Agree SA = Strongly Agree
1.	I feel confident that I understand computer capabilities well enough to maximize them in my classroom.	SD D NA/ND A SA
2.	I feel confident that I have the skills necessary to use the computer for instruction.	SD D NA/ND A SA
3.	I feel confident that I can successfully teach relevant subject content with appropriate use of technology.	SD D NA/ND A SA
4.	I feel confident in my ability to evaluate software for teaching and learning.	SD D NA/ND A SA

Continued

	SD = Strongly Disagree D = Disagree NA/ND = Neither Agree nor Disagree	A = Agree SA = Strongly Agree
5.	I feel confident that I can use correct computer terminology when directing students' computer use.	SD D NA/ND A SA
6.	I feel confident I can help students when they have difficulty with the computer.	SD D NA/ND A SA
7.	I feel confident I can effectively monitor students' computer use for project development in my classroom.	SD D NA/ND A SA
8.	I feel confident that I can motivate my students to participate in technology-based projects.	SD D NA/ND A SA
9.	I feel confident I can mentor students in appropriate uses of technology.	SD D NA/ND A SA
10.	I feel confident I can consistently use educational technology in effective ways.	SD D NA/ND A SA
11.	I feel confident I can provide individual feedback to students during technology use.	SD D NA/ND A SA
12.	I feel confident I can regularly incorporate technology into my lessons, when appropriate to student learning.	SD D NA/ND A SA
13.	I feel confident about selecting appropriate technology for instruction based on curriculum standards.	SD D NA/ND A SA
14.	I feel confident about assigning and grading technology-based projects.	SD D NA/ND A SA
15.	I feel confident about keeping curricular goals and technology uses in mind when selecting an ideal way to assess student learning.	SD D NA/ND A SA
16.	I feel confident about using technology resources (such as spreadsheets, electronic portfolios, etc.) to collect and analyze data from student tests and products to improve instructional practices.	SD D NA/ND A SA
17.	I feel confident that I will be comfortable using technology in my teaching.	SD D NA/ND A SA
18.	I feel confident I can be responsive to students' needs during computer use.	SD D NA/ND A SA
19.	I feel confident that, as time goes by, my ability to address my students' technology needs will continue to improve.	SD D NA/ND A SA
20.	I feel confident that I can develop creative ways to cope with system constraints (such as budget cuts on technology facilities) and continue to teach effectively with technology.	SD D NA/ND A SA
21.	I feel confident that I can carry out technology-based projects even when I am opposed by skeptical colleagues.	SD D NA/ND A SA

APPENDIX

2.B

Factor Analysis Results and Factor Loadings

Pre-Survey Scores (N = 280)

	Item Number	Stem	Loading
Factor 1 (alpha = .94) Computer Technology Capabilities and Strategies	1.	I feel confident that I understand computer capabilities well enough to maximize them in my classroom.	.84
	6.	I feel confident I can help students when they have difficulty with the computer.	.79
	2.	I feel confident that I have the skills necessary to use the computer for instruction.	.79
	5.	I feel confident that I can use correct computer terminology when directing students' computer use.	.75
	4.	I feel confident in my ability to evaluate software for teaching and learning.	.72
	3.	I feel confident that I can successfully teach relevant subject content with appropriate use of technology.	.71
	9.	I feel confident I can mentor students in appropriate uses of technology.	.69
	7.	I feel confident I can effectively monitor students' computer use for project development in my classroom.	.68
	11.	I feel confident I can provide individual feedback to students during technology use.	.64
	10.	I feel confident I can consistently use educational technology in effective ways.	.61
	18.	I feel confident I can be responsive to students' needs during computer use.	.60
	14.	I feel confident about assigning and grading technology-based projects.	.59
	12.	I feel confident I can regularly incorporate technology into my lessons, when appropriate to student learning.	.56
	13.	I feel confident about selecting appropriate technology for instruction based on curriculum standards.	.56
	16.	I feel confident about using technology resources (such as spreadsheets, electronic portfolios, etc.) to collect and analyze data from student tests and products to improve instructional practices.	.55
	8.	I feel confident that I can motivate my students to participate in technology-based projects.	.51

Continued

	Item Number	Stem	Loading
Factor 2 (alpha = .75) External Influences of Computer Technology Uses	21.	I feel confident that I can carry out technology-based projects even when I am opposed by skeptical colleagues.	.77
	20.	I feel confident that I can develop creative ways to cope with system constraints (such as budget cuts on technology facilities) and continue to teach effectively with technology.	.65
	15.	I feel confident about keeping curricular goals and technology uses in mind when selecting an ideal way to assess student learning.	.64
	19.	I feel confident that, as time goes by, my ability to address my students' technology needs will continue to improve.	.64
	17.	I feel confident that I will be comfortable using technology in my teaching.	.56

APPENDIX

2.C

Factor Analysis Results and Factor Loadings

Post-Survey Scores (N = 280)

	Item Number	Stem	Loading
Factor 1 (alpha = .96) Computer Technology Capabilities and Strategies	2.	I feel confident that I have the skills necessary to use the computer for instruction.	.81
	3.	I feel confident that I can successfully teach relevant subject content with appropriate use of technology.	.80
	14.	I feel confident that I can successfully teach relevant subject content with appropriate use of technology.	.80
	10.	I feel confident I can consistently use educational technology in effective ways.	.79
	8.	I feel confident that I can motivate my students to participate in technology-based projects.	.79
	6.	I feel confident I can help students when they have difficulty with the computer.	.79
	9.	I feel confident I can mentor students in appropriate uses of technology.	.78
	11.	I feel confident I can provide individual feedback to students during technology use.	.78
	18.	I feel confident I can be responsive to students' needs during computer use.	.78
	12.	I feel confident I can regularly incorporate technology into my lessons, when appropriate to student learning.	.78
	1.	I feel confident that I understand computer capabilities well enough to maximize them in my classroom.	.77
	16.	I feel confident about using technology resources (such as spreadsheets, electronic portfolios, etc.) to collect and analyze data from student tests and products to improve instructional practices.	.75
	13.	I feel confident about selecting appropriate technology for instruction based on curriculum standards.	.74
	4.	I feel confident in my ability to evaluate software for teaching and learning.	.74
	5.	I feel confident that I can use correct computer terminology when directing students' computer use.	.73
	7.	I feel confident I can effectively monitor students' computer use for project development in my classroom.	.73

CHAPTER

3

Measuring Teachers' Technology Uses: Why Multiple Measures Are More Revealing

Damian Bebell | Boston College

Michael Russell | Boston College

Laura O'Dwyer | Boston College

In the past 20 years, substantial investments have been made in educational technology. Not surprisingly, in today's zeitgeist of educational accountability there have been increasing calls for empirical, research-based evidence that these investments are affecting the lives of teachers and students. This paper examines the ways in which teachers use technology, with a specific emphasis on the measurement of teachers' technology use. Specifically, the survey responses of approximately 3,000 K–12 teachers are analyzed to examine the multidimensional nature of teachers' technology use. The findings provide insight into improved strategies for conceiving of and measuring teacher technology use.

Introduction

Over the past 20 years, substantial investments have been made in educational technology. Not surprisingly, in today's zeitgeist of educational accountability there have been increasing calls for empirical, research-based evidence that these massive investments are affecting the lives of teachers and students (McNabb, Hawkes, & Rouk, 1999). Although there is a strong desire to examine the effect of technology on student learning, effects on learning must be placed in the context of teacher and student use. In other words, before the outcomes of technology integration can be studied, there must first be a clear understanding of how teachers and students are using technology.

Currently, what is meant by *teachers' use of technology* varies widely. In some cases, teachers' use of technology is specific to their use while delivering instruction in the classroom. In other cases, teachers require students to use technology to develop products or to facilitate learning. In still other cases, teachers' use includes e-mailing, lesson preparation, and record keeping, as well as personal use. Despite the many ways in which teachers may use technology to support their teaching, research on technology often lacks a clear definition of what is meant by *teachers' use of technology.* In turn, a variety of approaches to measuring teachers' use have been employed, most of which group together different uses into a single dimension. Although defining technology use as a unitary dimension may simplify analyses, it complicates efforts by researchers and school leaders to do the following:

- provide a valid measure of technology use,
- interpret findings about the extent to which technology is used, and
- understand how to increase technology use.

In this chapter, we review the several ways in which technology use has been measured over the past two decades and then present data that demonstrate the utility of employing multiple measures of teachers' technology use.

Literature Review

The first large-scale investigation of educational technology occurred in 1986 when the U.S. Congress asked the federal Office of Technology Assessment (OTA) to compile an assessment of technology use in American schools. Through a series of reports (OTA, 1988, 1989, 1995), national patterns of technology integration and use were documented. In addition, a primary finding suggested that the extent to which technology is used is left largely to the teacher's discretion.

Ten years later, Congress requested OTA "to revisit the issue of teachers and technology in K–12 schools in depth" (OTA, 1995). In a 1995 OTA report, the authors noted that previous research on teachers' use of technology employed different definitions of what constituted technology use. In turn, these different definitions led to confusing and sometimes contradictory findings regarding teachers' use of technology. For example, a 1992 International Association for the Evaluation of Educational Achievement (IEA) survey defined a "computer-using teacher" as someone who "sometimes" used computers with students. A year later, Becker (1994) employed a more explicit definition of a computer-using teacher, for which at least 90% of the teachers' students were required to use a computer in their class in some way during the year. Thus, the IEA defined use of technology in terms of the teachers' use for instructional delivery, whereas Becker defined use in terms of the students' use of technology during class time. Not surprisingly, these two different definitions of a "computer-using teacher" yielded different impressions of the technology use. In 1992, the IEA study classified 75% of U.S. teachers as "computer-using teachers," whereas Becker's criteria yielded about one third of that (approximately 25%) (OTA, 1995). This confusion and inconsistency led the OTA to remark: "Thus, the percentage of teachers classified as computer-using teachers is quite variable and becomes smaller as definitions of use become more stringent" (p. 103).

During the mid-1990s, several advances in computer-based technologies came together and allowed teachers to use technology to support their teaching in an increasing variety of ways. Whereas instructional uses of computers had been limited largely to word processing and computer programming, teachers were now able to perform multimedia presentations and computer-based simulations. With the introduction of the Internet into the classroom, teachers were also able to incorporate activities that tapped the World Wide Web. Outside of class time, software for record keeping and test development provided teachers with new ways of using computers to support their teaching. In addition, the Internet allowed teachers access to additional resources when planning lessons (Becker, 1999) and allowed teachers to use e-mail to communicate with their colleagues, administrative leaders, students, and parents (Lerman, 1998). Naturally, as the variety of ways in which teachers could use technology increased, defining what was meant by technology-using teacher became more complicated. (For a complete review of the timeline of changes in the ways teachers use computers, see *Becker's Analysis and Trends of School Use of New Information Technologies*, 1994.)

Quantifying Teachers' Modern Technology Use (1994–2002)

Since 1994, the National Center for Educational Statistics (NCES) has conducted a series of surveys on public school teachers' access to and use of computers and the Internet.

In a 2000 report, the NCES differentiated among types of teachers' technology uses and reported that, although the vast majority of teachers were using technology for some aspects of their professional activities, noninstructive technology uses were pervasive. For example, the NCES reported that:

- 85% of teachers use a computer to create instructional materials at home and 78% do so at school.
- approximately half of all teachers use computers for administrative record keeping at school and at home.
- approximately half of all teachers use e-mail to "communicate with colleagues" and about a quarter of teachers communicate with parents by e-mail.
- approximately 20% of teachers post homework and assignments on the Internet.

Recognizing instructional use as a separate facet of technology use, the NCES also reported that 53% of all public school teachers who have a computer at school are using it for instruction during regular class time. In a summary report of the 2000 NCES document, Rowand (2000) articulated several facets of teacher technology usage that were measured by the NCES survey. These facets included the teacher using technology to/for the following (in descending order of frequency of use):

- creating instructional materials
- keeping administrative records
- communicating with colleagues
- gathering information for planning lessons
- presenting multimedia classroom presentations
- accessing research and best practices for teaching
- communicating with parents or students
- accessing model lesson plans

Besides the work by the NCES, perhaps the largest recent study of teachers' technology practices was the Teaching, Learning, and Computing (TLC) survey that was conducted in 1998 and has generated nine full reports, which detail the practices and beliefs of a representative sample of United States teachers (Becker, 1999; Ravitz, Wong, & Becker, 1998, 1999, 2000; Ravitz & Wong, 2000). Like the NCES, Becker and his colleagues documented that teachers' and students' use of computers was becoming more varied and more widespread. For example, 71% of Grade 4–12 teachers reported that they had their students use a computer at least once in some way during the 1997–1998 school year. Of those teachers who reported that they do not use technology with their students, three-fourths reported that they do use technology themselves for noninstructional purposes. In fact, the most frequent uses of technology across all subject areas was not instructional use but "professional uses of technology related to their day-to-day needs" (Becker, 1999, p. 31). One of the most frequent uses of technology reported by teachers was making handouts for class (66% of all teachers reported making handouts at least weekly). In addition, almost half of the teachers reported using a computer at least weekly for record keeping and student grading, two-thirds reported using the Internet for lesson planning, and 68% reported using e-mail for communication. In short, the 1998 TLC survey data indicated that the majority of teachers were using technology to support their teaching, but much of this use occurred outside of class time.

This finding was echoed by Cuban (2001), whose book *Oversold & Underused* has led many to question the impact of limited numbers of computers in classrooms on teaching and learning. It is important to note that when making the connection between technology use and teaching, Cuban separated technology use during class time and out of class time. Despite repeated efforts to distinguish between uses of technology during and outside of class time, when making the argument that computers are underused as instructional tools, Cuban employs a definition of technology use that is exclusive of technology for communication, lesson planning and preparation, grading, and record keeping. In other words, Cuban addresses the impacts (or lack thereof) of technology on instructional practices using a less than complete measure of what constitutes teachers' technology use.

It is clear, in both theoretical and investigative research, that defining and measuring teachers' use of technology has increased in complexity as technology has become more advanced, varied, and pervasive in the educational system. In actuality, very little has changed since the mid-1990s, when the U.S. Department of Education raised concern about the different ways in which technology use was being defined and measured. Today, several researchers and organizations have developed their own definitions and measures of technology use to examine the extent of technology use and to assess the impact of technology use on teaching and learning. Without question, instruments such as those developed by the CEO Forum and the International Society for Technology in Education (ISTE) appear to be effective in spurring reflection among school leaders and discussion regarding technology's impact in schools. Frequently these instruments collect information on a variety of different types of teachers' technology use and then collapse the data into a single generic "technology use" variable. Unfortunately, the amalgamated measure may be inadequate both for understanding the extent to which technology is being used by teachers and for assessing the impact of technology on learning outcomes. Moreover, there is a strong likelihood that the school leaders who rely on this information for decision making will interpret findings in a number of different ways. For example, some may interpret one measure of teachers' technology use solely as teachers' use of technology for delivery, whereas others may view it as a generic measure of the collected technology skills and uses of a teacher.

In recognition of the importance of how technology use is both defined and measured, the remainder of this chapter uses data collected as part of the Use, Support, and Effect of Instructional Technology (USEIT) Study to describe efforts to develop multiple measures of teachers' technology use and to provide examples of how a multifaceted approach to measuring teachers' technology use holds the potential to provide deeper insight into how technology use varies across settings. Based on the findings described here, implications for future definitions and measurement of technology use are discussed. Throughout the present work, the term *technology* refers specifically to computer-based technologies and includes personal computers, LCD projectors, and Palm Pilots. Before examining technology use, we provide a brief overview of the USEIT study sample and design.

Sample and Methodology

To explore the utility of a multidimensional definition of technology use, the analysis uses data collected as part of the USEIT Study. Working with 22 school districts located throughout Massachusetts, the USEIT Study examines the use of educational technologies by teachers and students, the factors that influence these uses, and the effect of these uses on student learning. The three-year study began during the spring of 2001 and included survey responses from 2,894 K–12 mathematics, English/language arts, science, social studies, and elementary school classroom teachers from schools across 22 districts. As described in greater detail by Russell, Bebell, and O'Dwyer (2003), the sample includes a broad spectrum of teachers across grade levels and school types (elementary, middle, and high school), with each grade level represented by at least 230 teachers. The sample also includes at least 470 teachers from each of the four main subject areas, as well as 1,279 self-contained elementary school classroom teachers who reported teaching multiple subject areas.

The USEIT teacher survey was developed based on current literature, was designed to focus on a broad range of issues related to teacher and student use of technology, and included 45 items that focused on uses of technology both in and outside of the classroom by both teachers and their students. Twelve of these items asked teachers about the frequency with which they used a specific piece of hardware, such as a desktop computer in their classroom, shared laptops, an LCD projector, or a scanner. Because these survey items did not specify whether it was the teachers or their students using the devices, they are excluded from the analyses that follow. Thus, these analyses began by focusing on the remaining 33 items, 21 of which were ultimately used to form seven separate scales of technology use.

Defining Technology Use as Multidimensional

Two approaches are often used to represent teacher technology use: (a) a composite measure that represents an index of general technology use is calculated, or (b) multiple measures, each of which represents a specific category or type of technology use, are generated. The first approach creates a single aggregate measure that represents the frequency with which a teacher uses technology for a variety of purposes. Because an increased value in a teacher's response to each survey item corresponds to more frequent use, the items are summed to generate a composite measure that represents the frequency of technology use.

A histogram of the summed composite measure of technology use for the sample of 2,628 teachers is displayed in Figure 3.1. As seen in Figure 3.1, the composite technology use measure is approximately normally distributed (skewness = –.04) with the majority of respondents clustered in the middle of the distribution and with a fairly equal number of respondents at the respective ends of the distribution.

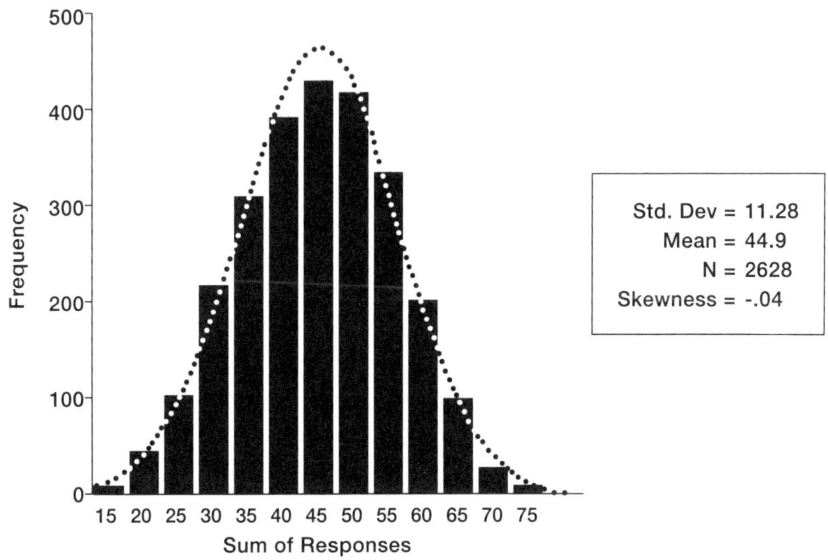

Figure 3.1 Single composite measurement of teacher technology use

The second approach to measuring teacher technology use involves examining the specific ways in which teachers make use of technology. In this case, multiple measures (i.e., scales) for the specific ways that teachers use technology are constructed from related survey items. As documented in Russell, O'Dwyer, Bebell, and Miranda (2003), principal component analyses were used to develop seven separate scales that measure teachers' technology use. These seven scales are as follows:

- Teachers' use of technology for class preparation (Preparation)
- Teachers' professional e-mail use (Professional E-mail)
- Teachers' use of technology for delivering instruction (Delivering Instruction)
- Teachers' use of technology for accommodation (Accommodation)
- Teacher-directed student use of technology during class time (Student Use)
- Teacher-directed student use of technology to create products (Student Products)
- Teachers' use of technology for grading (Grading)

These seven categories of teacher technology use are displayed in Figure 3.2 along with the distribution and mean response for each of the items used to form each of the seven scales.

As seen in Figure 3.2, the number of items used to form each category of use ranges from one to five. Also note that the distribution of responses and mean response varies considerably across the individual items. For example, the distribution of responses for the item that asks teachers how often they make handouts for students using computers is negatively skewed, with the vast majority of teachers reporting that they do this several times a week or several times a month. For this item, the mean response indicates that, on average, teachers often use computers to make handouts. In contrast, the distribution of responses for the item that asks teachers how often they have students perform research using the Internet or CDs during class time has a relatively normal distribution with a mean that is just below the midpoint of the scale. In further contrast, the item that asks teachers how often they ask students to produce multimedia projects has a large positive skew, with most teachers responding that they never have students create these type of projects.

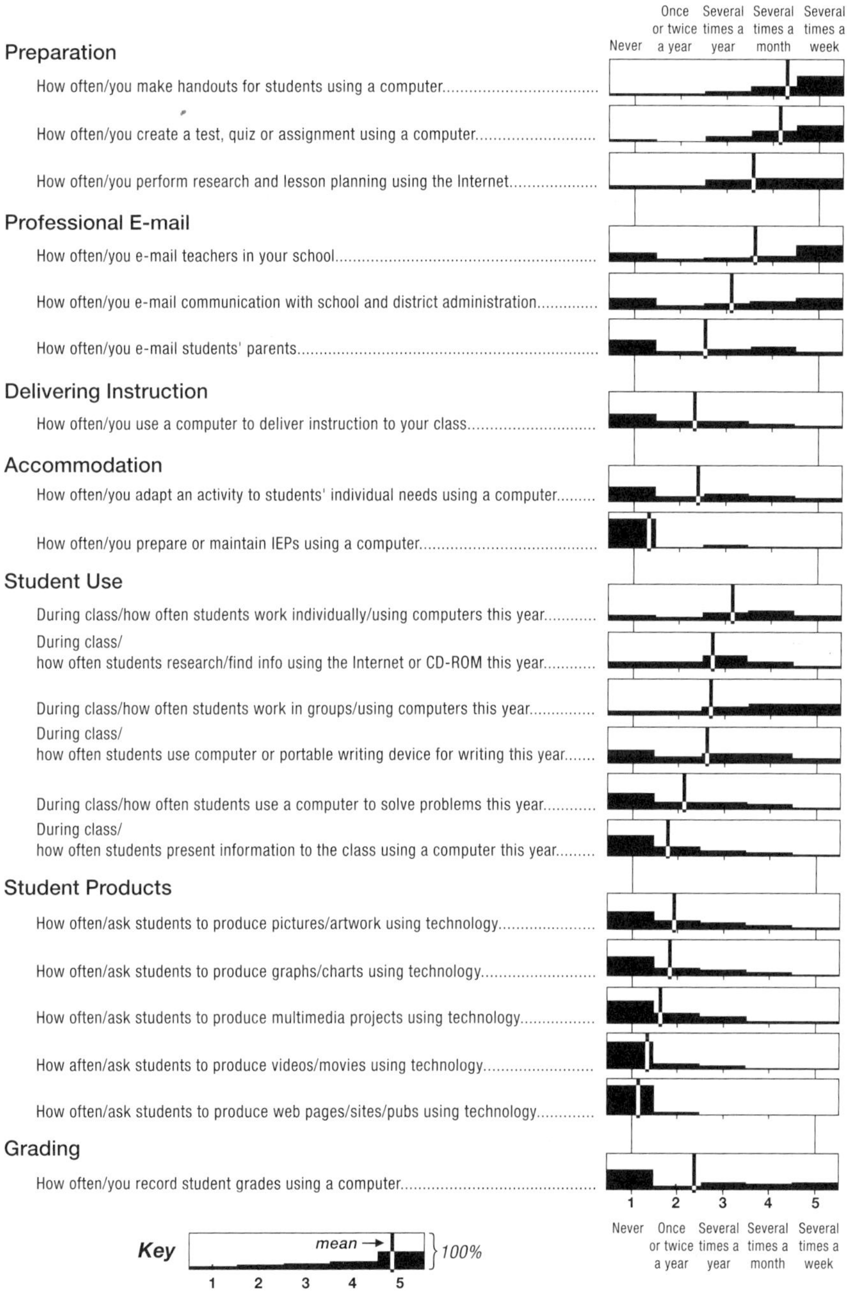

Figure 3.2 Distribution and mean frequency of use for items comprised in the seven categories of teacher technology use

Although examining teacher responses at the item level is informative and may reveal interesting patterns across items, patterns become easier to identify when items that focus on related uses of technology are combined into a single measure. As described previously, principal component analyses were used to identify the items that have strong intercorrelations and thus can be combined to form a single measure that represents a specific category of technology use. Furthermore, because the same 5-point response options, which correspond to the frequency of technology use, were used for all of the items that form the seven categories of technology use, an aggregate score for each category of use was calculated by summing each teacher's response across the survey items forming each category and then dividing by the number of items related to that category. The aggregate scores for each category of technology use are displayed in Figure 3.3.

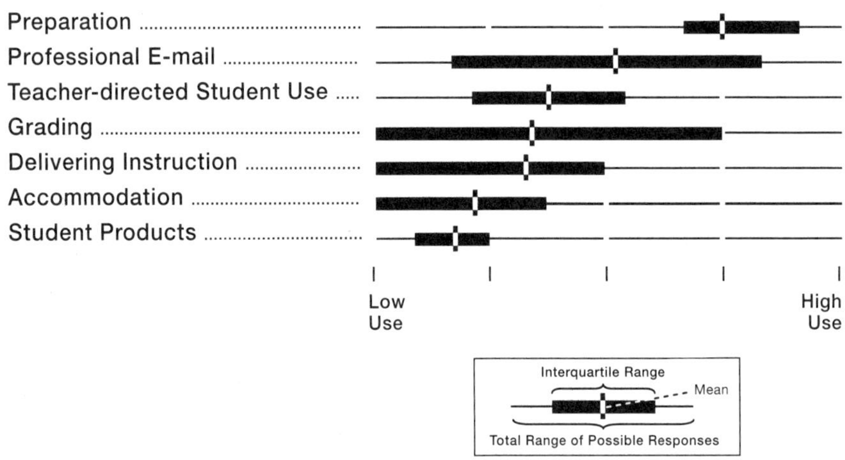

Figure 3.3 Degree of use for seven categories of technology use

As shown in Figure 3.3, teachers reported that the extent of technology use is highest for preparation. The next most frequent use is for e-mail, followed by teacher-directed student use of technology and the use of technology for grading. Note that with the exception of preparation, teachers (on average) report low to moderate levels of use for each category, with use for accommodation and for the creation of student products occurring least frequently. It is important to note, however, that the sample of teachers on which these analyses are based excludes special education teachers, who are perhaps more likely to develop accommodations for lessons.

Although it is procedurally easier to form a single composite score by combining responses across all items than it is to form multiple categories of use, a richer understanding of how technology is and is not being used by teachers results when multiple categories of use are employed. As an example, recall that the USEIT sample of teachers was normally distributed on the generic measure of technology use (Figure 3.1). This normal distribution indicates that most teachers are making moderate use of technology and that relatively few teachers are using technology heavily or not at all. The distribution of responses for the seven separate technology measures, however, suggest that the distribution of use varies dramatically across the separate categories of use. As shown in Figure 3.4, the distribution of teacher use of technology for instruction is positively skewed (skewness = 1.09) rather than normally distributed. This indicates that the majority of the teachers in this sample do not use technology for instruction very often. In fact, nearly 900 teachers indicated that they never use technology to deliver instruction.

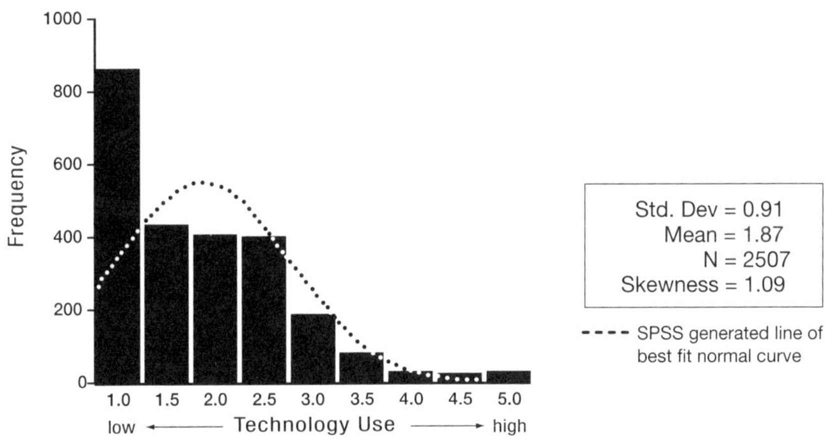

Figure 3.4 Histogram of teachers' use of technology for Delivering Instruction

In contrast, Figure 3.5 indicates that the use of technology for preparation is negatively skewed (skewness = −1.12), with most of the teachers reporting a high frequency of preparation use.

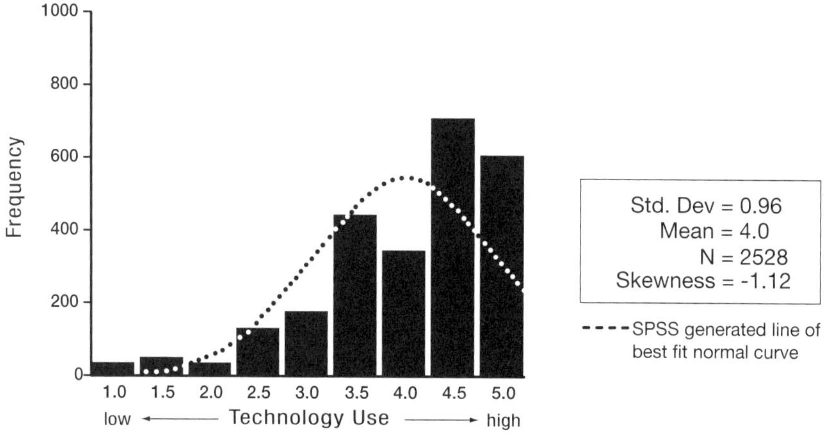

Figure 3.5 Histogram of teachers' use of technology for Preparation

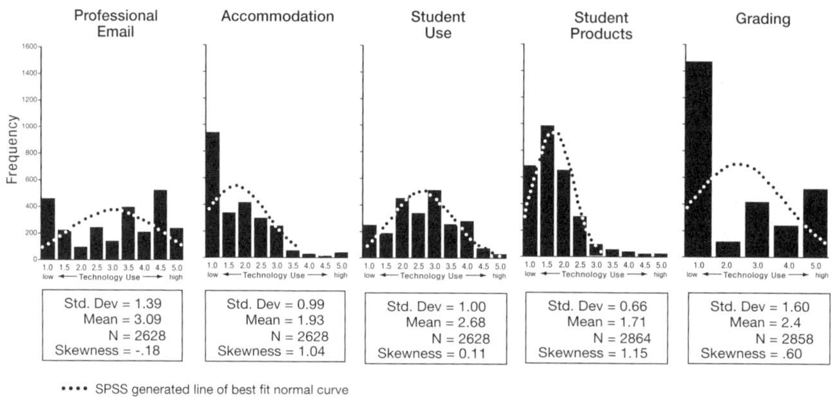

Figure 3.6 Histogram of the five remaining measures of teachers' technology use

Figure 3.6 displays the histograms for the five remaining technology use measures. As with Delivering Instruction, the distributions for Student Products use (1.15) and Accommodation (1.04) have large positive skews. Grading use (0.60) also has a weak positive skew, whereas teacher-directed Student Use during class time (0.11) is relatively normally distributed. Professional E-mail use (skewness = –0.18), however, appears bimodal, with a large percentage of teachers reporting frequent use and a large portion of the sample reporting no use.

In short, by measuring teachers' use of technology using specific measures, we see important differences in the frequency with which teachers use technology for a specific use as well as differences in how these uses vary across teachers. When compared to a single generic measure of technology use, multiple measures of specific technology use offer a more nuanced understanding of how teachers are using technology and how these uses vary among teachers.

Correlation among Technology Uses

By developing separate measures of teachers' technology use, we are not implying that each individual measure is unrelated to the other technology use measures. Indeed, it would be reasonable to assume that all of the measures have some degree of relation to each other. The strength of the relationships among the seven technology uses are examined via Pearson correlation coefficients, which are presented in Table 3.1.

Table 3.1 Correlation Table of the Seven Specific Teacher Technology Measures

	Accom.	Delivery	Prof. E-mail	Prep.	Student Use	Student Products	Grading
Accommodation	1.00						
Delivery	0.26	1.00					
Prof. E-mail	0.26	0.25	1.00				
Preparation	0.27	0.26	0.35	1.00			
Student Use	0.32	0.47	0.22	0.27	1.00		
Student Products	0.23	0.33	0.18	0.33	0.46	1.00	
Grading	0.11	0.17	0.15	0.24	0.07	0.00	1.00

Table 3.1 shows that the correlations among the seven teacher technology use measures are all positive, but generally indicate weak to moderate relationships. The positive intercorrelations suggest that teachers who use technology for one purpose are, on average, likely to use technology for other purposes. Likewise, a teacher who never uses one form of technology is likely to be an infrequent user of other technologies. However, the moderate to weak correlations also suggest that there is considerable variation between the extent to which teachers use technology for one purpose and the extent to which they use technology for another purpose.

Across the seven categories of technology use, the median correlation is 0.26. When examining the correlations between any two of the technology uses, two measures have intercorrelation coefficients that are larger than 0.4 (Delivery correlated with Student Use and Student Use correlated with Student Products). Aside from these relationships, there are four examples of correlations above 0.3 (Accommodation correlated with Student Use, Delivery correlated with Student Products, Preparation correlated with Professional E-mail, and Preparation correlated with Student Products). Again, it is logical that there is a positive relationship between these pairs of measures. Yet, the relatively weak to moderate correlations among each of the uses suggest that each teacher technology category does represent a separate aspect of technology use.

How Multiple Measures of Technology Use Improve Understanding

Although the seven teacher technology use measures are weakly to moderately related to each other, the analyses just presented provide evidence that (a) each measure does represent a separate and distinct category of technology use, and (b) the frequency and distribution of technology use varies considerably across the seven measures. In this section, we examine how the use of separate measures of technology use provides insight into the ways in which technology use varies across different groups of teachers. Specifically, we examine patterns of use for (a) teachers who have been in the profession for different lengths of time, (b) teachers who teach in different school types (i.e., elementary versus middle/high school), and (c) teachers who teach different subject areas (English/language arts, mathematics, social studies/geography, and science). These analyses are presented to illustrate how our understanding of technology use changes when a single generic measure of use versus multiple specific measures is used.

Technology Use by Years Teaching

It is commonly believed that as new teachers—who have grown up with and are comfortable using technology—enter the teaching profession, technology use in schools will increase (National Center for Education Statistics, 2000). When examining use of technology by teachers using a generic measure that comprises a variety of types of technology use, it appears that the frequency with which teachers use technology does not vary noticeably across the number of years in the profession. As seen in Figure 3.7, teachers who are brand new to the profession report almost the same amount of use as do teachers who have been in the profession for 11 or more years.

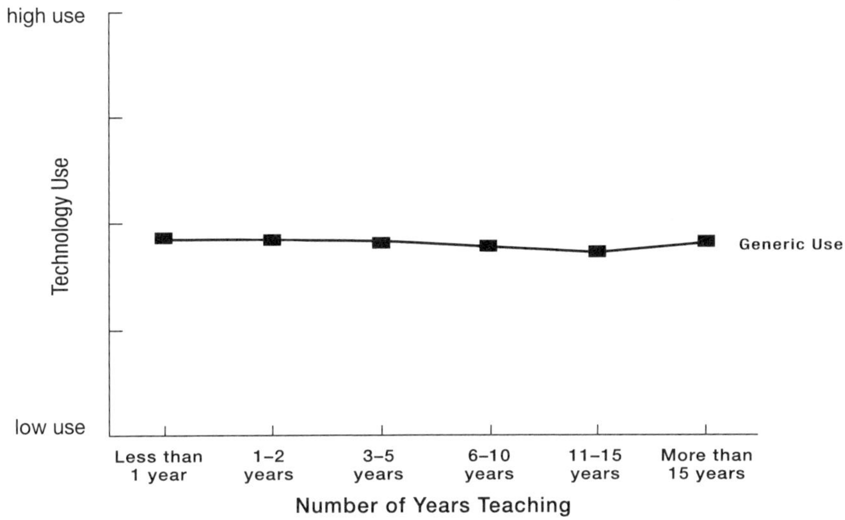

Figure 3.7 Comparison of generic technology use measure across the number of years teacher has taught

However, when multiple measures of technology use are employed, the pattern changes noticeably. As depicted in Figure 3.8, newer teachers report higher levels of technology use for preparation and slightly higher levels of use for accommodation than do more experienced teachers. Conversely, new teachers report less frequent use of technology for delivery and report asking students to use technology during class time less frequently than do their more experienced colleagues.

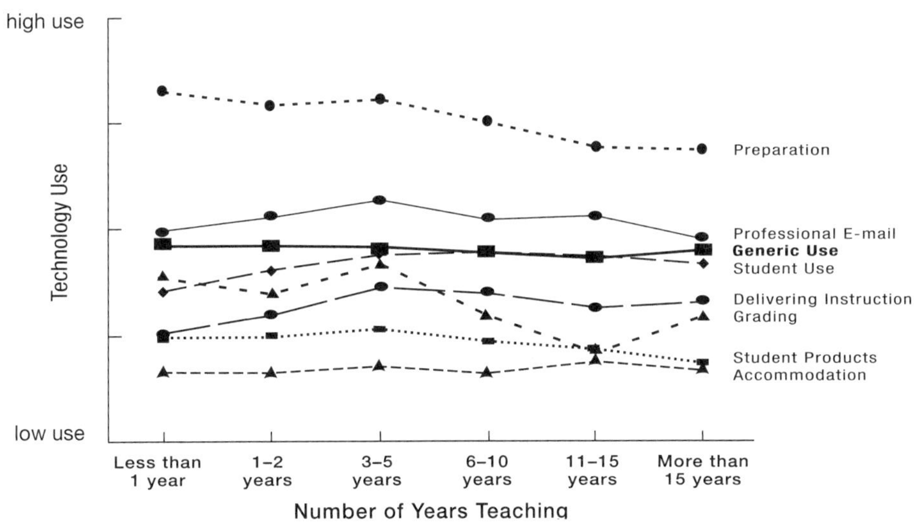

Figure 3.8 Comparison of multiple technology measures across the number of years teacher has taught

A similar pattern occurs when examining the relationship between technology use and school type. As shown in Figure 3.9, the frequency with which teachers report using technology appears to be nearly identical in elementary and in middle/high schools based on a generic measure of technology use. However, interesting differences appear when multiple measures of technology use are examined. Although teachers in both settings report about the same amount of use for Delivering Instruction, for Professional E-mail, and for Student Products, elementary teachers report using technology to accommodate lessons and asking their students to use technology during class time more frequently than do the middle/high school teachers. Conversely, the middle/high school teachers report using technology for preparation at a higher frequency than do the elementary school teachers. By far, however, the largest difference in use occurs for grading, which middle/high school teachers report occurring much more frequently than do their elementary school counterparts.

Although the differences are less dramatic across subject areas, the way in which technology use is defined also influences our perception of how technology use differs across subject areas. As seen in Figure 3.10, there appears to be little difference in the frequency of technology use across English/language arts, social studies/geography, and science teachers when technology use is defined with a generic measure. Using this generic measure, it also appears that mathematics teachers use technology less frequently than the other three groups of teachers. When employing multiple measures of technology use, we see a similar pattern for most uses, with mathematics teachers reporting the lowest levels of use for Preparation, Student Use during class time, and Student Products. For each of these uses, however, the difference in use between mathematics teachers and teachers of the other subjects is larger than it is for the generic use measure. However, mathematics teachers appear to use technology to deliver instruction about as frequently as any other group and report noticeably higher levels of use for grading. Although less dramatic, the way in which technology use differs between the other subject areas also changes when individual categories of use are examined. Perhaps most notably, whereas English, social studies, and science teachers appear similar with respect to the generic measure, English teachers report using technology for grading less and use technology for accommodations more than teachers of the other two subject areas.

Although there are many possible reasons that may explain the differences in use just noted, our purpose here for examining patterns of use is to demonstrate how these patterns differ depending on how one defines and measures technology use. Whereas there appears to be little difference in the frequency with which teachers use technology based on their years teaching, their school type, or across most subject areas (except mathematics) when a generic measure of technology use is employed, important differences appear when technology use is examined as a multidimensional construct.

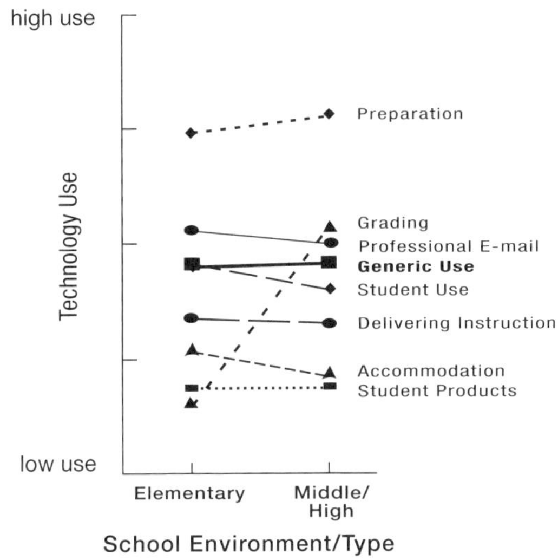

Figure 3.9 Comparison of different technology measures across school type

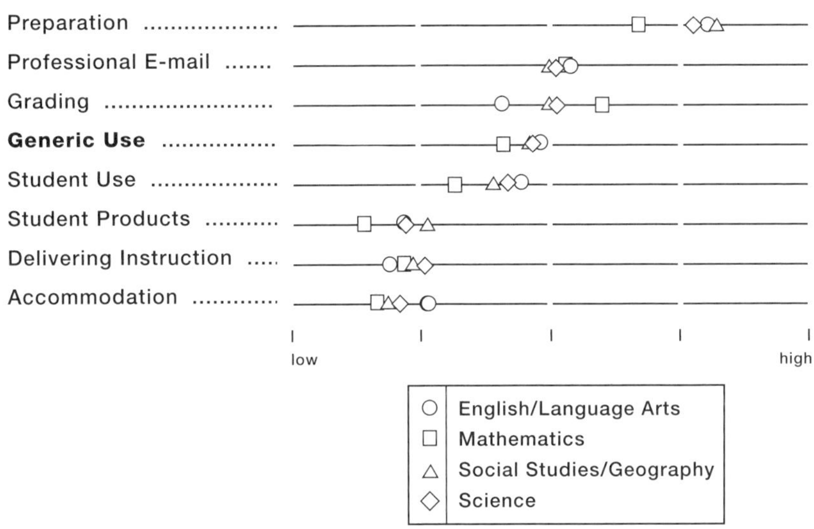

Figure 3.10 Comparison of different technology measures across subject areas

Discussion

Investments in educational technology have sparked important questions about the impact of technology on teaching and learning. In turn, leaders and researchers at the district, state, and national levels are making efforts both to increase use of technology by teachers and students and to examine technology's effects on student learning. In many cases, however, definitions of technology use vary substantially across settings and studies, and technology use is often examined in a generic fashion. The analyses presented here demonstrate the value of conceiving of technology use as multiple categories or types of use rather than a single generic construct. Using 21 survey items that focus on specific uses of technology, the analyses just presented demonstrate the following:

- Separate measures that represent distinct categories of technology use can be formed.
- Although these measures are correlated positively with each other, the relationships are weak enough to suggest that each category represents a separate and distinct type of use.
- The use of distinct measures versus a generic measure provides a richer, more nuanced understanding of how technology use differs across factors such as teacher tenure, school type, and subject area taught.

The implications of this approach are especially applicable to the future development of surveys and other research instruments designed to measure teachers' use of technology. For example, a district interested in documenting the extent to which teachers are using technology or the extent to which teachers' use of technology changes in response to the acquisition of more resources or the provision of professional development is likely to develop a richer understanding by collecting information about the specific types of teachers' technology use rather than simply measuring its generic presence or absence.

Using a multifaceted approach to measure teachers' use of technology also brings to bear the general issue of how complicated and varied technology use actually is in today's schools. In good faith, a principal can no longer evaluate a teacher based on whether the teacher is using technology or not, but rather the question should evolve to include *how* a teacher is making use of various technologies and for what purposes.

In fact, in keeping with previous research findings, our examination of educational technology use shows that the majority of teachers' use of technology goes on behind the scenes with lesson preparation, grading, and professional e-mail use rather than instructional use or teacher-directed student use (Becker, 1999; Cuban, 2001; Russell, Bebell, O'Dwyer, & O'Connor, 2003). For this reason, the traditional methodological tool of classroom observations would fail to capture these activities in an evaluation or research study. Similarly, studies that focus entirely on student-reported data (Edwards, 2002) would also fail to capture the most frequent and pervasive teacher uses of technology.

This point is also directly relevant when examining the relationship between technology use and its impacts on student learning. Although several studies have documented positive effects of technology use on student learning when the technology is used directly by students (see Goldberg, Russell, & Cook, 2003; Kulik, 1994; and Sivin-Kachala, 1998, for meta-analyses of nearly 700 studies), the analyses presented here suggest that teacher-directed student use of technology during class time represents just one category of use. Moreover, teacher-directed student use during class time is reported to occur less frequently in comparison to teachers' use for preparation or communication. Although it is unquestionably important to understand how student use of technology affects student learning, it is equally important to examine the relationship between student learning and other uses of technology by teachers that directly support instruction. Clearly, this type of analysis can only be conducted if multiple measures of technology use are employed.

Finally, it is important to recognize that although we strongly advocate for multiple measures of technology use, we are not suggesting that the uses we have employed represent a definitive body of uses or that the items used to form each measure are exhaustive. To the contrary, we believe that as researchers and educators who are familiar with educational technology consider the full range of ways in which technology is currently being used, additional categories of use will be identified. Similarly, as new technologies become available and as ubiquitous computing becomes more prominent in schools, specific uses of technology will emerge and categories of technology use will expand. Although it may seem efficient to "borrow" surveys or items that have been used for other research or evaluations, doing so may fail to capture the full range in which teachers are using existing and recently acquired technologies for a variety of purposes. It is for these reasons that we encourage schools, districts, and researchers who will be using surveys to document technology use to begin by defining the categories or types of use of interest, and to then develop items related to each category of use.

As an example, when developing the teacher survey for the USEIT Study, we theorized that teachers' technology use fell into four categories and developed several items related to each category. These theoretical categories included teachers' professional technology use outside of class time, teachers' use of technology during class time (including student-directed uses), teachers assigning work that required students to use specific technology, and teachers' communication through e-mail. As described earlier, our analyses of the teachers' responses to the survey led us to identify seven specific and independent uses of technology by teachers. This expansion occurred because three uses, which originally were subsumed within another category of use, were found to be independent. As an example, we had originally believed that grading was part of professional use outside of the classroom, and thus would be strongly related to creating tests, handouts, and using the Internet to prepare for lessons. Similarly, we believed that teachers' use of technology to deliver instruction and to make accommodations were components of technology use during class time. However, our analyses indicate that teachers' technology use for delivery and to accommodate lessons operated independently of teachers asking students to use technology during class time and that teachers' use of technology for grading operated independently of preparation. Having learned this, before conducting similar research in the future, we could increase the reliability of our measures and the amount of information provided about each category of use by developing additional items to measure the categories of use that have emerged from our analyses of the USEIT survey data.

In closing, during recent decades a wide variety of computer-based technologies that can and are being used for educational purposes have emerged. Without question, the variety of technologies and the multiple ways in which some technologies can be used for educational purposes complicate efforts to document technology use and the effect of these uses on teaching and learning. As we have shown using a limited number of survey items, simply conceiving of a variety of uses of technology as a single generic measure of technology use masks far more than it reveals.

Acknowledgments

This research was supported under the Field Initiated Study Grant Program, PR/Award Number R305T010065, as administered by the Office of Educational Research and Improvement, U.S. Department of Education. The findings and opinions expressed in this report do not reflect the positions or policies of the Office of Educational Research and Improvement or the U.S. Department of Education.

Author Update

In an effort to better define and measure the ways teachers use technology to support teaching and learning, we examined survey responses from more than 2,500 teachers using factor analytic techniques. Our analyses demonstrated that defining and measuring multiple, distinct technology uses was more informative than using a more general "technology use" metric. Specifically, our analyses suggested that teachers' use of technology is multifaceted and cannot be meaningfully collapsed into a single metric.

In the six years since the original 2004 *JRTE* publication, the possibilities for how teachers employ educational technology has only grown more nuanced (and complicated). Moreover, it's important to consider that the data we used in this chapter to demonstrate the multifaceted nature of teachers' technology use were collected in early 2001, from traditional K–12 learning environments. Indeed, since that time, the expectations of how (and why) teachers use technology has continued to evolve rapidly, as represented by the recent (2008) revisions to the ISTE National Educational Technology Standards for Teachers. Quite simply, the more types of educational technology infiltrate schools, the more potential ways there are for teachers to employ technology to support teaching and learning.

Similarly, the past decade has witnessed large increases in the number of schools that have adopted 1-to-1 technology access—providing environments where teachers can employ novel uses of technology with their students. Not surprisingly, one of the central themes to emerge from research into 1-to-1 settings has been the recognition of classroom teachers as critical gatekeepers to student technology use. Given this recognition of teachers and the importance of their technology-related practices in the classroom, it is vital that we, as researchers, find the best methods to recognize and measure the various ways in which teachers use technology.

References

Becker, H. (1994). *Analysis and trends of school use of new information technologies.* Washington, DC: Office of Technology Assessment.

Becker, H. (1999). *Internet use by teachers: Conditions of professional use and teacher-directed student use.* Irvine, CA: Center for Research on Information Technology and Organizations.

Cuban, L. (2001). *Oversold & underused: Computers in the classroom.* Cambridge, MA: Harvard University Press.

Edwards, V. (Ed.). (2002). Technology counts 2002 [Special Issue]. *Education Week, 21*(35).

Goldberg, A., Russell, M., & Cook, A. (2003). The effect of computers on student writing: A meta-analysis of studies from 1992 to 2002. *Journal of Technology, Learning, and Assessment, 2*(1). Retrieved October 21, 2003, from www.bc.edu/research/intasc/jtla/journal/v2n1.shtml

Kulik, J. (1994). Meta-analytic studies of findings on computer-based instruction. In E. Baker & H. O'Neil, Jr. (Eds.), *Technology assessment in education and training* (pp. 9–33). Hillsdale, NJ: Lawrence Erlbaum.

Lerman, J. (1998). *You've got mail: 10 nifty ways teachers can use e-mail to extend kids' learning.* Retrieved January 10, 2003, from www.electronic-school.com/0398f5.html

McNabb, M., Hawkes, M., & Rouk, U. (1999). *Critical issues in evaluating the effectiveness of technology.* Proceedings of the Secretary's Conference on Educational Technology: Evaluating the Effectiveness of Technology. Retrieved January 10, 2003, from www.ed.gov/Technology/TechConf/1999/confsum.html

National Center for Education Statistics, U.S. Department of Education. (2000). *Teachers' tools for the 21st Century. A report on teachers' use of technology.* Washington, DC: Author. Retrieved January 10, 2003, from http://nces.ed.gov/spider/webspider/2000102.shtml (Eric Document Reproduction Service No. ED 444599).

Office of Technology Assessment, U.S. Congress. (1988). *Power on! New tools for teaching and learning.* Washington, DC: U.S. Government Printing Office.

Office of Technology Assessment, U.S. Congress. (1989). *Linking and learning: A new course for education.* Washington, DC: U.S. Government Printing Office.

Office of Technology Assessment, U.S. Congress. (1995). *Teachers and technology: Making the connection,* OTA-EHR-616. Washington, DC: U.S. Government Printing Office.

Ravitz, J., & Wong, Y. (2000, April). How teaching philosophies relevant to computer use originate: Effects of educational background, teaching responsibilities, and computer experience. In H. Becker (Chair), *When does computer use contribute to pedagogical reform?* Paper presented at the annual meeting of the American Educational Research Association, New Orleans, LA.

Ravitz, J., Wong, Y., & Becker, H. (1998). *Teaching, learning, and computing: A national survey of schools and teachers describing their best practices, teaching philosophies, and uses of technology.* Irvine, CA: Center for Research on Information Technology and Organizations.

Ravitz, J., Wong, Y., & Becker, H. (1999). *Teacher and teacher directed student use of computers and software.* Irvine, CA: Center for Research on Information Technology and Organizations.

Ravitz, J., Wong, Y., & Becker, H. (2000). *Constructivist-compatible and practices among US teachers.* Irvine, CA: Center for Research on Information Technology and Organizations.

Rowand, C. (2000). *Teacher use of computers and the Internet in public schools. Stats in brief.* Washington, DC: National Center for Education Statistics.

Russell, M., Bebell, D., & O'Dwyer, L. (2003). *An overview of the USEIT study and the participating districts.* Boston, MA: Technology and Assessment Study Collaborative, Boston College.

Russell, M., Bebell, D., O'Dwyer, L., & O'Connor, K. (2003). Examining teacher technology use: Implications for preservice and inservice teacher preparation. *Journal of Teacher Education, 54*(4) 297–310.

Russell, M., O'Dwyer, L., Bebell, D., & Miranda, H. (2003). *The USEIT study technical report.* Boston, MA: Technology and Assessment Study Collaborative, Boston College.

Sivin-Kachala, J. (1998). *Report on the effectiveness of technology in schools, 1990–1997.* Washington, DC: Software Publisher's Association.

CHAPTER

4

Teacher Dispositions as Predictors of Classroom Technology Use

Rachel A. Vannatta | Bowling Green State University

Nancy Fordham | Bowling Green State University

This study examined various teacher dispositions that predict technology use among K–12 teachers. The Teacher Attribute Survey was administered to 177 K–12 teachers from six Northwest Ohio schools. This instrument measured a variety of teacher attributes, such as teacher self-efficacy, philosophy, openness to change, amount of professional development, and amount of technology use in the classroom. A forward multiple regression was conducted to identify the best combination of variables that predicts classroom technology use among K–12 teachers. Results indicate that the factor combination of amount of technology training, time spent beyond contractual work week, and openness to change best predicted classroom technology use.

Introduction

Although many preservice and inservice teacher programs have sought to improve the preparation of teachers to use technology as an effective instructional tool, many teacher educators and school administrators have realized that technology training alone does not create an effective technology-using teacher. Numerous studies have sought to better understand why some teachers use technology and others do not. However, much of the research has examined technology-specific variables (e.g., attitudes and beliefs toward computers, computer self-efficacy, technology proficiency) as predictors of technology use among teachers (Dupagne & Krendl, 1992; Marcinkiewicz, 1994; Milbrath & Kinzie, 2000). In contrast, the researchers were interested in examining how general or non-technology-specific teacher attributes work with technology training to predict classroom technology use.

Research has found that the personal beliefs and dispositions of teachers may relate to or predict successful technology integration. Honey and Moeller (1990) assert that teacher philosophy (student-centered versus teacher-centered) affected one's ability to effectively use technology in the classroom, in that student-centered teachers were more successful. MacArthur and Malouf (1991) determined in their case study that teacher beliefs and attitudes greatly influenced how computers were used in the classroom. Other personal variables, such as self-competence and willingness to change, have also been shown to be closely related to computer use among teachers (Marcinkiewicz, 1994). Albion (1999) states that teachers' beliefs, specifically self-efficacy beliefs, "are an important, and measurable, component of the beliefs that influence technology integration" (p. 2).

The researchers were also interested in how the construct of commitment to teaching improvement was a factor in predicting technology use among teachers. Although literature is limited on this proposed relationship, the researchers had observed in several teacher technology training programs that the teachers who took the time to "play" with technology and were interested in learning despite external rewards were the ones who made the greatest gains in technology use. With these observations and results in mind, the researchers sought to examine a broad array of teacher characteristics to better understand how these personal attributes work together to predict technology use in the classroom. Results from such a study could guide teacher educators and educational leaders in facilitating teacher dispositions that may improve the likelihood of technology integration in the classroom—integration that can be an awesome tool in enhancing student achievement (Schacter, 1999).

Methodology

This study sought to identify teacher dispositions as predictors of technology use in the classroom. The following research question guided the study:

Which combination of factors best predict classroom technology use among K–12 teachers: teacher self-efficacy, teacher philosophy, openness to change, amount of professional development, amount of technology training, years of teaching, hours worked beyond the contractual work week, and willingness to complete graduate courses without salary incentive?

PARTICIPANTS

Six northwest Ohio schools were asked to participate in the study. Four schools were elementary, two were high schools. These schools were selected because of their involvement in a Preparing Tomorrow's Teachers to use Technology (PT^3) grant at Bowling Green State University that provided a great deal of technology training to teachers over a three-year period. During this time, approximately eight teachers per school participated in the PT^3 training program. Because several studies have shown that teacher technology use at a typical school is quite low (PT^3, n.d.), the researchers hoped that the increased opportunities for technology training within the participating schools would help create a more normal distribution of classroom technology use within the sample. The total number of K–12 teachers employed at the six schools was 245. Teachers were asked to complete the survey during scheduled faculty meetings, held either before or after school during March/April 2002. The Teacher Attribute Survey (TAS) was completed by 177 teachers, 137 of whom were female. Whereas nearly 100% of the elementary teachers completed the survey, many high school teachers were unable to attend the scheduled meetings because of extracurricular activity supervision duties. After data were screened, a total of seven cases were eliminated as outliers, thus producing a sample of N = 170.

Two of the elementary schools were located in medium-sized, rural cities and were composed of primarily Caucasian staff and students. One elementary school was in a suburb and served a low number of minority students. The fourth elementary school was in a small rural city that includes a small percentage of immigrants. All participating elementary schools had four computers in each classroom. One of the participating high schools was located in a small rural town and had minimal technology resources available to faculty and students. The other participating high school was located in a suburban area and provided a technology-rich environment for faculty and students that typically included a teacher station and projection system in each classroom and access to multiple computer labs in the building.

INSTRUMENTATION

To measure the targeted teacher characteristics as well as classroom technology use, the Teacher Attribute Survey (TAS) was developed by the researchers to assess teacher self-efficacy, teacher philosophy, openness to change, amount of professional development, amount of technology training, years of teaching, hours worked beyond the contractual work week, and amount of teacher and student use of technology in the classroom (see Appendix 4.A). Although the authors were interested in measuring additional variables, such as attitudes and beliefs toward technology and technology integration, technology proficiency, personality types, and self-concept, they based the final selection of possible predictors on professional observation and literature support, previously presented. The 71-item survey consisted of items written by the researchers as well as revised items from existing instruments. Table 4.1 summarizes TAS as it presents the measured constructs, respective definitions, items, sources, scales, and reliability coefficients.

Items written by the researchers included amount of professional development and technology training, years of teaching, willingness to take graduate course without incentive, hours worked beyond contractual work week, and openness to change. Items that measured years of teaching and amount of professional development and technology training were open-ended, in that respondents wrote in the appropriate number. Although technology training is certainly a part of a teacher's professional development, one's professional development does not always include technology training. Thus, the researchers were interested in examining these two variables as distinct independent variables.

The construct of commitment to teacher improvement was measured by two variables. Willingness to take graduate courses without a salary incentive was addressed in item 31 and used the 6-point Likert scale ranging from strongly disagree (1) to strongly agree (6). Item 69 measured the number of hours one works beyond the contractual work week and provided six options: (1) none, (2) 1–5 hours, (3) 6–10 hours, (4) 11–15 hours, (5) 16–20 hours, and (6) 21 or more hours. Because this construct was measured with only two items, item results were treated separately and were not combined to create a factor.

The construct of openness to change was developed after a review of the literature. Five items (26–30) were created to measure one's comfort and excitement when trying new methods of instruction as well as willingness to take risks and make mistakes (Hurt, Joseph, & Cook, 1997; Marcinkiewicz, 1991, 1992). These items employed a 6-point Likert scale, ranging from strongly disagree (1) to strongly agree (6).

Several reliable existing instruments were utilized in the development of TAS. Woolfolk and Hoy's (1990) Teacher Efficacy Scale was adapted to measure one's belief in affecting student performance. These items (1–16) utilized a 6-point Likert scale. Items measuring teacher philosophy were adapted from Becker and Anderson's (1998) Teaching, Learning, and Computing Survey, Part J: Your Teaching Philosophy. The first set of items (17–25) measured teacher support of a teacher-centered or student-centered instructional environment and applied a 6-point scale. The second set of items (32–36) addressing teacher philosophy measured teacher adoption of a constructivist or a traditionalist environment. These items were similar to a semantic differential scale in which bipolar teacher statements regarding beliefs relative to teaching and learning were presented with a 5-point scale placed between opposing scenarios. Respondents were asked to check the box that best described their own beliefs. Because two different scales were applied in measuring teacher philosophy, two philosophy factors were created and utilized in the regression analysis.

The portion of the TAS that measured technology use was adapted from Vannatta and O'Bannon's (2002) Faculty Technology Survey. Items 37–51 measured teacher frequency of using a variety of tools/applications during the previous semester. Teacher use was defined as use during one's instruction (e.g., teacher demonstration, use of tool/application during presentation). A 4-point scale was applied: (1) none, (2) rarely—once or twice per semester, (3) moderate—several times per semester, and (4) high—almost weekly per semester. Student technology use was addressed in items 52–66 and was defined as frequency of student use in one's classes during the previous semester. The same scale found in teacher use was applied to student use.

After the TAS was developed, administration guidelines were written. School principals were contacted to arrange survey administration. In the meantime, the TAS was piloted with 20 K–12 teachers. Several items were revised for purposes of clarity. Instrument validation was also conducted through an expert panel review. Three scholars in the field of educational technology and/or measurement were asked to review the TAS. Definitions of factor constructs and a description of the instrument purpose were provided. Reviewers suggested minor revisions and supported the TAS in its content and purpose.

Survey administration was conducted during the month of April by the two researchers and a graduate assistant. Refreshments were provided during the meeting. In addition, participants were eligible for door prizes that consisted of restaurant gift certificates. Survey completion was voluntary and required approximately 15–20 minutes. Reliability of the TAS and each subscale was calculated using Cronbach's alpha (see Table 4.1). TAS reliability for the studied sample was $\alpha = .9083$. Such a high level of reliability is most likely due to the utilization of existing reliable instruments.

DATA ANALYSIS

Once data were collected, several items were recoded to create unidirectional variables (see Table 4.2). Factors were then generated by calculating the mean for the following groups of items: self-efficacy (items 1–16), philosophy 1 (items 17–25), philosophy 2 (items 32–36), openness to change (items 26–30), teacher use of technology (items 37–51),

Table 4.1 Variable Summary of Teacher Attribute Survey

Variable	Definition	Items	Source	Scale	Cronbach α
Teacher Self-Efficacy	Beliefs of ability to affect student performance	M (1–16)	Teacher Efficacy Scale (Woolfolk & Hoy, 1990)	1–6	.7287
Teacher Philosophy 1	Teacher-centered versus Student-centered	M (17–25)	Teaching, Learning, and Computing Survey, Part J: Your Teaching Philosophy (Becker & Anderson, 1998)	1–6	.6102
Teacher Philosophy 2	Constructivist versus Traditionalist	M (32–36)	Teaching, Learning, and Computing Survey, Part J: Your Teaching Philosophy (Becker & Anderson, 1998)	1–5	.6914
Openness to Change	Willingness to take risks and learn from mistakes	M (26–30)		1–6	.6919
Teacher Use of Tech	Frequency of instructor use of a variety of technology tools and applications in the classroom	M (37–51)	Faculty Technology Survey (Vannatta & O'Bannon, 2002)	1–4	.8516
Student Use of Tech	Frequency of student use of a variety of technology tools and applications in the classroom	M (52–66)	Faculty Technology Survey (Vannatta & O'Bannon, 2002)	1–4	.7966
Overall Use of Tech	Frequency of instructor and student use of a variety of technology tools and applications in the classroom	M (37–66)	Faculty Technology Survey (Vannatta & O'Bannon, 2002)	1–4	.8878
Continue Grad Course without Salary Incentive	Willingness to take graduate courses if no salary incentive was available	31		1–6	
Professional Development	# of actual hours in past two years	67		open	
Technology Training	# of actual hours in past two years	68		open	
# Hours beyond Work Week	# of hours one typically works beyond the contractual work week to prepare for teaching	69		1–6	
Gender	Male (1) or Female (2)	70		1–2	
# of Years Teaching		71		open	

student use of technology (items 52–66), and overall classroom use of technology (items 37–66). Descriptive statistics were calculated for each item and factor. Data were screened for possible outliers, linearity, and normality. One outlier was eliminated for the variable of technology training (that greater than 200 hours), and six outliers were eliminated for the variable of professional development (those greater than 400 hours). In addition, these two variables were substantially positively skewed and therefore were transformed using the logarithm. An ANOVA examined possible differences in overall technology use by school, as hardware accessibility varied by school. A forward multiple regression was conducted to identify the best combination of factors/variables that predict overall classroom technology use. Ten variables were entered into the equation: teacher self-efficacy, teacher philosophy 1, teacher philosophy 2, openness to change, willingness to complete graduate course without salary incentive, amount of professional development, amount of technology training, number of hours worked beyond work week, and number of years teaching. Gender was the only TAS variable excluded in this analysis for several reasons: categorical variables are not typically included in a regression analysis; gender is an innate characteristic that is unchangeable; and the researchers were aware of a possible gender difference in technology use for the sample because many of the participating males had also completed technology training with the authors.

Table 4.2 Means and Standard Deviations of Teacher Attributes

Variable	Recoded items	*M*	*SD*
Teacher Self-Efficacy	3, 4, 8, 10, 11, 12	3.90	.60
Teacher Philosophy 1	17, 18, 20, 21, 22, 23, 25	3.69	.93
Teacher Philosophy 2	32, 34, 35, 36	3.23	.75
Openness to Change	28	4.60	.75
Teacher Use of Tech		2.07	.61
Student Use of Tech		1.59	.53
Overall Use of Tech		1.83	.50
Continue Grad Course $		4.22	1.50
Professional Development		44.32	65.76
Technology Training		19.41	28.01
# Hours beyond Work Week		3.74	1.38
# of Years Teaching		16.11	9.50

Results

Descriptive statistics indicate that classroom technology use is fairly low among teachers and students (see Tables 4.3 and 4.4). In general, teacher use is higher than student use. Word processing, e-mail, and the Internet were the only applications utilized by teachers several times or more per semester. In addition, teacher use of digital cameras, database, spreadsheets, and presentation software slightly exceeded once or twice per semester. Unfortunately, students utilized only two applications—word processing and the Internet—at a frequency that exceeded once or twice per semester.

When combining student and teacher technology use to form overall classroom technology use, the researchers found a fairly normal distribution as revealed in Figure 4.1. Before conducting the regression analysis, the authors were also interested in determining if differences in overall classroom technology use differed by school, as schools had varying levels of hardware accessibility. ANOVA results indicated that the participating schools did not differ in classroom technology use: $F(5, 172) = 1.38, p = .233$.

Table 4.3 Teacher Use of Technology

Item	*M*	*SD*
Computer with Projection System	1.92	1.10
Digital Camera, Camcorder	2.14	1.03
Scanner	1.52	.87
Content-Specific Tools (e.g., digital microscope, graphing calculator)	1.52	.92
Word Processing	3.43	1.22
Database	2.15	1.17
Spreadsheet	2.15	1.17
Drawing/Graphics Programs (e.g., Photoshop, AutoCad)	1.90	1.28
Content-Specific Software (e.g., Inspiration, Accelerated Reader, Timeliner)	1.83	1.02
Presentation Software (e.g., PowerPoint, AppleWorks Slideshow)	2.02	1.13
Multimedia (e.g., HyperStudio, Kid Pix, iMovie, Adobe Premier)	1.89	1.05
E-mail/ Discussion Groups/E-mail Lists	3.22	1.13
Internet (web searches)	3.20	1.04
Class Website (communicate with students and/or parents)	1.85	1.17
Other, please list:	.26	.63
Overall Teacher Use	2.07	.61

Table 4.4 Student Use of Technology

Item	*M*	*SD*
Computer with Projection System	1.42	.77
Digital Camera, Camcorder	1.59	.86
Scanner	1.32	.71
Content-Specific Tools (e.g., digital microscope, graphing calculator)	1.30	.77
Word Processing	2.65	1.09
Database	1.55	1.90
Spreadsheet	1.54	1.46
Drawing/Graphics Programs (e.g., Photoshop, AutoCad)	1.49	.86
Content-Specific Software (e.g., Inspiration, Accelerated Reader, Timeliner)	1.68	.98
Presentation Software (e.g., PowerPoint, AppleWorks Slideshow)	1.71	1.19
Multimedia (e.g., HyperStudio, Kid Pix, iMovie, Adobe Premier)	1.82	1.03
E-mail/ Discussion Groups/E-mail Lists	1.66	1.20
Internet (web searches)	2.44	1.18
Class Website (communicate with students and/or parents)	1.25	.75
Other, please list:	.38	.74
Overall Student Use	1.59	.53

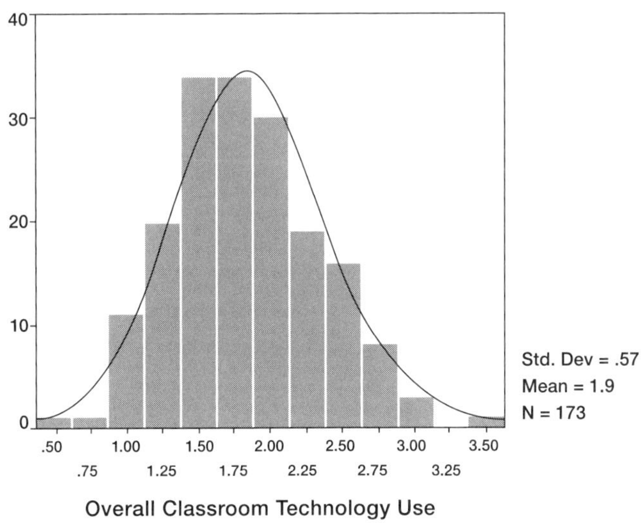

Figure 4.1 Histogram of Overall Classroom Technology Use

A review of the teacher attribute data revealed that the participating teachers had slightly above average self-efficacy, leaned slightly toward a student-centered and constructivist environment, and quite surprisingly were fairly open to change. In the past two years, the participating teachers averaged approximately 44 actual hours of professional development and 19 actual hours of technology training. In addition, the participants indicated that they spend 6–15 hours beyond the contractual work week for teaching preparation and had been teaching on average approximately 16 years.

A forward multiple regression produced a model of three factor/variables that best predicted overall classroom technology use: number of hours of technology training, number of hours worked beyond the contractual work week, and openness to change; $R^2 = .185$, $R^2_{adj} = .170$; $F(3, 166) = 12.54$, $p < .001$. This model accounted for over 18% of variance in classroom technology use. A summary of the model is presented in Table 4.5. In addition, bivariate and partial correlation coefficients between each predictor and the dependent variable are presented in Table 4.6.

Table 4.5 Model Summary

Step	R	R^2	R^2_{adj}	DR^2	F_{chg}	p	df_1	df_2
1. Hours Worked Beyond	.312	.097	.092	.097	18.12	< .001	1	168
2. Technology Training	.390	.152	.142	.055	10.83	.001	1	167
3. Openness to Change	.430	.185	.170	.032	6.59	.011	1	166

Table 4.6 Coefficients for Final Model

	B	b	t	Bivariate r	Partial r
Hours Worked Beyond	.005	.271	3.11*	.312	.285
Technology Training	.073	.199	2.99*	.264	.211
Openness to Change	.124	.185	2.64*	.257	.195

*Note: *Indicates significance at* $p < .01$

Discussion

Findings suggest that whereas technology training is obviously important in developing technology-using educators, a willingness to commit one's time "above and beyond the call of duty" and a risk-taking attitude are also essential. Although previous research has found that technology training and openness to change/innovation independently relate to or predict technology use among teachers (Marcinkiewicz, 1994; Vannatta & O'Bannon, 2002), such studies did not examine these variables together in predicting technology use. In addition, the relationship between time commitment in teaching and technology use has not been established in previous research.

In contrast, this study suggests that the teacher attributes of time commitment to teaching and openness to change *combine with* the amount of technology training to best predict classroom technology use. The process of learning to use technology requires time—time spent in training, but also time spent playing with and exploring technology. This willingness to commit time to the technology learning process may be represented by one's willingness and commitment to spend time beyond the typical work week to prepare instructional activities. As such, this result suggests that time is essential in becoming a technology using teacher, but also that technology use may predict time commitment to teaching.

Because technology is a dynamic innovation, learning to use it as a personal or instructional tool requires a willingness to make mistakes and learn from them and an ability to take risks—this study's definition of the variable, openness to change. As a result, a teacher who approaches technology professional development with an attitude that is open to change and is committed to spending time outside of training to further explore technology may be more likely to use technology in the classroom than one who attends training with ambivalence and a lack of time.

Interestingly, the other teacher attributes examined—teacher philosophy and self-efficacy, which have been found in previous research to predict teacher technology use—were excluded from the generated regression model (Albion, 1999; Becker & Anderson, 1998; Honey & Moeller, 1990). These results indicate that higher levels of classroom technology use were best predicted not only by the amount of technology training a teacher received, but also by the amount of time a teacher spends outside of class preparing for instruction and by a teacher's openness to change regardless of teaching philosophy or beliefs about one's teaching ability. Although research has shown that a constructivist teacher is more apt to utilize technology in the classroom, typically a constructivist teacher uses technology as a tool to advance constructive learning. Although the TAS measured the frequency of teacher and student technology use for a variety of applications, this instrument did not evaluate how technology was used (e.g., quality, student-centered, constructive applications) and therefore was not a focus of the study. The limitations of the TAS may also apply to the exclusion of self-efficacy from the regression model. For the purposes of this study, self-efficacy was defined as one's belief in affecting student performance. This variable was most likely eliminated from the model because the TAS focused on technology use and not on how that use influenced student outcomes.

Recommendations

RECOMMENDATIONS FOR FUTURE RESEARCH

This research suggests that the three teacher attributes of technology training, time commitment to teaching, and openness to change work together to predict overall classroom technology use among K–12 teachers. Because research to support this finding is limited, further study should be conducted on teacher attributes as predictors of classroom technology use. In addition, several limitations of this study have implications for future research: the limited sample with respect to size and heterogeneity, the measurement of frequency of classroom technology use and not quality of such use, and a regression model that accounts for a small portion of variance in classroom technology use. The development of a skilled, reflective technology-using teacher is a complex process. As a result, research that seeks to examine this outcome should take into account this complexity by: (1) studying a variety of teacher attributes (technology and nontechnology) in relation to technology use, (2) applying advanced statistical methods that analyze various combinations of independent variables, (3) utilizing random sampling methods to create a large, heterogeneous sample, and (4) creating valid and reliable instruments that measure the construct of classroom technology use as a whole, taking into account not just frequency but also quality, methods, outcomes, etc. Such research could provide a clearer and broader picture of the classroom technology use. In addition, further study should explore how administrators and teacher educators facilitate teacher attributes such as openness to change and time commitment to teaching.

RECOMMENDATIONS FOR TEACHER EDUCATORS AND ADMINISTRATORS

Teacher educators and administrators should not only provide extensive training on educational technology, but should also facilitate the dispositions of openness to change and commitment to teaching improvement. Clarke and Hollingsworth (2002) note that traditional models of professional development do not acknowledge the complexity of the growth/change process, nor do they reflect current learning theory and research. They add that the role of the environment is pivotal in motivating change behaviors: "The context in which teachers work can have a substantial impact on their professional growth" (p. 962). Hence, administrators in all settings and at all levels play key roles in establishing either "change" or "maintenance" cultures within their educational systems (Fullan, 1993; Sarason, 1990). To develop a culture that facilitates openness to change and commitment to teacher improvement among teachers and/or teacher candidates, the authors recommend that teacher educators and administrators provide teachers with the following:

- Technology training in which teachers personally experience technology's power as a learning tool (Guskey, 1986; Polonoli, 2001)
- Technology training combined with practitioner reflection and numerous demonstrations of effective technology-enhanced lessons
- Regular opportunities for collaboration and reflection with colleagues to discuss pedagogy, instructional practices, and research-based practices (Burns, 2002; Cobb, Wood, & Yackel, 1990; Johnson & Owen, 1986)
- Opportunities for discussion and reflection on one's dispositions and attributes that are brought to the teaching profession and how that affects student learning
- A positive leader who values teachers as learners, research-based practices, and informed risk-taking (Burns, 2002)
- Modeling of risk-taking behaviors with technology

In addition, the authors recommend that school administrators attempt to hire dynamic, reflective practitioners who are committed to ongoing improvement in one's teaching and students.

As the role of technology in society and education dynamically emerges, the adequate preparation of teachers in educational technology is integral to using such a tool effectively in the teaching and learning of our children. Although past literature and research have recommended extensive training in technology skills and pedagogy as the primary components of teacher preparation, this study suggests that technology training should be provided in conjunction with activities that facilitate the teacher dispositions of openness to change and time commitment to teaching improvement. Only in the hands of innovative, informed, and committed professionals in supportive educational cultures can technology serve as a medium for helping children advance confidently into the future.

Author Update

This chapter, first published in 2004, was one of the first to examine nontechnology factors in relation to classroom technology integration. The study was born out of years of working with and observing teachers using technology in the classroom. We were especially interested in examining what role teacher efficacy, philosophy, openness to change, and commitment in conjunction with technology variables predicted technology use.

In the past six years, the knowledge base in this line of research has greatly expanded. We now know that teacher technology use is very complex and involves a multitude of variables. The TPACK framework supports such findings, as it proposes that effective technology integration relies on more than just technology skills but also on pedagogy and content knowledge. The authors continue to explore how other teacher characteristics, such as risk-taking disposition and cognitive style, relate to effective classroom technology use. Another interesting aspect of this study was the measurement of technology integration, which was a major limitation of the study. Although teachers indicated the frequency of various types of technology uses for themselves and their students, the authors were very aware that the construct did not reflect quality of technology integration. This continues to challenge researchers as seen by the many journal issues dedicated to this topic. Currently, the authors are exploring methods in which various technology uses are weighted according to how the technology facilitates students' learning.

References

Albion, P. R. (1999). Self-efficacy beliefs as an indicator of teachers' preparedness for teaching with technology. *Technology and Teacher Education Annual 1999, (Society for Information Technology & Teacher Education)* (CD-ROM edition). Charlottesville, VA: Association for the Advancement of Computing in Education.

Ashton, P., & Webb, R. (1986). *Making a difference: Teachers' sense of efficacy.* New York, NY: Longman.

Becker, H. J., & Anderson, R. E. (1998). *Teaching, learning, and computing: 1998, A national survey of schools and teachers describing their best practices, teaching philosophies, and uses of technology.* Retrieved October 15, 2002, from www.crito.uci.edu/tlc/questionnaires/teachers_qs.pdf

Burns, M. (2002). From compliance to commitment: Technology as a catalyst for communities of learners. *Phi Delta Kappan, 84*(4), 295–302.

Clarke, D., & Hollingsworth, H. (2002). Elaborating a model of teacher professional growth. *Teaching and Teacher Education, 18*, 947–967.

Cobb, P., Wood, T., & Yackel, E. (1990). Classrooms as learning environments for teachers and researchers. In R. B. Davis, C. A. Mayer, & N. Noddings (Eds.), *Constructivist views on the teaching and learning of mathematics* (pp. 125–146). Reston, VA: National Council of Teachers of Mathematics.

Cohen, R. M. (2002). Schools our teachers deserve: A proposal for teacher-centered reform. *Phi Delta Kappan, 83*(7), 532–537.

Corcoran, T., Fuhrman, S. H., & Belcher, C. L. (2001). The district role in instructional improvement. *Phi Delta Kappan, 83*(1), 78–84.

Dupagne, M., & Krendl, K. A. (1992). Teachers' attitudes toward computers: A review of the literature. *Journal of Research on Computing in Education, 24*(3), 420–429.

Fullan, M. (1993). *Change forces.* London, UK: Falmer.

Guskey, T. R. (1986). Staff development and the process of teacher change. *Educational Researcher, 15*(5), 5–12.

Hargreaves, A., & Fullan, M. (1998). *What's worth fighting for out there.* New York, NY: Teachers College Press.

Henry, M. J. (1993). *Profile of a technology using teacher.* Paper presented at the Annual Convention of the Eastern Educational Research Association, February 17–23, Clearwater, FL.

Honey, M., & Moeller, B. (1990). *Teachers' beliefs and technology integration: Different values, different understandings* (Technical Report 6). New York, NY: Center for Technology in Education.

Johnson, N., & Owen, J. (1986). *The two cultures revisited: Interpreting messages from models of teaching and clinical supervision to encourage improvement in teaching.* Paper presented at the Australian Educational Research Association Annual Conference, Melbourne.

Levin, B. B. (1999). *Is the class of 1998 ready for the 21st century school? Longitudinal study of computer-using teacher candidates.* (ERIC Document Reproduction Service No. ED 432 556).

MacArthur, C. A., & Malouf, D. B. (1991). Teachers' beliefs, plans, and decisions about computer-based instruction. *The Journal of Special Education, 25*(5), 44–72.

Marcinkiewicz, H. R. (1994). Computers and teachers: Factors influencing computer use in the classroom. *Journal of Research on Computing in Education, 26*(2), 220–237.

Milbrath, Y. L, & Kinzie, M. B. (2000). Computer technology training for prospective teachers: Computer attitudes and perceived self-efficacy. *Journal of Technology and Teacher Education, 8*(4), 373–396.

The National Commission on Teaching and America's Future. (1996). *What matters most: Teaching for America's future.* Woodbridge, VA: Author.

Polonoli, K. (2001). Integrating technology into the classroom: Three questions concerned principals must ask. *Principal Leadership, 2*(4), 34–38.

Preparing Tomorrow's Teachers to use Technology (n.d). *21st century learners: The need for tech-savvy teachers.* Retrieved January 15, 2003, from www.PT3.org/technology/21century_learners.html

Sarason, S. (1990). *The predictable failure of educational reform.* San Francisco, CA: Jossey-Bass.

Schacter, J. (1999). *The impact of educational technology on student achievement: What the most current research has to say.* Retrieved July 14, 2003. from the Milken Family Foundation website: www.mff.org/pubs/ME161.pdf

Stoll, L., & Fink, D. (1996). *Changing our schools.* Buckingham, UK: Open University Press.

Vannatta, R. A., & O'Bannon, B. (2002). Beginning to put the pieces together: A technology infusion model for teacher education. *Journal of Computing in Teacher Education, 18*(4), 112–123.

Woolfolk, A. E., & Hoy, W. K. (1990). Prospective teachers' sense of efficacy and beliefs about control. *Journal of Educational Psychology, 82*(1), 81–91.

Willis, S. (2002). Creating a knowledge base for teaching: A conversation with James Stigler. *Educational Leadership, 59*(6), 6–11.

APPENDIX

4.A

Teacher Attribute Survey

PART A

Indicate how much you disagree or agree with the following statements by circling the appropriate number to the right of each statement.

1 = Strongly Disagree (SD)	4 = Slightly Agree (SLA)
2 = Moderately Disagree (MD)	5 = Moderately Agree (MA)
3 = Slightly Disagree (SLD)	6 = Strongly Agree (SA)

	Statement	Strongly Disagree SD	MD	SLD	SLA	MA	Strongly Agree SA
1.	When a student does better than usual, many times it is because I exerted a little extra effort.	1	2	3	4	5	6
2.	If one of my students could not do a class assignment, I would be able to accurately assess whether the assignment was at the correct level of difficulty.	1	2	3	4	5	6
3.	If parents would do more with their children, I could do more.	1	2	3	4	5	6
4.	If students are not disciplined at home, they aren't likely to accept any discipline.	1	2	3	4	5	6
5.	If a student masters a new concept quickly, it is probably because I knew the necessary steps in teaching that concept.	1	2	3	4	5	6
6.	If a student did not remember the information I gave in a previous lesson, I would know how to increase his/her retention in the next lesson.	1	2	3	4	5	6
7.	The influence of a student's home experience can be overcome by good teaching.	1	2	3	4	5	6
8.	The amount that a student can learn is primarily related to family background.	1	2	3	4	5	6
9.	When I really try, I can get through to the most difficult students.	1	2	3	4	5	6
10.	Even a teacher with good teaching abilities may not reach many students.	1	2	3	4	5	6
11.	A teacher is very limited in what he/she can achieve because a student's home environment is a large influence on his/her achievement.	1	2	3	4	5	6

Continued

	Item	SD (Strongly Disagree)	MD	SLD	SLA	MA	SA (Strongly Agree)
12.	The hours in my class have little influence on students compared to the influence of their home environment.	1	2	3	4	5	6
13.	If a student in my class becomes disruptive and noisy, I feel assured that I know some techniques to redirect him/her quickly.	1	2	3	4	5	6
14.	When a student gets a better grade than he/she usually gets, it is probably because I found better ways of teaching that student.	1	2	3	4	5	6
15.	When a student is having difficulty with an assignment, I am usually able to adjust to his/her level.	1	2	3	4	5	6
16.	When the grades of my students improve it is usually because I found more effective teaching approaches.	1	2	3	4	5	6
17.	Students are not ready for "meaningful" learning until they have acquired basic reading and math skills.	1	2	3	4	5	6
18.	Student projects often result in students learning all sorts of wrong "knowledge."	1	2	3	4	5	6
19.	Students will take more initiative to learn when they feel free to move around the room during class.	1	2	3	4	5	6
20.	Instruction should be built around problems with clear, correct answers, and around ideas that most students can grasp quickly.	1	2	3	4	5	6
21.	A quiet classroom is generally needed for effective learning.	1	2	3	4	5	6
22.	It is better when the teacher—not the students—decides what activities are to be done.	1	2	3	4	5	6
23.	Homework is a good setting for having students answer questions posed in their textbooks.	1	2	3	4	5	6
24.	Students should help establish criteria on which their work will be assessed.	1	2	3	4	5	6
25.	How much students learn depends on how much background knowledge they have—that is why the teaching of facts is so necessary.	1	2	3	4	5	6
26.	When exploring new instructional methods, I try to find ones that require little change.	1	2	3	4	5	6
27.	I am comfortable trying new things even when I will probably make mistakes.	1	2	3	4	5	6
28.	The instructional methods that I currently implement need little revision.	1	2	3	4	5	6
29.	I feel excited when I try new instructional techniques.	1	2	3	4	5	6
30.	I don't mind making mistakes since I can learn from them.	1	2	3	4	5	6
31.	I would continue to complete graduate courses even if they were not required for ongoing licensure OR rewarded with salary increase.	1	2	3	4	5	6

PART B

For each of the following pairs of statements, check the circle that best shows how closely your own beliefs are to each of the statements in the given pair. The closer your beliefs to a particular statement, the closer the circle you check. Please check only one circle for each pair.

32.	"I mainly see my role as a facilitator. I try to provide opportunities and resources for my students to discover or construct concepts for themselves."	○ ○ ○ ○ ○	"That's all nice, but students really won't learn the subject unless you go over the material in a structured way. It's my job to explain, to show students how to do the work, and to assign specific practice."
33.	"The most important part of instruction is the content of the curriculum. that content is the community's judgment about what children need to be able to know and do."	○ ○ ○ ○ ○	"The most important part of instruction is that it encourages 'sense making' or thinking among students. Content is secondary."
34.	"It is useful for students to become familiar with many different ideas and skills even if their understanding, for now, is limited. Later, in college, perhaps, they will learn these things in more detail."	○ ○ ○ ○ ○	"It is better for students to master a few complex ideas and skills well, and to learn what deep understanding is all about, even if the breadth of their knowledge is limited until they are older."
35.	"It is critical for students to become interested in doing academic work—interest and effort are more important than the particular subject matter they are working on."	○ ○ ○ ○ ○	"While student motivation is certainly useful, it should not drive what students study. It is more important that students learn the history, science, math, and language skills in their textbooks."
36.	"It is a good idea to have all sorts of activities going on in the classroom. Some students might produce a scene from a play they read. Others might create a miniature version of the set. It's hard to get the logistics right, but the successes are so much more important than the failures."	○ ○ ○ ○ ○	"It is more practical to give the whole class the same assignment, one that has clear directions, and one that can be done in short intervals that match students' attention spans and the daily class schedule."

PART C

Teacher Technology Use: Indicate the frequency that you used the following tools and applications in your instruction during this last semester. Examples of teacher use are: teacher demonstration, use of tool/application during lecture/presentation, etc.

1 = None	3 = Moderate (several times per semester)
2 = Rarely (once or twice per semester)	4 = High (almost weekly per semester)

37.	Computer with Projection System	1	2	3	4
38.	Digital Camera, Camcorder	1	2	3	4
39.	Scanner	1	2	3	4
40.	Content-Specific Tools (e.g., digital microscope, graphing calculator)	1	2	3	4
41.	Word Processing	1	2	3	4
42.	Database	1	2	3	4
43.	Spreadsheet	1	2	3	4
44.	Drawing/Graphics Programs (e.g., Photoshop, AutoCad)	1	2	3	4
45.	Content-Specific Software (e.g., Inspiration, Accelerated Reader, Timeliner)	1	2	3	4
46.	Presentation Software (e.g., PowerPoint, AppleWorks Slideshow)	1	2	3	4
47.	Multimedia (e.g., HyperStudio, Kid Pix, iMovie, Adobe Premier)	1	2	3	4
48.	E-mail/ Discussion Groups/E-mail Lists	1	2	3	4
49.	Internet (web searches)	1	2	3	4
50.	Class Website (communicate with students and/or parents)	1	2	3	4
51.	Other, please list:	1	2	3	4

PART D

Student Technology Use: For the following tools and applications, indicate the frequency of student use (demonstration, presentation) in your classes during this past semester.

1 = None	3 = Moderate (several times per semester)				
2 = Rarely (once or twice per semester)	4 = High (almost weekly per semester)				
52.	Computer with Projection System	1	2	3	4
53.	Digital Camera, Camcorder	1	2	3	4
54.	Scanner	1	2	3	4
55.	Content-Specific Tools (e.g., digital microscope, graphing calculator)	1	2	3	4
56.	Word Processing	1	2	3	4
57.	Database	1	2	3	4
58.	Spreadsheet	1	2	3	4
59.	Drawing/Graphics Programs (e.g., Photoshop, AutoCad)	1	2	3	4
60.	Content-Specific Software (e.g., Inspiration, Accelerated Reader, Timeliner)	1	2	3	4
61.	Presentation Software (e.g., PowerPoint, AppleWorks Slideshow)	1	2	3	4
62.	Multimedia (e.g., HyperStudio, Kid Pix, iMovie, Adobe Premier)	1	2	3	4
63.	E-mail/ Discussion Groups/E-mail lists	1	2	3	4
64.	Internet (web searches)	1	2	3	4
65.	Class Website (communicate with students and/or parents)	1	2	3	4
66.	Other, please list:	1	2	3	4

PART E

Background:

67. In the last two years, I have completed ___ (# of actual) hours of professional development. Note: One (1) graduate credit is equivalent to 15 hours of contact time.

68. In the last two years, I have completed ___ (# of actual) hours of training related to technology. Note: One (1) graduate credit is equivalent to 15 hours of contact time.

69. For an average week, how many hours do you work beyond the "contractual" teacher work week in order to adequately fulfill your teaching responsibilities?

    a. none
    b. 1–5
    c. 6–10
    d. 11–15
    e. 16–20
    f. 21 or more

70. Gender? ___ Male ___ Female

71. Number of years teaching? ___

CHAPTER

5

Impact of Problem-Based Learning (PBL) on Teachers' Beliefs Regarding Technology Use

Sung Hee Park | Ewha Womans University

Peggy A. Ertmer | Purdue University

Although computers are now commonplace within our lives, integration within schools is much less ordinary. While access and training are no longer considered significant barriers, attention has turned to the potential influence of teachers' beliefs. In response, problem-based learning (PBL) has been proposed as an effective approach for changing beliefs. This study investigated the impact of PBL on preservice teachers' beliefs regarding technology use and on their intended teaching practices. Participants included 48 preservice teachers enrolled in a one-credit educational technology course. Results showed that beliefs regarding technology use did not change significantly. However, participants significantly shifted their intended teaching practices from teacher-directed to student-centered learning. Implications for practice are discussed.

Although digital technologies have become common tools within our lives, teachers have yet to embed them within their daily teaching practices (Cuban, 2001). For example, after studying the technology uses of 78 K–12 teachers, Cuban reported that 80% of teachers used computers primarily for e-mail. Additionally, 65% never used computers for individual enrichment for advanced students, and 95% never used computers to facilitate student-to-student interaction.

There are many reasons why teachers do not use technology to its full potential, including limited classroom space, unwillingness to take students to labs, and lack of access at teachers' and students' homes. Other barriers include finding the time and resources to implement classroom technologies (Ertmer, Addison, Lane, Ross, & Woods, 1999; Parr, 1999; Vannatta & Beyerbach, 2000; Zhao & Frank, 2003).

Barriers to integration exist both within and outside of teachers. These internal and external barriers, as explored by Ertmer (1999), have different characteristics. External, or first-order, barriers include a lack of access to computers, software, planning time, or administrative support. Internal, or second-order, barriers relate to teachers' beliefs about instructional technology, preferred teaching methodologies, and willingness to make changes to classroom practices. First-order barriers are more easily recognized and easier to fix, whereas second-order barriers may require major changes in teachers' beliefs and daily teaching practices (Ertmer, 1999).

Because of the scope and cost of removing first-order barriers and the complexity of addressing second-order barriers, developing good technology use is a slow process. For example, a recent survey conducted by the U.S. Department of Education (2000) demonstrated that only one-third of teachers felt well prepared to use computers and the Internet in their classrooms, although 99% of public schools have Internet connections. That is, even after first-order barriers are removed, it is still difficult for teachers to integrate technology into the classroom, possibly because of second-order barriers. Sugar (2002) emphasized the importance of addressing teachers' beliefs about technology integration and removing second-order barriers to achieve technology integration. However, these internal barriers are persistent; teachers' beliefs regarding technology integration appear to be extremely difficult to modify (Ertmer, 2005).

Teachers' Beliefs about Technology

Teachers' beliefs refer to internal constructs that help teachers interpret experiences and that guide specific teaching practices (Nespor, 1987; Pajares, 1992). According to Fang (1996), a "teacher's beliefs are shaped by many factors. Among them are the influences of discipline subculture, the quality of preservice experience in the classroom, and the opportunity for reflection on the preservice experience" (p. 50). Although labeled a "messy construct" by Pajares (1992), beliefs are still considered the "best indicators of the decisions individuals make throughout their lives" (p. 307). Kagan (1992) cited significant evidence supporting the relationship between teacher beliefs and their decisions about classroom practice.

According to Miller and her colleagues (2003), teachers' beliefs about technology comprise three related, but independent components: pedagogical beliefs about teaching and learning, self-efficacy beliefs about technology use, and beliefs about the perceived value of computers for student learning. In a study by Russell, Bebell, O'Dwyer, and O'Connor (2003), these three components were found to be the main predictors of teachers' classroom technology use. In this study, we use these same three components to operationalize "teachers' beliefs about technology."

Pedagogical beliefs. Based on the results of a study with middle school teachers (Fulton & Torney-Purta, 2000), experiences during teacher preparation programs and early teaching assignments exert major influences on teachers' beliefs about teaching, learning, and technology. Wang (2002) examined preservice teachers' beliefs regarding their role in a classroom with computers. Results indicated that preservice teachers were more likely to use technology as a teacher-centered tool, based on the teaching methods from which they learned. Other studies have found similar results; when attempting to implement new methods without enough time to practice, preservice teachers tend to revert to traditional methods (Russell, O'Dwyer, Bebell, & Miranda, 2003).

According to Richardson (2003), belief change in preservice teachers is more important than knowledge transmission during teacher preparation because beliefs affect action in more critical ways. One recent study (Russell et al., 2004) suggested that changing teachers' beliefs about technology is needed to change teachers' classroom uses of technology.

It is generally acknowledged that preservice teachers come to their teacher education programs with an existing set of beliefs, based on their own experiences as learners, and that these experiences play a critical role in shaping their future practices (Kennedy, 1997; Richardson, 2003). In general, Becker (1999) suggested that teachers who have student-centered beliefs tend to use technology more frequently and to use it in more meaningful ways. That is, low-level technology uses (e.g., word processing, using technology to teach remedial skills) tend to be associated with teacher-centered practices, whereas high-level uses (e.g., engaging students in inquiry-based activities, collaborating with peers at a distance) tend to be associated with student-centered, or constructivist, practices. Consequently, to change teachers' practices, specifically where technology is involved, it may be important for teachers to embrace more student-centered beliefs, because teachers will base their practices on their beliefs (Albion & Ertmer, 2002; Kagan, 1992; Richardson, 2003).

Self-efficacy beliefs. Bandura (1997) defined self-efficacy as personal beliefs about one's capability to learn or perform actions at designated levels. In other words, teachers' self-efficacy beliefs comprise beliefs about what they are capable of doing with technology in the classroom as opposed to the knowledge they have about what to do (Ertmer et al., 2003). Researchers (Albion, 1999; Marcinkiewicz, 1994; Sheingold & Hadley, 1990) have found that teachers' self-efficacy beliefs regarding technology use are a critical predictor of their uses of technology in the classroom. According to the survey results of 72 teachers (Chen, Burnam, Howie, Aten, & Nambiar, 2003), teachers' self-efficacy beliefs regarding technology use were the strongest predictor of their classroom uses. Furthermore, Albion (2000) reported that preservice teachers' self-efficacy beliefs for technology use enhanced their expectations for using technology in their future classrooms.

Beliefs about the value of technology. According to Cuban (2001), teachers have received conflicting advice about how to integrate technology in the classroom and so are skeptical about the value that technology offers. Some researchers (Becker, 1999; Zhao & Frank, 2003) found that teachers who placed a more positive value on computers tended to use computers more frequently in their instruction. That is, beliefs about the value of computers greatly enhanced teachers' perceptions about the effectiveness of computers for teaching and learning. As such, the perceived relevancy of technology in the classroom can have significant impact on subsequent use in the classroom (Kellenberger, 1997).

Problem-Based Learning (PBL)

Current literature suggests that teachers' beliefs can be changed through practices that emphasize reflection on one's personal beliefs, hands-on experiences, and engagement in authentic problems from K–12 classrooms (Derry, Siegel, Stampen, & the STEP team, 2002; Ertmer, 2005; Tochon, 1999). For example, Derry et al. documented successful belief change after engaging preservice teachers in authentic displays of teaching (e.g., real cases, video cases). Through these authentic experiences, preservice teachers developed a better understanding of constructivist teaching practices, became more successful at implementing constructivist methods, and achieved meaningful reflections on the nature of teaching and learning.

As an authentic, hands-on teaching approach, problem-based learning (PBL) has been advocated as a potentially effective means for affecting teachers' beliefs (Derry et al., 2002). A PBL learning approach starts with an authentic, ill-structured problem that requires students to develop expertise in information seeking and decision making to solve problems. As such, PBL is believed to enhance students' critical thinking skills, increase motivation, and improve social skills through group work (Albion, 1999; Duch, Groh, & Allen, 2001; Sage, 2000).

In teacher education programs, a PBL approach using problems and issues from K–12 classrooms can help preservice teachers recognize different perspectives and encourage them to elaborate, defend, or modify their current beliefs about classroom practices. As a result, PBL can serve as a catalyst for shifting beliefs by helping preservice teachers reflect on their beliefs while obtaining new knowledge and engaging in problem solving, critical thinking, collaboration, and decision making (Levin, 2001; Lundeberg & Levin, 2003; Pierce & Lange, 2001).

Although some researchers have described strategies for changing preservice teachers' beliefs (Richardson, 2003; Tatto & Coupland, 2003), previous research has not investigated, specifically, how to change teachers' beliefs regarding technology use. Furthermore, little if any research has investigated how PBL might affect preservice teachers' beliefs regarding technology use. This study was designed to fill that gap. Specifically, this study asked:

1. What is the impact of problem-based learning on preservice teachers' beliefs regarding technology use? More specifically, what is the impact of PBL on preservice teachers' self-efficacy beliefs, pedagogical beliefs, and beliefs about the instructional value of computers?

2. How do preservice teachers' intended teaching practices change after participation in a PBL approach to technology integration?

Method

PARTICIPANTS AND COURSE

Participants were solicited from three intact sections of a one-credit educational technology course, *Classroom Applications of Educational Technology*, at a large Midwestern university. The course met once a week, for two hours, over the first eight weeks of the semester. From among the 50 students enrolled in the course in fall 2005, 48 students agreed to participate in the study and completed the pre- and post-surveys; 46 students also completed the pre- and post-lesson plans.

RESEARCH DESIGN AND IMPLEMENTATION PROCEDURES

This study employed a quasi-experimental research design using pre- and post-surveys and lesson plans to investigate the impact of problem-based learning on preservice teachers' beliefs regarding technology use. Two intact sections were assigned to the treatment condition (PBL: $n = 12$ and $n = 16$) and one to the control condition (control: $n = 20$). One instructor who had previous experience teaching the course, both traditionally and with PBL, taught all three sections. There was no relationship between the researchers and the instructor or students.

To initiate the PBL activity we used two 6-minute digital video clips of interviews with a middle school principal and the superintendent of a local school district. From these interviews, the students learned that the school district had recently purchased wireless laptops for all of their teachers and students. Now, the administrators needed to hire new teachers who could integrate technology into their classrooms. At the end of the interviews, the administrators announced that they would examine students' portfolios at the end of the term to identify the most promising teachers for the new positions.

In the first week of the course, the participants in the PBL group watched the digital video clips through the course website and then formed small groups of two or three students. This problem situation prompted a driving question for the class, "What does it take to be a successful teacher who integrates technology?" Each group "created" a potential teacher candidate, including the development of a web portfolio, to apply for the new position.

In the second week, each student submitted a lesson plan, which included the use of technology, following specific guidelines that required them to describe learners, goals, assessment methods, resources, and so on. Early lesson plans were compared with those developed at the end of the course to examine how students' intentions to use technology changed over time.

During the semester, students watched digital video cases of exemplary technology integration in K–12 classrooms, including interviews with teachers. After watching the digital video cases, students discussed classroom problems and the strengths and weaknesses of the solutions. Also, each group created artifacts related to the skills, knowledge, and attitudes required to succeed as technology using teachers in their content areas. In addition, students submitted reflections with each artifact as well as a final course reflection describing their PBL group experience.

Each small group created a digital portfolio to apply for the new positions in the school district. There were three main artifacts in each digital portfolio: (1) an artifact to demonstrate skills (e.g., digital curriculum vitae), (2) an artifact to demonstrate knowledge (e.g., lesson plans integrating technology), and (3) an artifact to highlight attitudes toward technology (e.g., an essay of teaching philosophy). At the end of the semester, each group made presentations to an interview panel composed of school administrators (including those who appeared in the initial video case) and content experts (e.g., professors and instructors in the College of Education). After each presentation, the interview panel asked questions about the candidates' portfolios. During this time, students in the other groups completed peer evaluations using an evaluation form.

The participants in the control group reviewed different multimedia programs used in the K–12 curriculum and evaluated them with a software evaluation form (not based on PBL). Course content was delivered mainly by the instructor. Two lesson plan projects, using web resources and instructional software, and one digital video development project were completed. The first two lesson plan projects were completed by individuals and the video development project was completed by a group. At the end of the course, the participants submitted their lesson plans for integrating technology.

DATA COLLECTION

Pre- and post-surveys were used to investigate the impact of problem-based learning on teachers' beliefs regarding technology use. Teachers' beliefs were examined via a 54-item survey, Teachers' Beliefs Regarding Technology Use Survey (TBTUS), composed of three components as suggested by the literature: teachers' pedagogical beliefs, teachers' self-efficacy beliefs for using technology, and teachers' beliefs about the perceived value of computers for instructional purposes. All items were presented in a 7-point rating scale; students were asked to rate their level of agreement from 1—completely disagree, to 7—completely agree (see Appendix 5.A at the end of this chapter).

Items used to measure teachers' pedagogical beliefs and teachers' self-efficacy beliefs had been widely used in previous research (Bai & Ertmer, 2008; Ertmer et al., 2003; McCombs, 2002). The pedagogical belief items (Appendix 5.A, items 1–35) were adapted from a three-factor survey developed by McCombs (2002) as a part of the Assessment of Learner-Centered Practice (ALCP) and had been field-tested and validated over a four-year time period. Bai and Ertmer (2008) conducted a confirmatory factor analysis on the scale with 230 students, and its results showed how well the proposed model (three-factor structure) fit the data. The model yielded a chi-square of 873.62 ($df = 557$, $p < .0001$) and the chi-square degrees of freedom (df) ratio was 1.57 (873.62/557= 1.57). The model was acceptable following the rule of thumb that a model fits if the ratio is less than 2 (Hatcher, 1994). Although the Cronbach reliability coefficients were somewhat low on the pre-test (from .56 to .74), results of the post-survey showed acceptable Cronbach coefficient alphas ranging from .72 to .88 ($n = 48$) on the three factors.

Items used to measure preservice teachers' self-efficacy for integrating technology (see Appendix 5.A, items 36–42) were adapted from Ertmer et al. (2003). The reliability of the items with the pre- and post-survey data ($n = 48$) showed a Cronbach alpha reliability coefficient of .97 on the pre-survey and .95 on the post-survey.

Items used to measure teachers' beliefs about the perceived value of computers for instructional purposes (see Appendix 5.A, items 43–54) were selected from surveys employed by practitioners in the field (Chen et al., 2003). All items were evaluated by an expert in the area of technology integration for preservice teachers and modified based on her suggestions, providing the instrument with a measure of content validity. The reliability of the items with the pre- and post-survey data (n = 48) showed a Cronbach alpha reliability coefficient of .82 on the pre-survey and .91 on the post-survey.

Pre- and post-course lesson plans were used to measure changes in participants' intended teaching practices. Participants' lesson plans were analyzed with a rubric, and the graders were blind to both the participant and the timing of the lesson plan. The rubric addressed seven categories: (1) teachers' roles, (2) students' roles, (3) curricular characteristics, (4) learning goals, (5) types of activities, (6) assessment strategies, and (7) types of technology (see Appendix 5.B). Each lesson plan was scored on each category according to a scale (1 = teacher-centered learning, 4 = student-centered learning). The seven category scores were added; possible scores ranged from 7 to 28. Two graders discussed what characterized a score of 1 through 4 while grading 10 sample lesson plans. Following that, each grader independently scored the same 30 lesson plans (30% of all the lesson plans) and discussed discrepancies. After reaching consensus, each grader graded 31 lesson plans individually, for a total of 62 additional plans and reached 91.47% agreement following recommended guidelines (Stemler, 2004).

DATA ANALYSIS

The data from the pre- and post-surveys were used to determine the impact of PBL on teachers' beliefs regarding technology use. An analysis of covariance (ANCOVA) was conducted, using the pre-survey as a covariate. Data from the pre- and post-course lesson plans were analyzed using the rubric developed. First, an analysis of covariance (ANCOVA) was used to determine the impact of PBL on teachers' intended teaching practices. The pre-course lesson plan score (total score) was used as a covariate. Second, a multivariate analysis of variance (MANOVA) was used to determine the overall impact of PBL on subcategories of teachers' intended teaching practices represented by the lesson plans. Because covariates with pre–lesson plan scores of each subcategory were not simultaneously significant, MANOVA was used instead of MANCOVA. Third, follow-up univariate analyses were conducted on each subcategory where significance was found, using the Bonferroni correction procedure to control for Type I error. That is, each subcategory was tested at the .007 alpha level (.05 divided by 7).

Results

TEACHERS' BELIEFS REGARDING TECHNOLOGY USE SURVEY

Overall, the pre-survey scores were significant as covariates in the ANCOVAs. However, the results of the survey showed that there were no significant differences between treatment groups in the categories of teachers' pedagogical beliefs, self-efficacy beliefs for technology integration, or beliefs about the perceived value of computers for instructional purposes.

Table 5.1 Analysis of Covariance (ANCOVA) of Lesson Plans (LP)

Source	Type III SS	*df*	Mean Squares	*F*	*p*
Covariate (pre-LP)	763.39	1	763.39	54.30	< .0001
Group	123.73	1	123.73	8.80	0.004

Table 5.2 Adjusted Means of the Lesson Plans

Group	*N*	Adjusted Means
Control	20	15.57
PBL	26	19.09

LESSON PLANS

The results of the ANCOVA showed a significant difference between groups in the amount of change demonstrated in intended teaching practices, $F(1, 43) = 8.80$, $p = .004$, $\eta^2 = .67$ (see Tables 5.1 and 5.2). Overall, participants in the PBL group showed greater change than participants in the control group in their intended teaching practices, moving from a teacher-centered to a student-centered learning approach. Table 5.3 presents the means for each of the seven subcategories of the lesson plans (pre- and post-course) for the two groups.

MANOVA results showed an overall effect of treatment on subcategories of lesson plans: Hotelling-Lawley Trace = .64, associated $F(7, 38) = 3.50$, $p = .0054$, $\eta^2 = .36$ (see Table 5.4). ANOVA indicated significant differences between groups, with the PBL group showing more student-centered learning approaches in four categories: (1) students' role, (2) curriculum characteristics, (3) learning goals, and (4) types of technology use. Each category is described in more detail in the following section.

Students' roles. Results revealed that PBL participants described students' roles in a more student-centered way, following treatment, than did students in the control group: $F(1, 44) = 11.37, p = .0016, \eta^2 = .21$. For example, on the pre-course lesson plans, participants in the PBL group described situations where the primary activity was for students to listen to a teacher's lecture, with no group work or follow-up activities. However, on the post-course lesson plans, participants described how students would participate in group work, have more choices for their research topics, and create different products based on collaboration. For example, a student's role was described in the pre-course lesson plan as "getting work done" during classroom activities that included research, presentation, and developing a poster. However, in the post-course lesson plan, the same participant described the student's role as the following:

> The students' role is to work with other students and learn how to be a team player. Teamwork is an important attitude to learn, as students will be using it for the rest of their lives. The students also need to be able to split up work evenly, so that work can be done in an effective way.

Curricular characteristics. Results revealed that PBL participants described curricular characteristics in a more student-centered way following treatment than did students in the control group: $F(1, 44) = 14.76, p = .0004, \eta^2 = .25$. On the pre-course lesson plans, participants described how the introduction of specific skills and knowledge followed a predetermined sequence. That is, the curriculum was structured such that all the students followed the same sequence. However, in the post-course lesson plans, curricula included more project-based approaches with multiple components, ranging from simple-level worksheets to higher-level products such as essays, reports, and hands-on projects, encouraging students to find their own paths through the learning process. For example, in a pre-course lesson plan about learning a piece of computer software, a participant described how a teacher would demonstrate the software menu and ask students to follow the step-by-step procedure described in a handout or manual. However, in the post-course lesson plan, the same participant described how a teacher would show multiple examples of projects created with the graphic program, show basic functions of the software, and demonstrate one example. Then, the teacher would allow each group to choose a project, based on their own needs and interests, to demonstrate their new skills. That is, students could use their own ideas to create an artifact instead of following one linear procedure established by the teacher.

Table 5.3 Means of Each Subcategory on Pre- and Post-Course Lesson Plans

	Control group (n = 20)				PBL group (n = 26)			
	Pre		Post		Pre		Post	
	Mean	SD	Mean	SD	Mean	SD	Mean	SD
Teachers' role	2.20	1.00	2.20	0.89	2.80	0.89	2.84	0.88
Students' role	2.05	0.82	2.10	0.85	2.57	0.85	2.92	0.79
Curriculum characteristics	1.95	0.94	1.95	0.82	2.30	0.97	3.07	1.09
Learning goals	1.80	1.00	1.65	0.98	2.30	1.01	2.76	1.10
Types of activities	2.20	0.69	2.05	0.82	2.42	0.75	2.80	0.98
Assessment strategies	1.90	1.11	2.00	1.07	2.73	1.21	2.88	1.14
Types of technology use	1.85	0.98	1.75	0.85	2.69	1.01	3.07	0.97

Table 5.4 Results of MANOVA on Lesson Plans

Subcategory	Hotelling's T	F	df	p	η^2
Students' role		11.37	1/44	<.007	.21
Curriculum characteristics		14.76	1/44	<.007	.25
Learning goals	.64	12.67	1/44	<.007	.22
Types of technology use	(p < .01)	23.29	1/44	<.007	.35

Learning goals. Results revealed that PBL participants described learning goals in a more student-centered way following treatment than did students in the control group: $F(1, 44) = 12.67, p = .0009, \eta^2 = .22$. Whereas they focused only on content-based learning goals in the pre-course lesson plans, participants looked beyond students' growth in subject content to problem solving, communication, or decision-making skills in the post-course lesson plans. For example, the topic of "ink-printing a t-shirt design" was described for an art class. In the pre-course lesson plan, the participant described how students would start the class either using computers to design an object to print onto their t-shirts, or finding an object to use from the Internet. However, in the post-course lesson plan, the participant described an instructional problem that involved the National Football League searching for a new symbol to replace the old one. Students were asked to design their own symbol to replace the old one. The preservice teacher expected to stimulate students' creativity, problem solving, and critical thinking through this process.

Types of technology use. Results revealed that PBL participants described uses of technology that were more student-centered following treatment, than did students in the control group: $F(1, 44) = 23.29$, $p < .0001$, $\eta^2 = .35$. Some technology uses were described in the pre-course lesson plans, such as using PowerPoint and an LCD projector to deliver a lecture. For example, to learn mechanics and the history of small engines in a technology education class, technology use was described in the pre-course lesson plan only in terms of teachers using technology to deliver a lecture as illustrated by this comment: "Teacher will have prepared an extensive PowerPoint presentation with slides that show motion and small video clips that last the duration of the first class period."

As another example, in a pre-course lesson plan about nutrition, a participant described how teachers used technology to demonstrate how to use a software program and students used a spreadsheet program to record numbers from the price tags on food items in the local grocery store. However, in the post-course lesson plan, a greater variety of technology was used for student learning. For example, after choosing a country or culture, students would do research on daily meals and find recipes for favorite dishes. Students would use the Internet for research and prepare a presentation based on their research. Although students would still learn about nutrition, the use of technology was different. Whereas in the pre-course lesson plans the technology was used solely by teachers to deliver a lecture or demonstration, in the post-course lesson plans it was used by students to both conduct research and to share research results.

Discussion

The purpose of this study was to investigate the impact of problem-based learning (PBL) on preservice teachers' beliefs regarding technology use and on their intended teaching practices as captured by detailed lesson plans. Our first research question examined the impact of problem-based learning on teachers' beliefs regarding technology use. This question was answered by examining beliefs in three subcategories: (1) teachers' pedagogical beliefs, (2) teachers' self-efficacy beliefs for technology integration, and (3) teachers' beliefs about the perceived value of computers for instructional purposes. No statistical significance was found on any measure related to beliefs. This means that, in this study, the use of problem-based learning, when compared to traditional teaching approaches (control), did not significantly affect preservice teachers' beliefs regarding technology use.

The lack of significant results on the TBTUS may be due to a number of reasons. First, intact classes may have caused sampling problems because random assignment of students to treatment conditions was not possible. Although it was necessary, for the purposes of this study, to use the same instructional method with the entire class, changes that occurred (or did not occur) in one class may have been due, not to the treatment, but to some other unique characteristic of the intact class (e.g., students in the earlier class may have been less engaged because of tiredness), thus making interpretation of the results more difficult.

Second, the instrument, TBTUS, may not have been sensitive enough to capture changes in preservice teachers' beliefs regarding technology use. Because preservice teachers' lesson plans showed significant changes in intended teaching practices, it may be that the TBTUS simply was unable to detect these types of changes in beliefs. However, more important to consider is the intrinsically difficult nature of measuring beliefs (Pedersen & Liu, 2003; Rokeach, 1968).

Third, the eight-week course may have been too short to affect teachers' beliefs regarding technology use. Because of the uniqueness of the one-credit course, the course was implemented as a weekly two-hour class over eight weeks. When considering that teachers' beliefs are described as a second-order barrier to the implementation of technology (Ertmer, 1999), changing them is likely to take a long time. Richardson (2003) pointed out that changing preservice teachers' beliefs is difficult during an academic course, especially one that is not accompanied by significant and structured involvement in a field experience.

The second research question, related to changes in intended teaching practices, yielded a statistically significant result. That is, this study supported the hypothesis that preservice teachers participating in PBL modify their intended teaching practices to reflect a more student-centered learning approach than those who do not participate in PBL. Specifically, preservice teachers in this study incorporated more student-centered strategies in their descriptions of (1) students' role, (2) curriculum characteristics, (3) learning goals, and (4) types of technology use.

It is likely that the preservice teachers' experiences during the PBL activities and their observations of the course instructor's approaches influenced their descriptions of their intended teaching practices. That is, during the semester, students participated in solving an authentic problem, observed exemplary teachers' practices, and engaged in group work, discussion, reflection, and presentation. Many of these same activities were included in students' post-course lesson plans. Engagement in PBL seemed to have affected preservice teachers' ideas of their own teaching practices, which were then captured in their final lesson plans.

Although it is possible that the participants' lesson plans reflected their "true" beliefs, it is also possible that they did not. That is, while it appears as though students' lesson plans were influenced by the PBL approach in which they were participating, this may have reflected only surface changes and students may have held stronger central beliefs regarding technology use that remained unaffected. For example, Ertmer (2005) explained:

> Although teachers may express the beliefs that technology is best used for high-level problem-solving activities, their day-to-day uses may include a large number of drill-and-practice applications, because they hold a more central belief that teachers are responsible for assuring that their students learn foundational, or prerequisite, skills. (p. 29)

Ertmer (2005) suggested three ways of scaffolding belief change in teacher preparation programs: (1) building collaborative structures, (2) modeling effective technology use, and (3) reflecting on current practices and beliefs. The results of this study suggest the possible importance of those approaches when embedded within PBL. Each component is described below.

First, a variety of collaborative activities were included within the PBL activities. Through group work and small and large group discussions, preservice teachers shared ideas about how to develop and improve their PBL artifacts. In addition, collaboration with the school administrators who provided the problem situation in the video clips, as well as the faculty members in the College of Education, increased the authenticity and value of the students' final presentations. The interview panel asked questions about students' portfolio presentations and provided meaningful feedback on their work. Also, preservice teachers posed questions for the interview panel as to actual expectations for new teachers and what types of preparation they needed before graduation. Through this collaboration with school administrators and faculty members, preservice teachers gained a clearer vision of the needs of the profession and how they might address them. In addition, the course instructor benefited from collaboration with two course supervisors and an instructional designer. This kept the course moving in a positive direction, provided prompt and improved support for preservice teachers during the PBL process, and supported the course instructor. Although it was not "inside-the-classroom" collaboration, this "outside-the-classroom" collaboration with PBL experts provided better solutions for managing the PBL process.

Second, the course instructor demonstrated effective use of technology as well as a student-centered learning approach during the PBL process. One interesting finding of this study was that participants in the PBL group designed post-course lesson plans that incorporated the features of PBL. This suggests that the course instructor's modeling activities influenced preservice teachers' intended teaching practices toward student-centered learning.

Third, opportunities for reflection were provided in the lesson plans. In both lesson plans, students were asked to provide a rationale for why they chose specific instructional approaches and why those choices would be effective. Through this process, preservice teachers reflected on their intended teaching practices. Furthermore, individual reflections on each artifact and on the PBL course were required of all preservice teachers. Although the artifacts were developed during group work, it was necessary for the students to reflect on the artifacts individually, considering what was done well and what needed to be improved. Furthermore, by reflecting on the PBL process at the end of the course, preservice teachers had the opportunity to connect and integrate their experiences with their current teaching ideas. Perhaps because of these reflection opportunities, PBL strategies were included in many post-course lesson plans.

As Ertmer (2005) summarized from other studies, beliefs are created through a process of enculturation and social construction; they can be shaped through an intense experience, or a series of events. In addition, change in teachers' beliefs may follow rather than precede teaching practices, and by helping teachers adopt new practices that are successful, the beliefs associated with these practices may also be changed.

The results of this study provide ideas about how PBL might be used to affect teachers' intended teaching practices. If preservice teachers were to participate in a series of student-centered approaches such as PBL, their intended teaching practices about teaching, learning, and technology may show changes during their teacher education programs. Then, over time, these intended practices may have an impact on preservice teachers' beliefs regarding technology use. Finally, these changed beliefs are likely to affect teachers' future teaching practices. Changes in intended teaching practices may be an important first step in changing teachers' beliefs regarding technology use and future teaching practices.

Author Update

The research reported in this chapter was based on efforts to use an innovative pedagogical approach (problem-based learning, or PBL) to address a persistent issue in teacher education: how to affect teacher beliefs. Without a doubt, researchers continue to examine the impact of PBL on student learning (for the most current research in this area, we encourage readers to access the *Interdisciplinary Journal of Problem-based Learning*—www.ijpbl.org); interest in the potential of this method continues to grow steadily among both educators and researchers. Additionally, research on teacher beliefs continues to be of strong interest to scholars today, with a number of important studies recently being completed by our European colleagues. For an updated summary of the research on teacher beliefs related to technology use, please see *Teacher Technology Change: How Knowledge, Confidence, Beliefs, and Culture Intersect*, by Ertmer and Ottenbreit-Leftwich, *JRTE, 42*(3), 2010.

Finally, although work is still being done on both of these fronts in the field today, we have seen little research that actually combines these two. Given the promising results of the study included here, we believe it is important that additional work be done that examines the relationship between these two (i.e., Can PBL positively affect teacher beliefs?). We welcome scholars to both the current conversation and ongoing work in this area.

Acknowledgments

This chapter was supported, in part, by the Purdue Research Foundation of Purdue University.

References

Albion, P. R. (1999). Self-efficacy beliefs as an indicator of teachers' preparedness for teaching with technology. *Computers in the Social Studies, 7*(4). Retrieved November 17, 2002, from www.cssjournal.com/albion.html

Albion, P. R., & Ertmer, P. A. (2002). Beyond the foundations: The role of vision and beliefs in teachers' preparation for integration of technology. *Tech Trends, 46*(5), 34–38.

Bai, H., & Ertmer, P. A. (2008). Teacher educators' beliefs and technology uses as predictors of preservice teachers' beliefs and technology attitudes. *Journal of Technology in Teacher Education, 16*(1), 93–112.

Bandura, A. (1997). *Self-efficacy: The exercise of control.* New York, NY: Cambridge University Press.

Becker, H. J. (1999). *Internet use by teachers: Conditions of professional use and teacher-centered student use.* Irvine, CA: Center for Research on Information Technology and Organizations. Retrieved October 12, 2003, from www.crito.uci.edu/tlc/findings/Internet-use/text-tables.pdf

Chen, E., Burnam, B., Howie, J., Aten, H., & Nambiar, V. (2003, April). *Predicting teachers' computer use in the classroom.* Paper presented at the annual meeting of the American Educational Research Association, Chicago.

Cuban, L. (2001). *Oversold & underused: Computers in the classroom.* Cambridge, MA: Harvard University Press. Retrieved July 12, 2004, from www.hup.harvard.edu/pdf/CUBOVE.pdf

Derry, S. J., Siegel, M., Stampen, J., & the STEP Research Group. (2002). The STEP system for collaborative case-based teacher education: Design, evaluation and future directions. In G. Stahl (Ed.), *Proceedings of computer support for collaborative learning (CSCL) 2002* (pp. 209–216). Mahwah, NJ: Erlbaum.

Duch, B. J., Groh, S. E., & Allen, D. E. (Eds.) (2001). *The power of problem-based learning.* Sterling, VA: Stylus.

Ertmer, P. A. (1999). Addressing first- and second-order barriers to change: Strategies for technology integration. *Educational Technology Research and Development, 47*(4), 47–61.

Ertmer, P. A. (2005). Teacher pedagogical beliefs: The final frontier in our quest for technology integration? *Educational Technology Research and Development, 53*(4), 25–39.

Ertmer, P. A., Addison, P., Lane, M., Ross, E., & Woods, D. (1999). Examining teachers' beliefs about the role of technology in the elementary classroom. *Journal of Research on Computing in Education, 32,* 54–72.

Ertmer, P. A., Conklin, D., Lewandowski, J., Osika, E., Selo, M., & Wignall, E. (2003). Increasing preservice teachers' capacity for technology integration through the use of electronic models. *Teacher Education Quarterly, 30*(1), 95–112.

Fang, Z. (1996). A review of research on teacher beliefs and practices. *Educational Research, 38*(1), 47–64.

Fulton, K., & Torney-Purta, J. (2000). *How teachers' beliefs about teaching and learning are reflected in their use of technology: Case studies from urban middle schools.* Paper presented at the International Conference on Learning with Technology, Temple University, Philadelphia, PA. Retrieved January 11, 2005, from http://l2l.org/iclt/2000/papers/126a.pdf

Hatcher, L. (1994). *A step-by-step approach to using the SAS(R) system for factor analysis and structural equation modeling.* Cary, NC: SAS Institute.

Kagan, D. M. (1992). Implications of research on teacher belief. *Educational Psychologist, 27*(10), 65–70.

Kellenberger, D. (1997). Predicting preservice teacher perceived computer use under differential access to resources. *Journal of Educational Computing Research, 16,* 53–64.

Kennedy, M. M. (1997). *Defining an ideal teacher education program.* Washington, DC: National Council for the Accreditation of Teacher Education. Retrieved August 24, 2004, from www.msu.edu/user/mkennedy/publications/Kennedy%20to%20NCATE.pdf

Levin, B. B. (Ed.). (2001). *Using problem-based learning in teacher education.* Alexandria, VA: ASCD.

Lundeberg, M. A., & Levin, B. B. (2003). Prompting the development of preservice teachers' beliefs through cases, action research, problem-based learning, and technology. In J. Rath & A. C. McAninch (Eds.), *Advances in teacher education series, 6* (pp. 23–42). Greenwich, CT: Information Age.

Marcinkiewicz, H. R. (1994). Computers and teachers: Factors influencing computer use in the classroom. *Journal of Research on Computing in Education, 26,* 220–237.

McCombs, B. L. (2002, March). *ALCP college survey validation results.* Denver, CO: University of Denver Research Institute.

Miller, S., Meier, E., Payne-Bourcy, L., Shablak, S., Newman, D., Wan, T. W., et al. (2003, April). *Technology as a catalyst for change: A leadership model for transforming urban teacher programs.* Paper presented at the annual meeting of the American Educational Research Association, Chicago, IL.

Nespor, J. (1987). The role of beliefs in the practice of teaching. *Journal of Curriculum Studies, 19,* 317–328.

Pajares, M. F. (1992). Teachers' beliefs and educational research: Cleaning up a messy construct. *Review of Educational Research, 62,* 307–332.

Parr, J. M. (1999). Extending educational computing: A case of extensive teacher development and support. *Journal of Research on Computing in Education, 31,* 280–302.

Pedersen, S., & Liu, M. (2002). The transfer of problem-solving skills from a problem-based learning environment: The effect of modeling an expert's cognitive processes. *Journal of Research on Technology in Education, 36,* 303–320.

Pierce, J. W., & Lange, H. G. (2001). Providing structure for analyzing authentic problems. In B. B. Levin (Ed.), *Energizing teacher education and professional development with problem-based learning* (pp. 38–55). Alexandria, VA: ASCD.

Richardson, V. (2003). Preservice teachers' beliefs. In J. Rath & A. C. McAninch (Eds.), *Advances in teacher education series, 6* (pp. 1–22). Greenwich, CT: Information Age.

Rokeach, M. (1968). *Beliefs, attitudes, and values,* San Francisco, CA: Jossey-Bass.

Russell, M., Bebell, D., O'Dwyer, L., & O'Connor, K. (2003). Examining teacher technology use: Implications for preservice and inservice teacher preparation. *Journal of Teacher Education, 54,* 279–310.

Russell, M., O'Dwyer, L., Bebell, D., & Miranda, H. (2004). *Technical report for the USEIT study.* Boston, MA: Boston College, Technology and Assessment Study Collaborative. Retrieved October 12, 2004, from http://escholarship.bc.edu/cgi/viewcontent.cgi?article=1024&context=intasc

Sage, S. M. (2000). A natural fit: Problem-based learning and technology standards. *Learning & Leading with Technology, 28(1),* 6–12.

Sheingold, K., & Hadley, M. (1990). *Accomplished teachers: Integrating computers into classroom practice.* New York, NY: Center for Technology in Education, Bank Street College of Education.

Stemler, S. E. (2004). A comparison of consensus, consistency, and measurement approaches to estimating interrater reliability. *Practical Assessment, Research & Evaluation, 9*(4). Retrieved April 5, 2005, from http://PAREonline.net/getvn.asp?v=9&n=4

Sugar, W. (2002). Applying human-centered design to technology integration. *Journal of Computing in Teacher Education, 19*(1), 12–17.

Tatto, M. T., & Coupland, D. B. (2003). Teacher education and teachers' beliefs: Theoretical and measurement concerns. In J. Rath & A. C. McAninch (Eds.), *Advances in teacher education series, 6* (pp. 123–181). Greenwich, CT: Information Age.

Tochon, F. V. (1999). *Video study groups for education, professional development, and change.* Madison, WI: Atwood.

U.S. Department of Education (2000). *Teachers' tools for the 21st century: A report on teachers' use of technology* (OTA-HER-616). Washington, DC: U.S. Government Printing Office.

Vannatta, R. A., & Beyerbach, B. (2000). Facilitating a constructivist vision of technology integration among educational faculty and preservice teachers. *Journal of Research on Computing in Education, 33*(2), 132–148.

Wang, Y. (2002). When technology meets beliefs: Preservice teachers' perception of the teachers' role in the classroom with computers. *Journal of Research on Technology in Education, 35*(1) 150–161.

Zhao, Y., & Frank, K. A. (2003). An ecological analysis of factors affecting technology use in schools. *American Educational Research Journal, 40,* 807–840.

APPENDIX

5.A

Teachers' Beliefs Regarding Technology Use Survey (TBTUS)

	Completely Disagree	Strongly Disagree	Somewhat Disagree	Undecided	Somewhat Agree	Strongly Agree	Completely Agree
1. Students have more respect for teachers they see and can relate to as real people, not just as teachers.							
2. There are some students whose personal lives are so dysfunctional that they simply do not have the capability to learn.							
3. I can't allow myself to make mistakes with my students.							
4. Students achieve more in classes in which teachers encourage them to express their personal beliefs and feelings.							
5. Too many students expect to be coddled in school.							
6. If students are not doing well, they need to go back to the basics and do more drill and skill development.							
7. In order to maximize learning, I need to help students feel comfortable in discussing their feelings and beliefs.							
8. It's impossible to work with students who refuse to learn.							
9. No matter how bad a teacher feels, he or she has a responsibility not to let students know about those feelings.							
10. Addressing students' social, emotional, and physical needs is just as important to learning as meeting their intellectual needs.							
11. Even with feedback, some students just can't figure out their mistakes.							
12. My most important job as a teacher is to help students meet well-established standards of what it takes to succeed.							

Continued

	Completely Disagree	Strongly Disagree	Somewhat Disagree	Undecided	Somewhat Agree	Strongly Agree	Completely Agree
13. Taking the time to create caring relationships with my students is the most important element for student achievement.							
14. I can't help feeling upset and inadequate when dealing with difficult students.							
15. If I don't prompt and provide direction for student questions, students won't get the right answer.							
16. Helping students understand how their beliefs about themselves influence learning is as important as working on their academic skills.							
17. It's just too late to help some students.							
18. Knowing my subject matter really well is the most important contribution I can make to student learning.							
19. I can help students who are uninterested in learning get in touch with their natural motivation to learn.							
20. No matter what I do or how hard I try, there are some students who are unreachable.							
21. Knowledge of the subject area is the most important part of being an effective teacher.							
22. Students will be more motivated to learn if teachers get to know them at a personal level.							
23. Innate ability is fairly fixed and some children just can't learn as well as others.							
24. One of the most important things I can teach students is how to follow rules and to do what is expected of them in the classroom.							
25. When teachers are relaxed and comfortable with themselves, they have access to a natural wisdom for dealing with even the most difficult classroom situations.							
26. Teachers shouldn't be expected to work with students who consistently cause problems in class.							
27. Good teachers always know more than their students.							
28. Being willing to share who I am as a person with my students facilitates learning more than being an authority figure.							
29. I know best what students need to know and what's important; students should take my word that something will be relevant to them.							

Continued

	Completely Disagree	Strongly Disagree	Somewhat Disagree	Undecided	Somewhat Agree	Strongly Agree	Completely Agree
30. My acceptance of myself as a person is more central to my classroom effectiveness than my teaching skills.							
31. For effective learning to occur, I need to be in control of the direction of learning.							
32. Accepting students where they are no matter what their behavior and academic performance makes them more receptive to learning.							
33. I am responsible for what students learn and how they learn.							
34. Seeing things from the students' point of view is the key to their good performance in school.							
35. I believe that just listening to students in a caring way helps them solve their own problems.							
36. I am confident that I can use technology as an effective teaching tool.							
37. I am confident that I can use one computer effectively during large group instruction.							
38. I am confident that I can develop effective lessons that incorporate technology.							
39. I am confident that I can use technology effectively to teach content across the curriculum.							
40. I am confident that I can overcome difficulties using technology in the classroom (time, scheduling, accountability).							
41. I am confident that I can manage the grouping of students while using technology as a teaching tool.							
42. I am confident that I can meet the challenges of technology integration.							
43. Computers can provide instruction suited to individual students' needs.							
44. Computer use promotes student-centered learning and self-discovery.							
45. Computers can enhance my students' creativity and imagination.							
46. Computers can engage my students in collaborative work.							

Continued

	Completely Disagree	Strongly Disagree	Somewhat Disagree	Undecided	Somewhat Agree	Strongly Agree	Completely Agree
47. My students can learn problem-solving more effectively with computers.							
48. Writing is easier for my students when they use computers.							
49. I encourage and model smart choices about the tools students might use to accomplish tasks, using books, a spreadsheet or digital information when each one is the best.							
50. I encourage students to use the Internet and e-mail to communicate with experts, other students, and people from around the world to enrich their learning.							
51. I expect students to organize their thinking using Inspiration and other software programs to make mind maps.							
52. I ask students to use networked computers to explore important questions and issues arising out of the content of my class.							
53. I am making more time now than I used to for students to do more of the thinking, analyzing, interpreting, inferring, and synthesizing of information.							
54. I am getting quite good at recognizing worthy uses of new technologies while avoiding the silly, trendy uses that waste time without delivering much of value.							

APPENDIX

5.B

Lesson Planning Rubric

	Teacher-centered Level 1: point 1	Mixed but more toward teacher-centered Level 2: point 2	Mixed but more toward student-centered Level 3: point 3	Student-centered Level 4: point 4
1. Teacher roles (Teacher activity)	Transmitter of knowledge; expert source; director of skill/concept development through structured experiences	Mixed role of lecturer and facilitator but more toward directed (i.e., prepare only single resource)	Mixed role of lecturer and facilitator but more toward constructivist (i.e., prepare various resources)	Guide and facilitator as students generate their own knowledge; collaborative resource and assistant as students explore topics
2. Student roles (Student activity)	Receive information; demonstrate competence; all students learn same material and complete same activities	Mixed role of receiver of content and active learner with/without collaboration but more toward directed (i.e., more passive way following teachers' structured instruction)	Mixed role of receiver of content and active learner through collaboration but toward constructivist (i.e., more active way to engage in different activities)	Collaborate with others; develop competence; students may learn different material or engage in different activities
3. Curriculum characteristics	Based on skill and knowledge hierarchies; skills taught one after the other in set sequence	Mixed methods but more toward directed and follow more hierarchies (i.e., structured research topic)	Mixed methods toward constructivist and more holistic approach (i.e., individual research)	Based on projects that foster both higher- and lower-level skills concurrently (i.e., multiple components, multiple learning paths)

Continued

	Teacher-centered Level 1: point 1	Mixed but more toward teacher-centered Level 2: point 2	Mixed but more toward student-centered Level 3: point 3	Student-centered Level 4: point 4
4. Learning goals	Stated in terms of mastery learning and behavioral competence in a scope and sequence (clearly stated skill objectives with test items matched to them) Teacher-selected goals	Mixed goals with mastery knowledge/skills and construction of knowledge but more toward directed (e.g., following more sequenced knowledge/skills)	Mixed goals with mastery knowledge/skills and construction of knowledge but more toward constructivist (e.g., more self-directed and their own research-based goal)	Stated in terms of growth from where student began and increased ability to work independently and with others (global goals that specify general abilities like proble solving and research skills) Student-selected goals and self-directed learning
5. Types of activities	Lecture, demonstration, discussions, student practice, seatwork, testing	Either group work or hands-on activities (i.e., more toward individual work with hands-on or more toward group work without hands-on activities)	Mixed activities of group work with hands-on activities (i.e., more toward group work and more toward hands-on activities)	Group projects, hands-on exploration, product development, problem solving activities with flexibility in grouping
6. Assessment strategies	Written tests and development of products matched to objectives; all tests and products match set criteria; same measures for all students	Mixed assessment with both written test and performance test but more toward directed (more test and less or performance test is not clearly described)	Mixed assessment with both written test and performance test but more toward constructivist (more performance test, but it is not clearly described with rubric)	Performance tests and products such as portfolios; quality measured by rubrics and checklists; measures may differ among students

Continued

	Teacher-centered Level 1: point 1	Mixed but more toward teacher-centered Level 2: point 2	Mixed but more toward student-centered Level 3: point 3	Student-centered Level 4: point 4
7. Types of technology use	Evident technology use based on teacher-centered learning (e.g., using drill-practice s/w, use single media to deliver lecture)	Mixed technology use based on both teacher-centered and student-centered learning but more toward directed (i.e., use tutorial style or information driven s/w, combine more lecture and technology use is more for teacher-centered and less student-centered)	Mixed technology use based on both teacher-centered and student-centered learning but more toward constructivist (i.e., combine less lecture and use multiple media, single media for constructivist way for more student-centered)	Evident technology use based on student-centered learning (i.e., problem solving method)
Total Score:				

CHAPTER

6

Preparing Teachers for the "Schools That Technology Built": Evaluation of a Program to Train Teachers for Virtual Schooling

N. E. Davis | Iowa State University

M. D. Roblyer | University of Maryland University College

As a result of the growth of virtual schools across the United States, K–12 school courses and diplomas are increasingly offered, either completely or partly, at a distance. In light of this increase, it is apparent that there will be demand for teachers who are prepared to teach from a distance and a complementary need for local counselors. The U.S. Department of Education agreed that the creation of a model for incorporating virtual schooling in preservice teacher education programs accompanied by appropriate assessment of the effect for a range of competencies would be a significant innovation. This article describes the planned model led by Iowa State University and the evaluation designed to establish its effectiveness, including dissemination through a national community of practice. For example, evaluation of the competence of counselors, who will be prepared to mentor K–12 students learning from a distant teacher, moves from a formative approach into scientifically based research with experimental and control groups. In addition, instruments to measure institutional adoption include a modified version of the CBAM instrument developed by Christensen and longitudinal surveys of preservice student teachers and graduates.

Introduction

VIRTUAL SCHOOLING: A GROWING PHENOMENON

The virtual schools movement, in which K–12 school courses and diplomas are offered either mostly or completely using distance technologies, is expanding rapidly, thanks in no small part to the success of web-based distance learning in post-secondary education (Clark, 2001; Loupe, 2001; Roblyer, 2003; Setzer, Lewis, & Green, 2005; Zucker & Kozma, 2003). A just-released report on K–12 virtual schooling from the National Center for Education Statistics (NCES) (Setzer et al., 2005) says that about one-third of U.S. public school districts—representing 9% of public schools—had students enrolled in distance education courses during the 2002–2003 school year. According to Wood (2005), this translates to about 300,000 students attending online classes in this time period.

This is a remarkable growth rate for a phenomenon whose web-based incarnation only emerged around 1996. Although technologies such as broadcast radio and television had enabled distance learning in school programs in the United States and elsewhere for many years, pilot projects by the Concord Consortium in Massachusetts and Florida's Virtual School marked the beginning of an organized effort to offer K–12 distance courses using the Internet (Roblyer, 2005). According to Revenaugh (2005), nearly half of U.S. states now offer "statewide supplementary online programs, full-time cyber-schools, or both" (p. 25). In addition, a variety of presecondary schools in Canada, Australia, the United Kingdom, and elsewhere have opened their "virtual doors" (Roblyer, 2003; Zucker & Kozma, 2003). The NCES study (Setzer et al., 2005) reported that two-way interactive video is the technology most often cited as a primary instructional delivery system in small districts, but in large districts, web-based systems are used to offer the majority of programs.

Although many of these enterprises have been in operation less than a decade—and some only a few years or less—students seem to be flocking in record numbers to the "schools that technology built." Virtual schools that use the Internet began with high school students taking individual web-based courses, but now many of them offer complete high school diploma programs, and some provide instruction for middle school and even elementary school students.

The demand for virtual schools seems to be growing in response to a variety of needs, some that existed before 1996 when the K–12 web-based movement began, and some that have emerged as a by-product of our ever more technological society. The vision that drove the first virtual schools was that of more affordable, consistent, and equitable access to high-quality educational opportunities for students who need them most: rural, underserved, and at-risk populations. However, today's virtual school student is just as likely to be one who prefers the self-pacing and flexibility of virtual learning as one who lacks local access to courses needed for graduation (Wood, 2005).

The demand for virtual schools is driven at least in part by fundamental changes in our society and the students who inhabit it. As ubiquitous communications and immediate access to information have become more common, learners recognize that learning can be an anytime-anywhere experience. They want educational opportunities that reflect these characteristics. The disconnect between many current educational methods and those possible in an information-connected environment is becoming increasingly obvious. A new kind of student requires a new kind of schooling.

A PROGRAM TO PREPARE VIRTUAL TEACHERS

Just as today's virtual student differs in fundamental ways from those of the past, virtual teachers must also reflect different qualities. Virtual school experiences of the past 10 years have demonstrated that students who have been successful in traditional classrooms are not always as accomplished in virtual ones (Roblyer & Marshall, 2003). Those who succeed in online learning possess a set of skills that enables them to thrive in the rich atmosphere of cyberspace. It has become apparent that successful online teachers also require a unique set of skills. Wood (2005) quotes Blomeyer's observation that, "(there is a) persistent opinion that people who have never taught in this medium can jump in and teach a class.... A good classroom teacher is not necessarily a good online teacher" (p. 36).

Although much of the experience that defines competencies required for effective virtual teachers is anecdotal, there is widespread agreement on many of these skills. Roblyer and McKenzie (2000) found that many of the factors that make for a successful online instructor are the same as those for any successful instructor: good communication and classroom organization skills. However, a review of research by Cyrs (1997) identified several areas of unique competence for distance instructors, all of which require experience with distance learning environments:

- Course planning and organization that capitalize on distance learning strengths and minimize constraints
- Verbal and nonverbal presentation skills specific to distance learning situations
- Collaborative work with others to produce effective courses
- Ability to use questioning strategies
- Ability to involve and coordinate student activities among several sites (p. 17)

Easton's (2003) study of skills required by distance learning instructors supports the observations of both Cyrs (1997) and Roblyer and McKenzie (2000). She found that many communication skills required of the online instructor are similar to those needed for effective classroom teaching. However, she also pointed out that the online instructor's role requires a paradigm shift in perceptions of instructional time and space, virtual management techniques, and ways of engaging students through virtual communications.

In light of the increasing demand for virtual courses and the rapid expansion of schools to meet the demand, it is apparent that there will be a parallel need for teachers who are prepared to teach at a distance from their students. There will also be an equivalent need for counselors and other support personnel who understand the unique benefits of this new medium and are prepared to meet its needs and requirements. Research in K–12 virtual schooling (VS) shows that a "distant" teacher should be complemented with a local counselor and, better still, guidance from each student's homeroom teacher. That is, good practice in VS has local as well as distant components (Aronson & Timms, 2003; National Education Association, n.d.). Therefore, this rapidly developing facet of K–12 education is more likely to have a beneficial effect if all K–12 teachers become competent as VS counselors.

To help meet this demand, a consortium of universities led by Iowa State University is developing a model program to train personnel qualified to counsel, support, and teach K–12 virtual school students. This article will describe the Iowa State program, the evaluation designed to establish its effectiveness, and methods anticipated to disseminate the model.

A National Model to Integrate Virtual Schooling into Preservice Teacher Education

The U.S. Department of Education agreed that a model for incorporating VS in preservice teacher education programs, accompanied by appropriate assessment of the range of acquired competencies, would be a significant and much-needed innovation. In fall 2004, a project was funded to create a model to integrate a comprehensive VS curriculum into four diverse programs of preservice teacher education for the first time. Led by a land grant university (Iowa State University [ISU]), the project aims to spread to a large public southern university (University of Florida [UF]), a highly selective eastern university (University of Virginia [UVA]), and a liberal arts college (Graceland University [GU]) with several Midwest campuses, including a virtual campus. This creation of an innovative and transferable model of curriculum for more than 1,000 teachers' colleges across the United States will be supported by collaborating virtual schools, consultants, and a community of practice.

The context of VS provides significant challenges to preservice teacher education, beyond those of technology integration that will continue to challenge sustainability

(Davis, 2003). Virtual schools do not have physical premises to visit because courses, classrooms, and their administration have been adapted with technology specifically to disperse teachers and students for some or all of their time in VS. In addition, simultaneous renewal of teacher education and K–12 education is necessary (Goodlad, 1994; Thompson, Schmidt, & Davis, 2003) at a time when many K–12 schools and services are in the early stages of developing policy and practice for VS (Setzer et al., 2005). The challenges to teacher education include finding ways to expose examples of effective VS curriculum and practice so that preservice teachers may study the whole educational process and develop their own reflective practice.

The goal is for all teacher candidates to learn how to counsel a student who is participating in VS. In addition, the provision of guided observations and effective mentoring to develop the candidates' practice in live K–12 virtual classroom(s) needs to be creatively developed, so that some beginning teachers join the profession with an ability to assist other teachers in VS or have teaching experience in VS. The project will also add an advanced course in which teacher candidates design part of a course for K–12 students, similar to a course provided by a virtual school for its teachers. In all, the project aims to affect a total of four courses during the next three years and to assess the development of candidates' competence in the four roles listed in Table 6.2 (see page 136), namely Counselor, Assistant, Teacher, and Designer. The goal is to integrate competence of VS Counselor into all four preservice programs for all students, but only a few teacher candidates will be advised to take additional courses that develop competence in the other three teaching roles. This follows existing policy. For example, ISU's approach to developing competence as a VS teacher will build on its policy for student teaching abroad, through which strong teacher candidates suited to the experience are selected and carefully prepared for K–12 teaching experience in a foreign culture.

The Teacher Education Goes Into Virtual Schooling (TEGIVS) project has three complementary strategies to address these problems and build a model:

- Curriculum development in teacher education to map VS into the four programs and adapt or create selected courses that will include assessment of VS competence against standards. This will be underpinned by strategic professional and organizational development.

- Tools to expose VS will be created. For example, shell software will be created to provide a means for preservice students, faculty, and staff to select and explore particular instances of VS, drawing on related software design such as the goVHS tour (www.govhs.org), and the eDoc electronic portfolio project in ISU (Hassall, Nilakanta, Sheppard, & Wang, 2005).

- A national community of VS practice in teacher education is being developed to facilitate adoption of VS into teacher education nationwide.

Comprehensive evaluation within the project will inform the project development and assist in its dissemination. The plan has been accepted by the Fund for the Improvement of Postsecondary Education (FIPSE), which is using the project's evaluation plan as a model to inform other projects.

Evaluating the Virtual Schooling Preservice Program

A theme that runs throughout the design of the TEGIVS project is "planned innovation." The methods used to evaluate the success of the project are designed to match and reflect the innovative nature of the instructional strategies themselves. A team of internal and external evaluators is working together to develop creative ways of assessing the project's success in developing and implementing the training program. Formative assessments throughout the project also will help identify and guide needed modifications to strategies. Described here are the goals, strategies, and instrumentation that have been planned to carry out the evaluation.

EVALUATION OBJECTIVES

The goal of the project is to prepare preservice teachers in the four cooperating institutions to implement effective VS curricula at four levels of competence: counselor, assistant, teachers, and designer. The evaluation plan described here focuses on formative and summative measures of the implementation, results, institutionalization, and effect of three major project objectives that lead to this goal. These objectives, framed as research questions, are:

- ***VS competence:*** Do preservice teachers in the member institutions demonstrate competence in each of four levels of VS instruction?
- ***VS tools:*** Has the project developed effective tools for VS preservice teacher education?
- ***Community of practice:*** Are personnel inside and outside the project using project methods and procedures and working together to enhance them?

Project personnel will use formative data to guide development of the curriculum, tools, and courses and to improve dissemination methods, as needed. Summative data will be documented in final project reports to project staff, to the consortium members, and to the funding agencies.

EVALUATION STRATEGIES

The evaluation plan consists of the following activities designed to address each of the three objectives:

1. ***Strategies to evaluate objective 1.*** In keeping with new federal requirements to use scientifically based research in evaluation methods, evaluators will employ a quasi-experimental design, using a control group to provide comparisons with groups trained in the project. A test consisting of web-based scenarios is being developed to integrate with the curriculum. For example, VS Counselors at ISU will be trained in six labs with 15–20 students each. Three labs, chosen randomly, will participate as the experimental group and three will serve as the control group. Testing at the other consortium members will replicate this evaluation strategy as much as is possible in light of their course structures.

2. ***Strategies to evaluate objective 2.*** Three types of activities will be used to assess accomplishment of this objective. First, formative evaluation will review documentation of the software development, using evaluation procedures described by Hix and Hartson (1993). This procedure calls for identifying the benchmark tasks and usability specifications, and then using "critical incidents" observation as students perform benchmark tasks. These observations will be reported in cost/importance tables, with data analyzed to produce a priority ratio and priority rank for each critical incident. Incidents with a sufficiently high priority rank or ratio will identify areas in need of revision. Second, summative evaluation will consist of survey and observation of the student and instructor users about the usability of the software during pilots and field trials; observations, based on the pre-identified benchmarks, will include one-to-one evaluation first, then small groups, and then field trials. The benchmarks are typically more carefully defined in one-to-one evaluation and become more loosely defined as the software matures and users' utilization of it becomes more representative of real-world use. Third, summative evaluation of Objective 2 will occur when the tools are used as part of the intervention evaluated for Objective 1 with the quasi-experimental design.

3. ***Strategies to evaluate objective 3.*** Summative evaluation for this objective will use a set of checklists to monitor milestones met, logs of participant data, and a modified version of the *Concerns-Based Adoption Model (CBAM)* instrument, developed by Rhonda Christensen in conjunction with the Institute for the Integration of Technology into Teaching and Learning at the University of North Texas (see www.iittl.unt.edu/surveys/demos/CBAM.htm). Data logs will be kept on participants in conferences, workshops, and websites; use of digital library items; and minutes of meetings in which new courses and certificates are approved.

ASSESSMENT INSTRUMENTS AND RESOURCES

Materials to carry out the project evaluation are developed by the external and internal evaluators with the help of the project management team, and the external evaluator will establish instrument validity and reliability. Instruments will include:

> ***Pre- and post-course evaluation Likert scale.*** These instruments will provide formative, self-report data from students on all aspects of course satisfaction. Students will complete pre-course and post-course evaluations, and results will be compared for a match between anticipated and achieved results.
>
> ***VS scenario rubrics.*** Scenarios will challenge students to respond with best practices in various virtual instructional situations; rubrics will measure their success in choosing most appropriate responses for each situation.
>
> ***Post-course rubric for online instruction.*** Developed by faculty and staff at California State University, Chico, this instrument is designed to aid both the development and evaluation of online courses. (See the rubric at: www.csuchico.edu/celt/roi)
>
> ***Tool ratings checklists.*** Ratings checklists will assess usefulness and ease of use of each tool developed by the project. Checklists will be completed by instructors and preservice students at all four institutions.
>
> ***Modified* CBAM.** This instrument has been modified to focus specifically on faculty's awareness and adoption of TEGIVS resources and methods, as opposed to awareness and adoption of technologies in general. (See the JRTE website [www.iste.org/jrte] for a copy of the draft instrument.)
>
> ***Preservice and postgraduation follow-up survey items.*** To assess students' post-course and post-program perceptions of how well the program prepared them for work in virtual school environments, items will be added to two surveys used by ISU: the existing survey of students on teaching practice and the graduate follow-up survey. These surveys also provide an opportunity to sample the presence of VS in K–12 schools as perceived by ISU students and graduates.

In addition to the formal evaluation evidence just described, the project encourages faculty and graduate students to undertake complementary research. This will be facilitated by a code of practice that respects all participants and stakeholders, plus ongoing mandatory regulation by the Institutional Review Board in ISU.

Table 6.1 summarizes these evaluation instruments. Instrumentation currently under development is indicated with an asterisk.

Table 6.1 Evaluation Instruments in the TEGIVS Project

Project Objectives	Instrumentation					
	Coursc Evaluation Likert Scale (pre/post)*	VS Scenario Rubrics*	Rubric for Online Instruction	Tool Ratings Checklists*	Modified *CBAM*	Post-graduation Follow-up Survey Items*
1: Teaching competence	X	X	X			
2: Effective tools				X		
3: Active community					X	X

Conclusion: Plans for Disseminating Results

The goal of the project goes beyond the small representative sample of participating teacher education programs to create a model for all U.S. programs. One of the strategies is to create a national community of practice building on existing structures. In this way, early milestones have been achieved on target within the first six months. One example is the creation of the first version of the VS standards by building on ISTE's National Education Technology Standards (NETS) for Teachers (2004). ISTE's NETS have been widely adopted across the United States, and NETS for Teachers (NETS•T) are part of the accreditation process mandated by the National Council for Accreditation of Teacher Education (NCATE). The published literature and participants' experience in VS were used to redraft a set of competencies for each VS role. (See Table 6.2.) Working through existing national communities in professional associations is a second example of the project building on existing national structures. The project held a session at the 2005 annual conference of the Society of Information Technology in Teacher Education (SITE), where the vision and the first version of the VS competencies were validated with peers in the United States and worldwide (Davis, Niederhauser, Compton, Lindstrom, & Schoeny, 2005). The SITE committee for distance education discussed the challenges of VS, and that committee welcomed ongoing dialogue with the project through its online discussion board and conference sessions.

Table 6.2 The Four Roles (Levels) of VS Competence Planned for Preservice Teachers

Roles	Types of Competence
VS Counselor	Advise and support K–12 students participating in VS
VS Assistant	Assist a teacher providing a VS course
VS Teacher	Teach a VS class
VS Designer	Design and teach a VS course

The project will make extensive use of the Internet for dissemination. The project's website (www.ctlt.iastate.edu/research/projects/tegivs/homepage.html) will be complemented by pushing information to locations where teacher educators tend to seek it. Resources developed by the project will be shared through the digital library of the Association for the Advancement of Computing in Education (AACE). These will include VS curriculum materials, tools, case studies, and evaluation instruments. Collaboration with leading-edge publishing expertise in AACE will enable the development of appropriate procedures and protocols to archive curriculum materials and other media, including the open-source software of the VS tools. This approach aims to be sustained after the funded project's completion. The inclusion of the evaluation instruments in the digital library also answers calls to improve research into technology in teacher education using multiple sources of data and shared research instruments (Thompson, 2005).

The authors welcome correspondence and plan to link readers' communications with the dissemination strategies discussed earlier. We recognize that the virtual schools movement brings many challenges to K–12 education and to teacher preparation. Goodlad's (1994) view of simultaneous renewal serves as a reminder that innovations in K–12 education must be matched by innovation in preservice teacher education—one cannot come before the other, because both must change together. We plan for this change to be carefully evaluated to inform the development of a model, to sustain VS in the collaborating programs of teacher education, and to inform and support its dissemination nationwide. With continuing evaluation and revision, the project will yield a model for how to prepare teachers and support staff who are both comfortable and competent with "the schools that technology built."

Author Update

The rapid coevolution of educational practices and digital technologies continues to fuel the exponential growth of virtual schooling, both in the United States and abroad—including New Zealand, where the first author has relocated. The products of our federally-funded project Teacher Education Goes into Virtual Schooling are archived in the project's website at http://ctlt.iastate.edu/~tegivs/TEGIVS/homepage.html. The evaluation of our national project to include this new mode of schooling within all four universities' preservice teacher education programs measured statistically significant, albeit highly variable, changes in student teachers' perceptions of and competence in virtual schooling. Data collection using the modified *Concerns-Based Adoption Model (CBAM)* instrument for the diffusion of this innovation was most problematic because of the sensitivity of surveying faculty. An innovative aspect of the project was the design and pilot of an early field experience course with a virtual school and an online teacher. Qualitative evidence indicated substantial progress in preservice teachers' understanding of virtual schooling and willingness to engage with it.

Effective practice for virtual schooling is evolving rapidly and with a variety of benefits to teachers, schools, and education systems (Sampson-Gruener, Roblyer, Bielefeldt, & Schneidmiller, 2009). The second author, now at the University of Tennessee in Chattanooga and an external evaluator for the Alabama ACCESS virtual school system, recently reported findings that virtual teaching has a reverse impact on improving teachers' in-person teaching (Roblyer, Porter, Bielefeldt, & Donaldson, 2009). Professional practice is, however, highly variable, as shown in a recent editorial for a special issue of the *Journal of Technology and Teacher Education* (Davis & Ferdig, 2009). This continuing evolution has resulted in additional research into perceptions of virtual schooling using evidence gathered with the TEGIVS Lab Tool and related rubric (Charania, 2010) and the additional innovation of a field experience in virtual schooling (Compton, Davis, & Mackey, 2009).

Acknowledgments

The contents of this chapter were partly developed under a grant from the Fund for the Improvement of Postsecondary Education (FIPSE), U.S. Department of Education. However, these contents do not necessarily represent policy of the Department of Education, and no one should assume endorsement by the federal government. We also wish to acknowledge support from all participating organizations.

References

Aronson, J., & Timms, M. (2003). *Net choices, net gains: Supplementing the high school curriculum with online courses.* San Francisco, CA: WestEd.

Charania, A. (2010, in preparation). *Are preservice teachers ready for virtual schooling?* Unpublished PhD dissertation, Iowa State University.

Clark, T. (2001, October). *Virtual schools: Trends and issues.* Report commissioned by the Distance Learning Resource Network, a WestEd Project; co-sponsored by the Centre for the Application of Information Technologies at Western Illinois University. Available at: www.dlrn.org/trends.html

Compton, L. K., Davis, N. E., & Mackey, J. (2009). Virtual field experience in virtual schooling. *Journal of Technology and Teacher Education, 17*(4).

Cyrs, T. E. (1997). Competence in teaching at a distance. In T. E. Cyrs (Ed.), *Teaching and learning at a distance: What it takes to effectively design, deliver, and evaluate programs* (pp. 15–18). San Francisco, CA: Jossey-Bass.

Davis, N. E. (2003). Technology and teacher education in the USA: What makes for good sustainable practice? *Technology, Pedagogy and Learning, 12*(10), 59–84.

Davis, N. E. & Ferdig, R. (2009). Editorial: What is special about teacher education for Virtual Schooling? *Journal of Technology and Teacher Education, 17*(4).

Davis, N. E, Niederhauser, D. S., Compton, L., Lindstrom, D., & Schoeny, Z. (2005, March). Virtual Schooling lab practice: Case studies for teacher preparation. In C. Crawford, R. Carlsen, I. Gibson, K. McFerrin, J. Price, R. Weber, & D. A. Willis (Eds.), *Society for Information Technology & Teacher Education International Conference Annual* (pp. 342–345), Phoenix, AZ. Charlottesville, VA: Association for the Advancement of Computing in Education.

Easton, S. (2003). Clarifying the instructor's role in online distance learning. *Communication Education, 52*(2), 87–105.

Goodlad, J. (1994). *Educational renewal.* San Francisco, CA: Jossey-Bass.

Hassall, L., Nilakanta, R., Sheppard, M., & Wang, Y. (2005, March). eDoc: Innovation in electronic portfolio design and development. In C. Crawford, R. Carlsen, I. Gibson, K. McFerrin, J. Price, R. Weber, et al. (Eds.), *Society for Information Technology & Teacher Education International Conference Annual* (pp. 96–100), Phoenix, AZ. Charlottesville, VA: Association for the Advancement of Computing in Education.

Hix, D., & Hartson, H. R. (1993). *Developing user interfaces: Ensuring usability through product and process.* New York, NY: Wiley.

International Society for Technology in Education. (2004). *National educational technology standards for teachers: Preparing teachers to use technology.* Eugene, OR: Author.

Kosma, R., Zucker, A., & Espinoza, C. (1998, October). *An evaluation of the virtual high school after one year of operation.* Arlington, VA: SRI International. Available at: http://vhs.concord.org

Loupe, D. (2001). Virtual schooling: A new dimension to learning brings new challenges for educators. *eSchool News, 4*(6), 41–47.

McLester, S. (2002). Virtual learning takes a front row seat, *Technology &Learning, 22*(8), 24–36.

National Education Association. (n.d.). *Guide to online high school courses.* Washington, DC: Author. Available at: www.nea.org/technology/distanceed/highschool/

Revenaugh, M. (2005). Virtual schooling: Legislative update. *Technology & Learning, 25*(9), 20–25.

Roblyer, M. D. (2003). Virtual high schools in the United States: Current views, future visions. In J. Bradley (Ed.), *The open classroom: Distance learning in and out of schools* (pp. 159–170). London, UK: Kogan Page.

Roblyer, M. D. (2005). Real issues for virtual schools. *The International Principal, 8*(3).

Roblyer, M. D., & Marshall, J. (2003). Predicting success of virtual high school distance learners: Preliminary results from an educational success prediction instrument (ESPRI). *Journal of Research on Technology in Education, 35*(2), 241–255.

Roblyer, M. D., & McKenzie, B. (2000). Distant but not out-of-touch: What makes an effective distance learning instructor? *Learning & Leading with Technology, 27*(6), 50–53.

Roblyer, M. D., Porter, M., Bielefeldt, T., & Donaldson, M. B. (2009). Teaching online made me a better teacher: Studying the impact of virtual course experiences on teachers' face-to-face practice. *Journal of Computing in Teacher Education, 25*(4), 121–126.

Sampson-Gruener, G., Roblyer, M. D., Bielefeldt, T., & Schneidmiller, J. (2009). *Report on the Alabama Connecting Classrooms, Educators, & Students Statewide (ACCESS) distance learning program.* Montgomery, AL: Alabama State Department of Education. Retrieved from http://accessdl.state.al.us/Documents/ISTE/ISTEREPORTONACCESSYR3FinalRevised.pdf

Setzer, C., Lewis, L., & Greene, B. (2005). *Distance education courses for public elementary and secondary school students: 2002–2003.* Report No. NCES 2005–101. Washington, DC: National Center for Education Statistics.

Thompson, A. D. (2005). Scientifically based research: Establishing a research agenda for the technology in teacher education community. *Journal of Research on Technology in Education, 37*(4), 331–337.

Thompson, A. D., Schmidt, D. A., & Davis, N. E. (2003, January). Technology collaboratives for simultaneous renewal in teacher education. *Educational Technology Research and Development, 51*(1), 71–87.

Wood, C. (2005). Highschool.com. *Edutopia, 1*(4), 32–37.

CHAPTER

7

The Diffusion of Electronic Portfolios in Teacher Education: Issues of Initiation and Implementation

Neal Strudler | University of Nevada, Las Vegas

Keith Wetzel | Arizona State University

This descriptive study investigates the diffusion of electronic portfolios in preservice teacher education by documenting the context and emergent practices in six programs identified as mature in their implementation. Context variables examined include prior use of paper portfolios, pressures for standards-based assessment, and leadership and governance issues. Variations in program implementation are also explored, including the portfolio tools employed, artifact selection, evaluation of student work, and the role of reflection. Findings of the study suggest that amid the common themes across programs, there are numerous variations in approaches to e-portfolio use. The authors conclude that further research is needed to examine the future directions for e-portfolios envisioned as well as specific advice for those in earlier stages of adoption or implementation.

Introduction

This study investigates the diffusion of electronic portfolios in preservice teacher education by documenting emergent practices in their use and the process by which those practices are adopted and implemented. The focus of this study is to examine mature, well-articulated efforts in programs in which faculty and students have used electronic portfolios program-wide for two or more years. Specifically, it seeks to answer the following two research questions:

1. What was the situational and historical context in which electronic portfolios were adopted and implemented?
2. What do the various facets of the electronic portfolio process look like as implemented?

PORTFOLIOS IN TEACHER EDUCATION

The use of portfolios has a rich history in teacher education. In a survey of schools, colleges, and departments of education (hereafter referred to as colleges of education), Salzman, Denner, and Harris (2002) found that 89% reported using portfolios for some type of assessment. As technology has advanced, some institutions are moving from or are considering moving from hard copy to electronic portfolios (Bartlett, 2002; Gathercoal, Love, Bryde, & McKean, 2002; Smith, Harris, & Sammons, 2001; Williams, Wetzel, & Wilhelm, 2004; Yancey, 2001). Colleges of education have marshaled resources to help them prepare for and develop electronic portfolio programs, as demonstrated by the fact that 50% of the 400 U.S. Department of Education's Preparing Tomorrow's Teachers to use Technology (PT^3) grant programs focused at least in part on implementing digital portfolios in teacher education (Britten, Mullen, & Stuve, 2003). An examination of the annual proceedings of the Society for Information Technology and Teacher Education (SITE) revealed 52 papers presented in 2003 and 56 in 2004 that focused on electronic portfolios in preservice education.

WHAT ARE PORTFOLIOS AND WHY ARE THEY USED?

Shulman, an early proponent of educational portfolios, defines the teacher's working portfolio as a "structured documentary history of a set of coached or mentored acts of teaching, substantiated by samples of student portfolios, and fully realized only through reflective writing, deliberation, and conversation" (1998, p. 37). Preservice student portfolios document their journey in becoming a teacher. Preservice students select, share, and reflect on artifacts such as educational philosophies, classroom management plans, unit and lesson plans, plans to meet the needs of diverse and special needs pupils, and video clips of practice teaching. Portfolios make learning visible, and thus faculty members and students focus on learning in new ways (Yancey, 2001). In general, such learning portfolios are based on a constructivist philosophy. Students may be expected to take responsibility for selecting artifacts, making connections to standards, and interpreting their own learning.

Portfolios can also be used to promote or market students for employment opportunities. The hiring or employment portfolio includes work samples that showcase students' preparation to be teachers. It is designed to help students secure teaching positions. The audience is school district principals or others involved in selecting teachers.

Other approaches to portfolios are primarily designed to meet the needs of the programs or institutions (Barrett, 2004; Fagin, Hand, & Boyd, 2004). Teacher education programs are increasingly being asked to align curriculum and student outcomes with state and national teacher education standards. For programs, faculty, and preservice students, standards provide direction for artifact selection and organization of the electronic portfolio. Students thus create these portfolios to satisfy outside readers. Often rubrics are used to evaluate the included items. The evaluation data are aggregated and disaggregated to demonstrate that a program is meeting the necessary standards. Colleges of education also use the data to show where improvements are required.

In addition, portfolios can be used to determine whether individual students meet the requirements for certification and graduation. Portfolios assessed for these purposes can be considered high-stakes assessments. Several states mandate portfolios for this purpose.

WHAT TOOLS ARE USED TO CREATE ELECTRONIC PORTFOLIOS?

Colleges of education are selecting one of two routes to portfolio creation. Some use off-the-shelf tools such as Microsoft Office and various web authoring applications. Others use commercial web-based systems (e.g., Chalk & Wire, Johns Hopkins' Portfolio System, Live Text, Professor Portfolio, and TaskStream). Off-the-shelf programs are productivity tools that students use to design their electronic portfolios. Commercial systems are web-based and assist students with the construction of their electronic portfolios as well as provide for the storage and managing of the information in the portfolios.

Theoretical Framework

The theoretical framework of this study is grounded within the change theory of Fullan (2001) and Hall and Hord (2001). Together these bodies of work serve as a lens for analyzing specifics of the change process. A discussion follows of selected themes of that work that are especially relevant to this study.

PHASES OF THE CHANGE PROCESS

Fullan (2001) outlined three broad phases of the change process:

1. Initiation or Adoption—consisting of the process that leads up to and includes a decision to adopt or proceed with a change
2. Implementation—usually the first two or three years of use, involving the first experiences of attempting to put an idea or reform into practice
3. Continuation or Institutionalization—referring to whether the change gets built in as an ongoing part of the system

Fullan notes, however, that these phases offer a simplified version of a "detailed and snarled process" (p. 50). He adds that the process is not necessarily linear, "but rather one in which events at one phase can feed back and alter decisions made at previous stages" (p. 50). For example, a decision made at the adoption phase to use a particular program may be later modified during implementation.

CHANGE IS A COMPLEX, SOCIOCULTURAL PROCESS THAT TAKES TIME

Hall and Hord (2001) view change in education as a complex process that takes a minimum of three to five years, with large-scale innovations taking longer. Fullan concurs that the "total time frame from initiation to institutionalization is lengthy; even moderately complex change takes 3 to 5 years, while larger scale efforts can take 5 to 10 years with sustaining improvements still being problematic" (p. 52). One explanation for this difficulty is that an organization will not change until individuals within it change (Hall & Hord, 2001). Furthermore, the culture of the organization can present a major obstacle to implementing new ideas and practices. Fullan (2001) quantifies this challenge in what he calls the *25/75 Rule for Educational Change* in which "twenty-five percent of the solution is having good directional ideas; 75% is figuring out how to get there in one local context after another" (p. 269). Fullan (2001) supports this view in citing the work of Senge, a prominent theorist on organizational change. Senge wrote, "The fundamental flaw in most innovators' strategies is that they focus on their innovations, on what they are trying to do—rather than on understanding how the larger culture, structures, and norms will react to their efforts" (Senge et al., 1999, p. 99). Hall and Hord (2001) agree that most change efforts overly emphasize development at the expense of implementation.

GOVERNANCE ISSUES

In view of the challenges of implementing large-scale educational change, one might ask what governance structures best address these challenges. Primarily referring to

K–12 schools, Hall and Hord (2001) assert, "Although top-down and bottom-up change can work, a horizontal perspective is best" (p. 10). Interestingly, both Hall and Hord and Fullan (2001) acknowledge that top-down change—that is, change mandated from administration—can be effective. Hall and Hord qualify that mandates can lead to successful change if accompanied by support, training, and an understanding of the change process. While noting that top-down change often leads to resistance during implementation, Fullan writes that administrative mandates can have positive results if the proposed change is indeed a good idea and is "combined with empowerment and choices as the process unfolds" (p. 67). In summary, the literature supports a horizontal or balanced approach to governing change that depends on administrators' support and assistance in securing resources as well as the eventual "buy-in" from those who will be most involved in implementing the change.

Method

This study employs case methodology (Yin, 1989) to investigate the adoption and implementation of electronic portfolios within teacher education programs. During the first phase of the study (Wetzel & Strudler, 2005), the researchers sought to identify teacher education programs in which the use of e-portfolios is well articulated and mature and optimally in place for a minimum of two or three years. A call for nominees was posted on several electronic mailing lists pertaining to teacher education and technology, including AERA, SIGTE, and AACE. The call stated:

> We are conducting a study on the use of electronic portfolios for teaching, learning, and assessing in preservice teacher education. We will survey, interview, and then visit selected teacher education sites to investigate current and emergent practices in the use of e-portfolios. For this study we are seeking nominations of institutions that are accomplished users of electronic portfolios. Programs that you recommend should be well articulated and mature with faculty and students who have optimally used portfolios program-wide for a few years. You may self-nominate your program.

In addition, we reviewed related literature and polled experts in the field. Twenty-six programs were nominated by one or more of their peers or were self-nominated. The nominees represented 25 universities in 15 U.S. states and one Australian university. As programs were identified through the various methods described, a letter of nomination accompanied by a brief survey was sent out to deans to gather information about the 26 programs nominated, including purposes for electronic portfolio use and the dates of program-wide adoption. A follow-up reminder was sent to deans or the deans' designees of the programs nominated who did not complete the survey within two weeks. Twenty-three of the 26 deans or their designees completed the survey.

The 15-item questionnaire was administered using Survey Monkey's online survey tool (The survey is available at http://coe.nevada.edu/nstrudler/survey3.pdf). On analysis of the surveys, phone interviews were then employed to gather more data to inform the final selection of six programs for the case studies. The primary criteria for selection were the length of time that the electronic portfolio program had been in place and the extent to which it was a program-wide venture that involved a large percentage of faculty and other personnel. Beyond seeking programs that are advanced in their use of electronic portfolios, cases were selected based on variations in their emphases and approaches. Variables considered were differing purposes for the portfolios (e.g., accreditation or accountability versus learning and reflection); low versus high stakes in terms of exit requirements; prior history with print-based portfolios; the size of the program; public versus private universities; and the employment of off-the-shelf applications versus commercial systems for creating portfolios.

DATA SOURCES AND ANALYSIS

Based on surveys, phone interviews, and review of websites and relevant documents, six programs were selected: California Lutheran University (CLU), Eastern Kentucky University (EKU), Indiana University of Pennsylvania (IUP), Johns Hopkins University (JHU), University of Rhode Island (URI), and University of Iowa (Iowa). Site visits were scheduled for the research team during November and December 2004 for approximately three days each. During that time, semistructured interviews were conducted with teacher education faculty, university administrators, teacher candidates, recent graduates, and technology support providers. We opted for a nonrandom, purposeful sample of informants arranged with the help of one or more people serving in a liaison role at each of the universities. In some cases additional interviews were scheduled during the site visits based on information gathered during those visits. It was our intent to interview a cross section of informants that reflected a range of perspectives and participation in the process. Overall, we conducted 80 interviews of individuals and small groups with 124 informants in all. The interviews ranged from 15 to more than 90 minutes in length. The average interview took approximately 45 minutes.

In addition, we reviewed supporting artifacts and observed various facets of the implementation process, taking field notes throughout the visit. As with the interviews, in addition to classroom observations scheduled by our hosts, impromptu observations were arranged during our interactions with various informants.

During unscheduled intervals during the visits and subsequent to the daily schedule, the researchers discussed reactions to the interviews and observations. Notes were recorded, and any unanswered questions were noted for follow-up in subsequently scheduled interviews. It was our goal in each of the site visits to probe into any unclear areas so that by the end of the visits, we arrived at a clear picture of each program and how it was perceived by the various stakeholders.

All interviews were audiotaped and transcribed, and then analyzed using Hyper-RESEARCH Qualitative Analysis Tool. Using the constant comparative method (Strauss, 1987), data analysis began as data were first collected and continued throughout the study. Data were triangulated as our review of documents and field notes from observations served to confirm the trustworthiness (Lincoln & Guba, 1985) of the interview data.

We began by reading and rereading our field notes and transcriptions of the interviews. Guided by the research questions, we coded the data, beginning with a common set of codes established by the researchers. As the study progressed, we revised our codes as needed to reflect the data gathered. Eventually we arrived at 50 unique codes, a subset of which was employed for this chapter.

Drafts of individual case summaries were written for three of the sites visited. Because of time constraints, the remaining cases were summarized through discussion among the researchers. Then, based on the cross-case analysis, drafts of the chapter were written and sent to key informants at each site to check for accuracy of the data and feedback on our analysis. Corrections and modifications were then made to the chapter as needed.

Results

1. What was the situational and historical context in which electronic portfolios were adopted and implemented?

As previously described, sites for the case studies were selected for the degree of program-wide implementation of electronic portfolios and for variations in terms of the mission and size of the universities, and their approaches to and goals for electronic portfolio use. Table 7.1 provides a summary of program characteristics of the six sites visited. Further elaboration on selected data from Table 7.1 follows, organized by the following themes: prior experience with paper portfolios, impetus for adoption of electronic portfolios, leadership and governance, and grants.

Table 7.1 Summary of Program Characteristics

	CLU	EKU	IUP	JHU	Iowa	U of RI
Approx. # Teachers Certified Annually	80	800	500	200	385	250
Public or Private	Private	Public	Public	Private	Public	Public
Carnegie Classification (2000)	Masters I	Masters I	Doctoral/ Research Intensive	Doctoral/ Research Extensive	Doctoral/ Research Extensive	Doctoral/ Research Extensive
Primary Certification Program	5th Year Initial Licensure	Undergrad	Undergrad	Master's	Undergrad	Undergrad
National Accreditation Body	NCATE	NCATE	NCATE	NCATE	NCATE	NCATE
Program-Wide Paper Portfolio/ Initial Purpose	Yes/State Standards (CSTP)	Yes/State Standards (KERA)	Yes/Job Seeking	Yes/INTASC	No/Using in some courses	Yes/State Standards (RI-BTS)
Grants to Support Planning	PT^3 (1999)	PT^3 (2000)	PT^3 (1999)	PT^3 (1999); Title II	No PT^3; Funding sources not specified	PT^3; 3 State Grants
Primary Tools	ProfPort, commercially distributed	Templates, Front Page	Template, HTML editors	JHU system, commercially distributed	Templates, HTML editors	In-house system

BACKGROUND: PRIOR EXPERIENCE WITH PAPER PORTFOLIOS

In analyzing data across cases, we looked for factors that led the various programs toward their early adoption of electronic portfolios. We found that five of the six sites selected had substantial program-wide experience with paper portfolios before working with electronic portfolios. Furthermore, we found that several of the programs were strongly influenced by their state standards for beginning teachers. Cal Lutheran had a history of use of paper portfolios throughout the teacher education program starting around 1995–96. The portfolio artifacts supported the California Standards for the Teaching Profession (CSTP), which evolved from six standards to the current number of 13. Similarly, Eastern Kentucky initiated paper portfolios to address new teacher standards that were enacted by the Kentucky Reform Act (KERA) in 1990. The first paper portfolio required of students included a resume, sample lesson plans, a teaching philosophy, and introductory material. University of Rhode Island enacted requirements for paper portfolios in the late '80s, based on work that led to the Rhode Island Beginning Teacher Standards (RI-BTS), which were derived largely from the INTASC principles. At Johns Hopkins, in 1995, faculty started looking at INTASC principles and developed a process for paper portfolios.

An administrator from Rhode Island described their initial efforts with paper portfolios:

> It began in student-teaching and methods block, when we had much of the same discussion that we had today, to tell you the truth—what are some of the types of tasks that someone would accomplish to show that they are a competent planner, that they can manage a classroom, that they can assess students.... There was a state group that was meeting at the same time and we sort of had some synergy here on campus with that state group. And we began to utilize those in student teaching and in methods ... and it was, you know, a unit plan, and an assessment of student work, and what we called a context statement, where, you know: "Describe a district and its key variables or factors which influence student learning, SES, etc., etc., state testing." So we had these series of tasks, and students then completed these paper portfolios.

At IUP, the initial impetus for electronic portfolios was to aid in students' seeking jobs. Explained an administrator, "The paper portfolio that they had was intended more to guide the students toward the creation of a job-hunting portfolio when they were to complete the program." At University of Iowa, paper portfolios were used in courses such as the student teaching seminar or as a culminating experience in art education, but were not implemented across an entire program.

IMPETUS FOR INITIATION OF ELECTRONIC PORTFOLIOS

Each case has its own unique interaction of factors that led to initiating their respective electronic portfolio programs. In this section we discuss themes identified in various programs as the main impetus for adopting electronic portfolios. Related factors such as governance, leadership, and grants are discussed in subsequent sections.

Transition from Paper Portfolios. As described previously, a primary impetus for initiating paper portfolios at several sites was to meet state standards for beginning teachers. With that approach already established, it follows that the implementation of paper portfolios would pave the way for initiating electronic alternatives. Interview data suggest that paper portfolios posed several logistical problems that needed to be addressed. Faculty alluded to the onerous task of lugging around and sharing large paper portfolios. A professor at Cal Lutheran explained, "You had these rooms full of these four and five inch thick portfolios that we had to go through, so they were physically unwieldy." Another Cal Lutheran faculty member added, "We typically collected them at the end of the semester, so we had this truckload of binders that we needed to go through. It was a very laborious proposition." Another recalled, "We used to have portfolios lining the walls. Every student had one and we would pass them from faculty member to faculty member. Sometimes they even got lost. And that was sad but true."

An administrator from Rhode Island concurred,

> I'm sinking under the paper. Which ones do you keep? Which ones don't you keep? And you began to think about electronic portfolios. And we got some seed money to begin to develop that concept.

A professor from Eastern Kentucky reflected on the transition to electronic portfolios from paper to make it so that binder portfolios would become broadly viewable.

> The binder had not been around that long to say it was a permanent part of the education program. Then putting it into the e-portfolio form just seemed like a logical next step with the development of the World Wide Web and the ability to access things from remote locations. That's a large part of it.

To varying degrees, paper portfolios provided alternatives for faculty and students in terms of how student learning was evaluated. A director at Cal Lutheran noted that due to the prior paper portfolio use, the move to electronic portfolios "was a technological leap but not necessarily a conceptual one in terms of assessment." He added, "If you're not into authentic assessment, then you're probably not going to appreciate what a web folio system can do for you."

Standards and Accreditation. Whereas state standards were prominent in decisions to adopt paper portfolios, electronic portfolios were initiated in large part to address NCATE requirements for documenting teacher candidates' attainment of standards. A dean from one of the programs articulated what several others had noted:

> The impetus, to some extent, maybe more of an extent than I'd want to admit, is continuing NCATE accreditation, and the need to have very extensive, clearly archived records of how well students ... are achieving the goals of the program.

A [department] chair at Johns Hopkins explained their approach to implement electronic portfolios that would serve in lieu of a traditional thesis for their master's program. She stated that it was an exit requirement that became driven by needs of accountability and accreditation:

> When you are up against NCATE standards and specialty organization standards, how do you show evidence of this and this? You can point to some of it from observations in classrooms, but a fair amount of it can be hinged on their portfolios.

An administrator at Johns Hopkins stated that they developed an electronic version for their portfolio based on a structure already in place. Fortunately, Johns Hopkins had access to the necessary expertise in the Center for Technology in Education, an entrepreneurial unit housed within the college of education.

Although Iowa had initial plans for electronic portfolios to support the professional placement of their teacher candidates (i.e., marketing/hiring), it became a means for addressing state and national mandates for standards-based performance assessment. Stated a University of Iowa administrator, "Obviously, it's a tool for moving through accreditation." A Rhode Island administrator discussed the challenge of tracking student progress across programs and the potential of electronic portfolios to help:

> I think that the requirement that you will have data across programs, and you've got to keep that straight in some fashion. Every program has a different task and a different rubric and a different scaling system, you're really talking about some resources to be able to give any judgments about how well are students doing.

LEADERSHIP AND GOVERNANCE

Leadership for electronic portfolios can come from the top (i.e., administration) or from faculty and staff. Although the literature supports the effectiveness of a combination of top-down and bottom-up leadership, it also suggests that administrative mandates can work when accompanied by the allocation of resources and meaningful faculty input over time. Clearly, data in this study suggest that the approaches to leadership and governance are key variables in how the initiation of electronic portfolios were received by faculty and ultimately implemented. Although it is beyond the scope of this paper to explore leadership and governance issues in depth for each case, selected themes are described.

Respect and Vision. Interview data illustrate many examples in which informants recognized the influence and leadership of those who are respected by others. One University of Iowa professor noted:

> The discussion of the e-portfolio was spearheaded by [a staff member and administrator]; they're the ones who really got that going. They're both very well respected here, and if somebody else had come in with this idea, it might not have gone over so well, but they're both very well respected and they're good at building consensus and making adjustments.

A University of Iowa faculty member confirmed this regarding that particular administrator. She explained, "Everybody has such respect for ____ that they're going to do it [electronic portfolios].... But I never got the impression that anyone's passionate about it like, for example, their research."

When asked about influential leaders, a Rhode Island faculty member noted:

> He was one of those faculty members that everybody looked to and was respected and known across the university.... He was always good at sort of cutting through the b.s., you know, "Folks, you can gripe all you like, but you're just wasting our time."

There were several comments about the vision of particular administrators and the respect that they command pertaining to electronic portfolios:

> We have a dean who saw the value of this, who was able to look in a crystal ball and see this is coming down the road. We have an associate dean who was nationally known in accreditation and standards movements, he's nationally known as a visionary in how this should be done. So we're very fortunate.

Selling the Vision. Part of leadership is communicating and "selling the vision" to others. One administrator commented on the effect of a faculty leader for electronic portfolios at Cal Lutheran:

> I think there's no doubt that [his] force of personality has made things happen around here because he doesn't take no for an answer. It's kind of funny and wonderful. The real impetus came from [him]. He knew about it. He was in love with it. He sold it.

A University of Iowa administrator elaborated on the importance of helping others establish a vision for electronic portfolios and spread their enthusiasm:

> Part of it was also a little-kid-like enthusiasm about look what we've got here! And see this again is where [two leaders] were so critical because they developed the frameworks that we could demonstrate to faculty even before we asked them to get started, so we could show them how user-friendly it was going to be, how relatively simple it was going to be, for them to upload their syllabi and to design their assignments that were standards based, and how easy it was going to be for the students to follow up on that. So, there was a kind of gee whiz factor involved, and nobody wanted to say, "I don't get this. I don't want to do this."

One of the University of Iowa leaders described their leadership strategy for selling their vision by working with those who are most ready in large groups, small groups and one-to-one, with the hope that word will spread:

> We don't just bring it all together at one time. We try to start off with pioneers, like Art Education was one of our early pioneers.... Elementary Ed faculty seem to be really in tune to ePortfolios, and so now we're putting in the pieces for our secondary education program. But you just can't do all of this at once. Incremental implementation and especially trying to find pioneer peers that the faculty respect and will follow is really key.

Finally, another electronic portfolio proponent at University of Iowa reflected on their commitment to develop and disseminate their electronic portfolio system:

> You couldn't pay someone to spend as much time as we did, but it was our baby—it was our passion. We knew it helped students, who thanked us endlessly for giving them these tools. And I don't know if an institution can really generate this kind of program without serious collaboration from the top to the very bottom.

Allocation of Resources. Resource allocation is a major prerogative of administration that clearly affects users' perceptions about particular initiatives. A large majority of the informants across cases noted the successful acquisition of technology resources as evidence of administrative support and leadership. At Eastern Kentucky, although faculty appeared to lead the effort to design the paper portfolio system, the primary leadership for the electronic portfolio efforts was reported to have come from the dean and other administrators. A chair assesses the effects of that leadership:

> It was an administrative decision. The leadership that we had at that time believed in technology, believed in the paperless format, and provided opportunities and resources for us to be able to move forward with that. But it took the right leadership at the top, all the way down. We had, during that time, a change of president; we had a change in the provost level, and a change in the dean of our college. All three very much aligned with the use of technology and moving forward. They moved the university forward very quickly in a short period of time. That was most helpful in that initial process to get it going.

In addition to obtaining technology resources, securing adequate human resources in the form of staff and faculty is critical. Several informants made note of efforts by administrators to fund the personnel necessary to support the respective electronic portfolio programs. For example, one chair alluded to their dean's effective leadership in securing resources to hire a technology coordinator for their college.

Involving Faculty. Inclusive and productive faculty governance can be a key component in contributing to faculty participation and satisfaction with the electronic portfolio program. Consistently, informants cited Cal Lutheran's collaborative culture and its positive effect on the adoption and implementation of electronic portfolios. A Cal Lutheran professor recalled the process in which electronic portfolios were discussed and adopted by the faculty:

> No, no. There was never a vote on that....These are our goals. If anyone has a problem with it, speak now or forever hold your peace. Because if we get this [grant], we will do it. And we got it, so we did it. But I think going and asking for buy-in, it then wasn't this top down thing because we had a committee that was working on this grant that included our partners in K–12 schools, and they all were in on this thing.

When asked if she was involved in conceptualizing and planning the electronic portfolio system, a Cal Lutheran administrator replied:

> We were all involved in those workshops where we talked about what it might be and what it could do, and here is how it works. And because we had the PT^3 grant, it gave us an opportunity to really delve in and work with it.

Although there were several comments about collaborative governance at the various sites, sometime committees were not involved in the initiative until after administrative decisions were made. As Fullan (2001) noted, however, administrative mandates can have positive results if the proposed change is a good idea and is "combined with empowerment and choices as the process unfolds" (p. 67). Interview data include many references to committees and other governance structures to get faculty input and potentially empower faculty in the process. For some faculty, that scenario worked, whereas others expressed dissatisfaction. For example, Eastern Kentucky faculty differed on their perception of the governance of the electronic portfolio process. Some faculty thought that the leadership did not sufficiently seek out their input, and others thought that input was adequately sought and it was time to move on and start implementing.

Along that vein, a University of Iowa professor acknowledged the mandate to implement electronic portfolios and reflected:

> We'll continue it [use of electronic portfolios] now because it's turned out to be a good way to show what we're doing in the program. But we also had this standards-based program dumped on us, and we had to figure out what to do with it.

In this particular case, the professor saw the value of the electronic portfolio program and suspended resistance in favor of program implementation.

An administrator at IUP summed up the pros and cons of the collaborative process:

> It's sometimes slower and more painful than to just put up the sign on the wall that says, "By Monday, the following will happen." But that would be a very unrealistic thing for me to do here—probably would be anywhere with faculty. But because they're not going to do anything this significant [implement electronic portfolios] unless they genuinely believe that this is the right thing to do. And I think that the support for the idea is built.

GRANTS

As reflected in Table 7.1 and in the prior narrative, PT^3 and other grant awards had a huge effect on electronic portfolio implementation across cases. Clearly, initiatives of this scope cannot be successfully implemented without adequate resources. In most cases, programs used the awards to fund the development of electronic portfolio software or templates, and in all cases funds were secured to provide critical training and support.

In some cases, the grants specifically were focused on electronic portfolios. For example, a faculty leader at Cal Lutheran recalled:

> Our dean came back from a conference and she said there's money available and you're going to write the grant. I said thanks. And so I immediately started getting school people together and we met in groups and we decided on goals and things that we would like to do, and included in that, one of them was that we will establish an electronic portfolio system and throughout teacher preparation.... Then we got the grant and it was sufficient that we would employ Doug and Jerry as consultants and they would come in and we would set this up. We had enough money to buy our own server.

At Eastern Kentucky, an administrator brought colleagues together from Arts & Sciences and Education to write the implementation PT^3 grant. The first major component was to integrate technology and good pedagogical skills into general education classes, and to do this with teams from across the colleges. The second major component was to develop and implement an electronic portfolio program.

At other programs, their PT^3 grants did not explicitly focus on electronic portfolios at first, though they did later on as the project evolved. Overall, all of the other programs secured PT^3 grants and/or other major funding to support the level of change embodied in the large-scale implementation of electronic portfolios.

2. What do the various facets of the e-portfolio process look like as implemented?

A number of decisions must be made as colleges of education bring the electronic portfolio from an idea to implementation. For example, what electronic tool will be used? What will be included in the electronic portfolio and who will make the decision? How will the electronic portfolio be introduced to students? How will it be assessed? To answer the research question, these issues are addressed.

THE TOOLS SELECTED

There was significant variation in the types of tools that were employed to construct the electronic portfolio. At three colleges (Eastern Kentucky, IUP, and Iowa), students built electronic portfolios using templates and HTML tools (hereafter, "tools approaches"). Two others (Johns Hopkins and Rhode Island) designed their own systems. At Johns Hopkins, students used a web-based integrated system designed by the university that is now being made available commercially to others. Rhode Island developed its own system, but is examining other systems to replace it. Cal Lutheran collaborated with a university-based software developer to tailor a commercially available system to their needs. Although the electronic portfolios varied across cases, the template designers reported that their tools approaches met their program goals. To provide an overview of the tools approach, we will explain an electronic portfolio using examples from Iowa and IUP. The Iowa electronic portfolio system has three components: (a) the Digital Backpack containing standards, performance assessments and artifacts, and links to course syllabi, (b) a collection of best work for employment, and (c) The Cyber ToolBox, which stores materials for use after graduation (Achrazoglou, Anthony, Jun, Marshall, & Roe, 2002).

An Iowa faculty member explained that for their electronic portfolios, students download templates for each course.

> For example, here's one of our programs, these are index pages for Early Childhood, and here's the template, linked to the standards page ... and here are all the classes that have portfolio elements in Early Childhood, so you can see that it's quite lengthy. So students don't have to ask, "Well, for what classes in Early Childhood do I have to upload artifacts?" This is the index page.... Likewise, if you're in secondary English, this is what your index page would look like ... and again a link to a standards page.

An IUP student explained the technical aspects of building an electronic portfolio using templates and common tools:

> I created them in Word and I saved them as Web pages ... and then I just linked them. I used Word as my editing tool for my web pages.

> And I scanned some things in, like my clearances, or some documents that I didn't have saved electronically.

The Johns Hopkins University Center for Technology in Education (2002) provides an overview of their commercially available system and describes the student electronic portfolio as an organized collection of student work to show progress toward a set of standards. The system has three interfaces: working portfolio, reviewer, and presentation. Integrated features include an electronic filing cabinet, a journal tool, and a message center.

Although the commercially available web-based systems are comprehensive in scope, the template-based electronic portfolios also have links to standards, course materials, artifacts, and rubrics. In fact, we found the distinction between the commercial systems and tools approaches to be somewhat blurred. Each approach allows students to upload/attach artifacts and align them to specific standards. While the tools approaches require that students learn to create hyperlinks, both approaches require students to use technology skills such as scanning, editing and sizing digital graphics, and converting documents to PDFs. Although the commercial integrated systems include data collection and analysis tools, designers of the tools approach could add a database and aggregate data from evaluation rubrics. Generally, the commercial systems tend to involve more integrated components such as communication systems and online grading in addition to the electronic portfolio construction and viewing sections. For both approaches, study participants had recently developed or were planning to develop their data collection and analysis tools.

DESCRIPTION OF THE ELECTRONIC PORTFOLIO PROCESS

Colleges of education made three major decisions about the electronic portfolio process: (a) who controls the content of the electronic portfolio, (b) the point at which faculty evaluate the artifacts that are placed in the electronic portfolio, and (c) the role of student reflection in the learning and evaluating process.

Artifact Inclusion Decision. Cal Lutheran, Eastern Kentucky, and Johns Hopkins asked students to make decisions about and select their best work demonstrating progress toward the standard. These programs provided explicit guidelines for the self-selection of artifacts for the electronic portfolio. Typically, the guideline included the standard and performance objectives that must be met and the minimal number of artifacts to be used to demonstrate the competence as well as the student's statement as to the reasons that these artifacts were selected and how they meet the standards. Other guidelines included whether the artifacts (e.g., a lesson plan) had to be implemented in a practicum setting and whether one artifact could be used as evidence for more than one standard. A Johns Hopkins faculty member explained the support they provide for students in selecting artifacts and providing the rationale for selection:

> We begin talking about the INTASC principles in every course … in each one of those seminars they address an INTASC principle, they talk about the strategies … for how they will go about writing their rationale for selecting that assignment … [they also] need to reflect on the breadth of what they have done.

On the other hand faculty at Iowa, IUP, and Rhode Island specified the artifacts that students were to include in the electronic portfolio. An IUP faculty member stated:

> We have just really gone through, within the whole College of Ed., and identified for every class at least one artifact that would fit and meet one of the standards—whether they're professional ones or under INTASC, that would actually fit. And so, when the students get a copy of the syllabus, they will see the breakdown and what objectives meet what standard. And then there will be at least one key artifact, and possibly up to three that they know goes with what standard.

This decision about who chooses the artifacts reflects philosophical beliefs as well as assessment considerations. On the one hand, assessment may become more difficult when students choose the artifacts that they think best meet the standards rather than when the assignments that meet the standards are prescribed for them. On the other hand, student selection of artifacts may lead to a deeper learning experience as they wrestle with understanding the connections between what they do and the standards. In addition, they may have a deeper belief that the electronic portfolios belong to them rather than just the college. Each of the study programs made decisions that matched their beliefs and purposes.

Electronic Portfolio Evaluation: Course or Checkpoint. Faculty may evaluate electronic portfolio artifacts as part of a course or at checkpoints to determine student progress toward the standards. If students self-selected the artifacts for their electronic portfolios, faculty (and others, e.g., student teaching supervisors) examined them at each of several checkpoints or at the end of the program. With the exception of Johns Hopkins, at a minimum the checkpoints occurred before and after student teaching. If the education faculty specified the artifacts to be included, the evaluation of the artifact occurred as part of the regular course grading procedure. This means that faculty members did not conduct a formal evaluation of the electronic portfolio outside of the typical grading procedures.

All programs that followed the checkpoint procedures discussed the time involved in conducting the reviews. Although the extensiveness of the evaluation of each student's portfolio varied across the sites, all checkpoint systems require faculty time to set them up, develop standard procedures for evaluating the portfolios, provide rater feedback for students, provide opportunities for students to address concerns raised, and provide for the raters to reevaluate the portfolio.

For Johns Hopkins, a student's electronic portfolio is completed in lieu of his/her master's thesis. The electronic portfolio is a culminating event and is assessed during the final semester of the student's program. Although there is one checkpoint, faculty commented on the commitment of time required for this extensive review.

Role of Reflection. In both instances—evaluation within courses and at checkpoints—programs required that students reflect on their work. The nature of the reflection differed across the sites. At a minimum, students were asked to discuss what they learned as a result of doing the work, what they learned from implementation in the practicum, and what they would do differently. At a minimum, faculty reported that they checked to see if the reflection was present, but with less attention to the substance of the reflection. At other sites, faculty reported that the role of reflection was substantive. For example, at Johns Hopkins, several faculty and students explained a theoretical model for reflection that required analysis beyond the basic questions discussed earlier.

In a similar vein, a Rhode Island faculty member described the reflection process in elementary education:

> Our final reflection is structured for them to go back … through their entire portfolio, look at what they had completed for tasks over the student-teaching semester and, if appropriate, prior to, and reflect on what it has meant in terms of their development as teachers. The idea is to get them to really state where they are right now. How far have you come? How did you get there? And then to take the next step and say "What is this going to mean for your first couple years of teaching? What are you going to have to focus on? What do you think your professional development's going to need to look like? What are your strengths and weaknesses?"

The Rhode Island electronic portfolio system kept track of all student reflections and responses. In addition, the written student reflection and faculty responses cycles were analyzed as part of the process of gathering data for program and accreditation review.

Similarly, at Cal Lutheran, informants reported that reflection was an important part of each assignment but also a special feature of the checkpoint review. As part of the professional development plan that accompanied the artifacts, students specified the areas they needed to address during the following semester and before the next checkpoint review. At the next review they would report on their progress toward the professional goals and add their goals to address before the next review.

INTRODUCTION OF THE ELECTRONIC PORTFOLIO AND SUPPORT

As is the case with technology skills in general, programs had different approaches to teaching their students how to construct the portfolios. Iowa and IUP had a required educational technology course that students completed at the beginning of their programs. The educational technology course taught students the technology and pedagogical skills needed to design the electronic portfolio and add the artifacts required from each course taken during that semester. At the completion of this course, typically students reported that they were comfortable with their electronic portfolios and their ability to design their initial portfolio. On the other hand, Johns Hopkins, Cal Lutheran, Eastern Kentucky, and Rhode Island did not have a required educational technology course. Their approaches to helping students learn to use the electronic portfolio system varied. Often they reported a combination of two methods: introduction during regular teacher education courses and labs with specific hours for electronic portfolio construction.

With respect to the specific skills required for the portfolio, most had developed a step-by-step tutorial or guide that students could print or access online. Cal Lutheran offered tutorials online with short videos illustrating each electronic portfolio step and phone support along with optional weekend sessions. Throughout their programs, students reported that they were most satisfied when general education faculty took a few minutes of class time to discuss the artifacts that they might include from their classes, the standards that they met, and the placement in the electronic portfolio, and modeled the procedure for uploading and commenting on artifacts. For those programs requiring specific artifacts from each class, students voiced their appreciation if all instructors would check to make sure the correct artifacts were in the right place. Students also reported helping each other construct their electronic portfolios. Most preferred learning from another student rather than attending an out-of-class session.

Generally, students reported that technical support and access to technology were adequate. However, there were exceptions. Across most cases, informants reported that students often saved their electronic portfolio work until the end of the semester or program. This was particularly problematic at the conclusion of student teaching when many artifacts were due or a checkpoint was pending. Often students reported that the electronic portfolio labs were full and they had to wait in line to complete their work.

ASSESSMENT OF ELECTRONIC PORTFOLIOS

The nature of the evaluation process differed across the sites. Johns Hopkins' electronic portfolio was the comprehensive examination for their MAT program. The checkpoint occurred at the conclusion of the program and included an evaluation of the electronic portfolio and an oral defense.

Eastern Kentucky, Cal Lutheran, and Rhode Island reported that they used three benchmark checkpoints to assess student progress toward the standards at each of three checkpoints. For each checkpoint, there was a standard rubric used for evaluation. The rubrics were aligned with the standards and the performance objectives. A mastery learning approach was employed; that is, if students did not meet an acceptable level, they were allowed to address the rater's concerns and resubmit.

For those without benchmark checkpoints, artifacts were assignments that were assessed as part of the course. For multiple sections of the same course, none of the programs reported training instructors to rate assignments across courses with consistency. Further, they reported that they had not established interrater reliability among all instructors.

In both cases (for individual assignments and benchmark checks), programs rarely reported providing rater training. Most programs with checkpoints reported that they had more than one scorer for the checkpoint and the scorers came to an agreement about the final score. However, they had not established procedures for consistency of scoring of an electronic portfolio across all raters and had not established interrater reliability among all scorers. Leaders representing each program participating in the study indicated that this was an area that they hoped to address in the future.

Discussion

In analyzing data across cases, it was interesting to note common themes that led to program-wide adoption of electronic portfolios. Consistent with the literature (Gathercoal et al., 2002), prior experience with paper portfolios in this study was an important factor in the successful implementation of e-portfolios, especially for those programs with a greater emphasis on performance assessment and student reflection.

In exploring the impetus for the adoption of e-portfolios across cases, we also found quite a bit of common ground. Although each case has its own unique flavor, much of the momentum for the initiation of e-portfolios was influenced by new requirements from accrediting bodies to document teacher candidates on a range of performance standards. Clearly, top-level support for portfolios was affected by these requirements. Also in line with the literature, there was ample evidence of strong dean-level leadership that included substantial allocation of resources to support faculty and students in their use of portfolios. This involved securing grants and obtaining internal funding within the university.

Overall, the cases selected for this study nicely illustrate Fullan's (2001) assertion that effective change requires a combination of both pressure and support. Pressure, in this case, refers to expectations that faculty will participate in the electronic portfolio program and support students in their use. Support encompasses both the human and technological infrastructure that facilitates the implementation of e-portfolios. Fullan explains that pressure without support leads to resistance and alienation, whereas support without pressure can lead to drift or waste. Data from the present study suggest that effective, large-scale implementation of e-portfolios benefits from a good balance of both pressure and support.

It is interesting to note that the pressure for change with technology in the current study was greater than what is typically cited in the technology and teacher education literature. For example, in a prior study by the authors on exemplary integration of technology in teacher education, when reflecting on the notion of pressure and support, we wrote:

> Pressure for technology implementation, however, does not appear to be effective when it comes in the form of a mandate. Rather, as a faculty leader at the University of Virginia stated, the pressure for change should be like the wind at your back. (Strudler & Wetzel, 1999, p. 79)

The mandate in this case was not for electronic portfolios per se, but for some type of standards-based performance assessment. This requirement, however, was a major factor that led to initiation and implementation of e-portfolios in all of the programs. Although the level of support was clearly acknowledged and appreciated, some faculty and students expressed negative views toward the pressure for implementation. As opposed to the supportive image of a gentle breeze at your back, the pressure for using e-portfolios was seen by some as an unwelcome gust. This, however, can be expected when moving to mandatory participation in a large-scale change effort. Although most prior efforts to integrate technology in teacher education have been on a voluntary basis, the implementation of e-portfolios represents a new level of technology-based initiatives that have required program-wide participation.

Finally, it should be noted that each of the programs in the current study has plans to fine-tune its approaches to better meet the needs of the various stakeholders. To help us understand these new directions, we asked informants about the "next steps" that they envisioned for their electronic portfolio programs. Their responses provide a nice window from which to view how the stakeholders perceive the program and where they would like to see it go. Furthermore, we asked for their recommendations for other programs in earlier stages of adoption or implementation of electronic portfolios. Again, informants' advice provides valuable insights into what the stakeholders value and what might prove useful for others just getting started with e-portfolios. Answers to both of these questions will be addressed in Chapter 8 based on an extension of the data set explored in this study.

Acknowledgments

The authors would like to thank participants from each of the six sites for graciously agreeing to share their insights and experiences with us. We especially would like to thank those who helped arrange and facilitate the respective site visits. Without their contributions this study would not have been possible.

References

Achrazoglou, J. Anthony, R., Jun, M., Marshall, J., & Roe, G. (2002). *A white paper on performance assessment in teacher education: The Iowa ePortfolio model.* Iowa City, IA: College of Education, University of Iowa.

Barrett, H. (2004). Differentiating electronic portfolios and online assessment management systems. In C. Crawford, N. Davis, J. Price, & D. Willis (Eds.), *Technology and Teacher Education Annual* (pp. 210–213). Norfolk, VA: Association for the Advancement of Computing in Education.

Bartlett, A. (2002). Preparing preservice teachers to implement performance assessment and technology through electronic portfolios. *Action in Teacher Education, 24*(1), 90–97.

Britten, J., Mullen, L., & Stuve, M. (2003). Program reflections on the role of longitudinal digital portfolios in the development of technology competence. *The Teacher Educator, 39*(2), 79–94.

Fagin, R., Hand, D., & Boyd, K. (2004). Electronic portfolios for aggregating and disaggregating data: Measuring a transformed life. In S. Van Kollenburg (Ed.), *Promoting Student Learning and Effective Teaching: Vol. 3. Assessment of Student Learning.* Chicago, IL: The Higher Learning Commission.

Fullan, M. (2001). *The new meaning of educational change* (3rd ed.). New York, NY: Teachers College Press.

Gathercoal, P., Love, D., Bryde, B., & McKean, G. (2002). On implementing Web-based electronic portfolios. *Educause Quarterly, 2,* 29–37.

Hall, G. E., & Hord, S. M. (2001). *Implementing change: Patterns, principles, and potholes.* Needham Heights, MA: Allyn & Bacon.

The Johns Hopkins University Center for Technology in Education (2002). CTE applications for education. Available at: http://cte.jhu.edu.

Lincoln, Y. S., & Guba, E. G. (1985). *Naturalistic inquiry.* Beverly Hills, CA: Sage.

Salzman, S., Denner, P., & Harris, L. (2002). *Teaching education outcomes measures: Special study survey.* Paper presented at the Annual Meeting of the American Association of Colleges of Teacher Education, New York.

Senge, P. M., Kleiner, A., Roberts, C., Roth, G., Ross, R., Smith, B. (1999). *The Dance of Change.* New York, NY: Doubleday.

Shulman, L. (1998). Teacher portfolios: A theoretical activity. In N. Lyons (Ed.), *With portfolio in hand: Validating the new teacher professionalism* (pp. 23–37). New York, NY: Teachers College Press.

Smith, P., Harris, C., & Sammons, L. (2001). Using multimedia portfolios to assess preservice teacher and P–12 student learning. *Action in Teacher Education, 22*(4) 28–39.

Strauss, A. (1987). *Qualitative analysis for social scientists.* New York, NY: Cambridge University Press.

Strudler, N. & Wetzel, K. (1999). Lessons from exemplary colleges of education: Factors affecting technology integration in preservice programs. *Educational Technology Research and Development, 47*(4), 63–82.

Wetzel, K. &. Strudler, N. (2005). A survey of colleges of education thought to be accomplished users of electronic portfolio programs. In C. Crawford, R. Carlsen, I. Gibson, K. McFerrin, J. Price, R. Weber, & D. A. Willis (Eds.), *Technology and Teacher Education Annual* (pp. 208–214). Norfolk, VA: Association for the Advancement of Computing in Education.

Williams, M., Wetzel, K. &. Wilhelm, L. (2004). Trials and tribulations of reflective practices in preservice teacher electronic portfolios. In C. Crawford, N. Davis, J. Price, & D. Willis. (Eds.). *Technology and Teacher Education Annual* (pp. 301–306). Norfolk, VA: Association for the Advancement of Computing in Education.

Yancey, K. (2001). Introduction: Digitized student portfolios. In Barbara Cambridge (Ed.), *Electronic portfolios: Emerging practices in student, faculty, and institutional learning.* Washington, DC: AAHE.

Yin, R. K. (1989). *Case study research: Design and methods* (rev. ed.). Newbury Park, CA: Sage.

CHAPTER

8

The Diffusion of Electronic Portfolios in Teacher Education: Next Steps and Recommendations from Accomplished Users

Keith Wetzel | Arizona State University

Neal Strudler | University of Nevada, Las Vegas

The previous chapter addressed issues of electronic portfolio adoption and implementation in preservice teacher education; this chapter documents next steps and key recommendations by informants from the six programs studied. Next steps included streamlining requirements, addressing reliability of technology and access, and planning for data aggregation and program evaluation. Key recommendations were to involve a broad base of participants in the planning process, clarify the purposes for electronic portfolios, move forward incrementally, and provide sufficient technology access, training, and support. The study concludes that a range of research is needed to inform future decisions pertaining to the large-scale implementation of electronic portfolios in teacher education.

Introduction

Chapter 7 addressed the conditions that led to the initiation and implementation of the diffusion of electronic portfolios in teacher education (Strudler & Wetzel, 2005). Our focus was to examine mature, well-articulated efforts in programs in which faculty and students have used electronic portfolios program-wide for two or more years. Using the same theoretical framework on educational change (Fullan, 2001; Hall & Hord, 2001), This chapter documented the "next steps" planned and the recommendations of stakeholders at selected universities. Specifically, the study sought to answer the following two research questions:

1. What are the "next steps" envisioned for the electronic portfolio program?

2. What recommendations do experienced users of e-portfolios have for programs in earlier stages of adoption or implementation?

Sites were identified and visits were conducted by the research team during November and December 2004 for approximately two to three days each. During that time, semistructured interviews were conducted with teacher education faculty, university administrators, teacher candidates, recent graduates, and technology support providers. It was our intent to interview a cross section of informants that reflects a range of perspectives and participation in the process. Subsequently, all interviews were transcribed and then analyzed using the constant comparative method (Strauss, 1987). Interview data were triangulated using field notes from observations and a review of available documents to confirm the trustworthiness (Lincoln & Guba, 1985) of the findings. Further details about the methods employed can be found in Strudler and Wetzel (2005).

Findings

1. What are the "next steps" envisioned for the electronic portfolio program?

Consistent with the notion that change is a complex, sociocultural process that takes time (Fullan, 2001; Hall & Hord 2001), the universities selected for this study experienced many challenges as they planned and implemented complex electronic portfolio systems that served multiple purposes. Some of the challenges have been resolved, but for others, university personnel developed short- and long-term plans to address them. We asked stakeholders at each institution about the next steps that they envisioned for their electronic portfolio program. The responses fell into three categories: issues that related to the streamlining of their programs, issues of reliability and access, and the need for data aggregation and program review.

STREAMLINING PROGRAMS

Several of the sites assessed student progress toward the standards and benchmarks at periodic checkpoints. The nature of the checkpoints and their timing differed, but they all had certain due dates—for example, before student teaching, when at least one faculty member examined a student's portfolio and evaluated his/her progress toward the teaching standards.

In each of these cases, faculty and administrators commented on the amount of time required to implement the checkpoint procedures. We illustrate this challenge by focusing on California Lutheran University. Here there were three checkpoints after students were admitted to their teacher education program, called CLUES B, C, and D. Each involved a face-to-face meeting with each student by one or more faculty members and sometimes, depending on the checkpoint, a student teaching supervisor. Students would prepare their portfolios and present oral defenses of their progress and their professional development plans.

A director explained that these checkpoints have been increasingly difficult to perform:

> Until recently, each of the checkpoints—CLUES B, C, and D—was evaluated by a team consisting of faculty members and supervisors. With increased student enrollment and change in the state standards (new standards were added) it has been difficult to ask faculty members and supervisors to read and evaluate each part of the student's portfolio.

A chair explained the demands on faculty and possible modifications at California Lutheran:

> I liked the interview. However, first of all, they were all during exam week or previous to that, and we didn't have time. It was a terrible load on professors. Some people did it, some people chose not to. Also, some faculty members felt that it was a little too labor-intensive—[more] than it needed to be.

The chair also explained the plan to reduce the demands on faculty time:

> So this time … we're going to divide up the people and each professor will be assigned three or four people to read. But it would be one full faculty professor analyzing the benchmark. There would not be a team. Not with a face-to-face meeting. Now part of the thinking here is that [students are] interacting with professors on a weekly basis. So they were being monitored all the way through the process by the individual instructors.

At this time, the fourth checkpoint—the exit interview—would continue to include the oral presentation to the raters and peers. However, changes regarding the fourth checkpoint were also being discussed.

Eastern Kentucky also employed similarly timed checkpoints to evaluate student progress toward state standards. Elementary and middle school education faculty members were responsible for evaluating the electronic portfolios of students at certain checkpoints. Faculty members reported that it was difficult to conduct a substantive evaluation of each student's portfolio at the checkpoints. Some faculty members have a 10-minute interview with each student, and others have an interview only with students who are experiencing difficulties. Checklists are used to determine if the necessary artifacts and reflections are present. A senior faculty member explained the time constraints:

> I have nearly 100 portfolios and we are just desperately trying to get the student to get them done so we can evaluate them. To stop them and say "whoops" you really need to stop and spend a little more time on reflection [is not possible] when in fact students are scrambling just to get them done. So I think there hasn't been an emphasis on reflection.

In both of the foregoing cases, faculty time to complete checkpoints was an issue. The core of this next step is consistent with the observation of Shulman (1998) that

> Portfolios done seriously take a long time. They are hard to do. Teaching is a job that occupies every waking and nonwaking moment of a good teacher. Given such demands, the question is: Is it worth it? And if it is, is there any chance of reorganizing the life of teachers so they can do this hard work without killing themselves? (p. 35)

The comments of the stakeholders at these institutions indicated they took seriously the demands on faculty time and were contemplating strategies that would lead to streamlined procedures without losing the benefits of their checkpoints.

The programs also recognized challenges regarding efficient use of students' time to complete the electronic portfolio. University of Iowa and Johns Hopkins provide particularly apt examples. A University of Iowa faculty member stated that the student time required should be reconsidered:

> And we've worked with the teachers of those courses to try to create a more realistic amount of stuff that the students would have to upload, that would still be enough to try to demonstrate that they know what they're doing as teachers, but not so much that it begins to seem like busy work to them.

A Johns Hopkins faculty member in the MAT program explained a new pilot study to determine if new procedures streamline the electronic portfolio requirements for students and the review process for faculty:

> [In regard to INTASC principle one, two, and three], you identify the things that you have done that meet those particular INTASC principles. [In each of those categories] there are what we call required elements that need to go in the certain sections. We are toying with having one artifact address multiple INTASC principles to bring more synthesis and reflection to it. So instead of saying okay you have to have three things in for INTASC principle number 1, and two things in principle number two, show us in three maybe four big artifacts that you have developed, how you have met a variety of the principles. Because if you are using a unit plan you should be able to demonstrate within that unit how you addressed maybe nine or ten [of the INTASC principles, not just one].
>
> ...[M]y group again is going to be piloting these new versions of it in May so that we can see the changes in the amount of time it takes students and amount of time it takes faculty in the review process, whether or not it is really easier to score and get a painted picture of who these folks are as teachers.

RELIABILITY AND ACCESS

Informants also raised concerns related to technical issues. Although University of Rhode Island stakeholders addressed issues related to the server and technical support and Eastern Kentucky raised issued related to the tool students use to create their electronic portfolios, both cases illustrate next steps related to technology.

Originally, University of Rhode Island created an electronic portfolio system that was difficult to maintain and support. An administrator explained one part of the main problem, the server:

> If that goes down at the end of the semester on a weekend and you have a major crisis with students and their confidence in the system and their ability to move forward with their lives and upload things, and you know, you have them trying 20 times in the weekend to see if the thing's up, that's a problem.

Their next step was to select a new electronic portfolio system that is robust and supported by the university, not just by the college. The same administrator explained:

> What I'm trying to do is get the University commitment to a system here on campus and provide resources for that system and support for that system.

A University of Rhode Island faculty member explained the differences between the previous and new systems:

> Differences will be that there is going to be 24/7 support that's outsourced; there will be someone else—at least initially—maintaining the hardware side of it; and there will be an increased ability—as I perceive it and I think this is one of the main reasons we want to go outside of what we're doing now, aside from the lower cost—to get our data back out in a way that we want.

Eastern Kentucky stakeholders explained the impact of students' backgrounds and their access to software to build electronic portfolios. Eastern Kentucky has the lowest tuition of any public institution of higher education in Kentucky and many students come from lower income families. The challenge and next step for Eastern Kentucky reflects this circumstance. Many of the stakeholders at Eastern Kentucky noted access issues affected by several factors. Students reported that they could not work on their electronic portfolios at home because they did not have Microsoft Front Page, the necessary software. Consequently, they were required to do their electronic portfolio work at the labs on campus. In addition, some students were completing course work at satellite campuses and at student teaching assignments some distance from campus. These students would save their electronic portfolio work until the end of the semester and attempt to make one trip to campus to complete it. The labs would be swamped with students late in the semester. As described in our prior article, the Eastern Kentucky electronic portfolio program was based on templates with links that students modify using Microsoft's FrontPage, an HTML editor. An administrator explained a possible solution to this challenge:

> The reason why we're doing some rethinking now is because while we had Front Page available here and the students have it, many schools don't. For a while Front Page was something you could get free. Now it's part of the Office package but many people use other products than Office. You have to buy Office with Front Page. We're experimenting. My guess is that the folks who are working on it will come up with new and creative ways to do it for less of a cost to the student and allow them to maintain it through more commonly used programs.

We found that technical issues such as server reliability and software accessibility affected time requirements for faculty and students and motivated faculty members and administrators to address them.

In summary, these universities were examining the amount of work that their electronic portfolio programs required for students and faculty and were reconsidering the number of artifacts, the type of artifacts, and the depth of reflection needed for students to demonstrate mastery of a standard. Further, they were considering strategies enabling students to use one assignment to meet multiple standards. Finally, they were addressing technical concerns that would make their electronic portfolio systems more user-friendly for faculty and students and sustainable by the school or college.

DATA AGGREGATION AND PROGRAM REVIEW

All of the programs were planning to gather data from their analysis of student portfolios to use for program review and accreditation purposes. Once again they were in different stages of preparation to mine the data from the scoring of entries in the electronic portfolios. Three cases, Johns Hopkins, IUP, and University of Iowa, will be used to illustrate the next steps in data aggregation.

Johns Hopkins was constructing a tool to help colleges of education capture key data and analyze it. A Johns Hopkins chair explained their purpose and their data analysis needs:

> It is an exit requirement that becomes driven by needs of accountability and accreditation. When you are up against NCATE standards and specialty organization standards and how do you show evidence of this and this? You can point to some of it from observations in classrooms, but a fair amount of it can be hinged on their portfolios.

The comments of the two IUP administrators are particularly illustrative of their future plans. IUP has immediate and longer-range goals for the use of the electronic portfolio system for program review and accreditation. The first administrator explained the plans they were beginning to implement including the database they were constructing to help them prepare for their NCATE review:

> We have seven different gates for our initial and advanced programs, and one of the databases, which we'll begin using at the end of this semester, is related to the course assessments. So as faculty at the end of the semester begin using this key assessment system, they will go into Banner [the campus student information system] just as if they were entering final or midterm grades, and then instead of selecting the link to final grades, they have another link to access the key assessment component. And then, depending on whether or not the course has one, two, or three key assessments identified, there will be one, two, or three key assessment evaluation columns displayed by each student's name. Once again, the drop-down menus provide opportunity for entering unacceptable, acceptable, or target performance. Now that's the collection mechanism for the data.

The same administrator also explained the plan to use data for the NCATE review:

> Behind that we have built mapping tables, and the mapping tables were determined by taking the individual key assessment matrices that were identified within each course. We've compiled those into program matrices, and the program matrices show whether or not we do have full coverage, over 10 to 12 courses that make up a particular program, of the program standards, as well as the unit standards. Now, we'll be using the information from that course—in effect course-evaluation system—as one piece of the evidence that will be provided back to NCATE relative to the student's accomplishment of … well, standard number one—the content standard, standard number two—the use of the unit assessment system. The way that we've designed the system, too, we're providing drill-down capabilities for the board of examiners. So we start off by providing a global view of student performance in the entire unit relative to the accomplishment of the standards and the individual descriptors of the standards. And then within each of those, we're providing additional linking capabilities to go to the program level, and then also to the course level.

In addition to these technical issues regarding tools and procedures, the bigger questions that need to be addressed are: What is good teaching? What is the domain to be measured? How valid are the artifacts and judgments? The second IUP administrator explained their long-range plan for the use of the electronic portfolio system for assessment:

> So I think that the issue for us here is that, probably over the next four or five years, we'll see another level of development of these portfolios … I think questions about what do those artifacts tell you about the ability of our students to teach those children or youth, that one, I think, is still very open. I know NCATE's ambition here was to have us know by now very precisely [and be] able to define what that meant: what is the specific set of competencies that causes a new teacher to be able to get students to learn. I have to tell you that I think we're still working on that, and we will be for a while.

A major purpose of the electronic portfolio system at Iowa was program evaluation and accreditation. Faculty teams determined the artifacts from each course that would show evidence that the student was meeting each standard. However, an administrator discussed moving from an initial step, aligning artifacts with each standard, to the next step, determining the degree to which all of the artifacts aligned with the standard demonstrate that the student has achieved the performance. An administrator explained the first stage of their data collection and recommended a next step:

> We do now have artifacts that are associated with standards, but the next step is to have some shared understanding of what quality looks like when you're looking at a particular standard...."Okay, let's take a look at assessment, let's take a look at planning, and let's see what the students have uploaded, and let's see if we can come to a consensus to which of these is really good." But it's above the artifact level, the important thing is the preponderance of evidence within a standard.

Although all of the programs were in different stages of development in their use of electronic portfolio data for program review and accreditation, they clearly were planning to continue to improve the processes for mining data.

2. What recommendations do experienced users of e-portfolios have for programs in earlier stages of adoption or implementation?

In answer to this question, many of the informants presented recommendations that related to leadership and fostering faculty support for the electronic portfolios. In addition, it was recommended that the proponents of electronic portfolios need to be clear about the purposes for using them, and they need to plan for the necessary training, support, and technology infrastructure.

LEADERSHIP TO INVOLVE OTHERS

Earlier we reported that sites in this study had strong dean-level support for the initiation of their electronic portfolio programs. However, informants also recommended that a broad spectrum of stakeholders be involved in the decision making and planning processes. This recommendation is consistent with the literature that encourages a combination of top-down and bottom-up planning as the optimal approach for effective implementation (Fullan, 2001; Hall & Hord, 2001). An IUP faculty member suggested that this involvement is necessary to build support for electronic portfolios:

> You need to figure out a way to be subversive and get it going from the grassroots so it's their idea. That ownership is crucial, and if there's no ownership there—true ownership, not forced, not placed on them, not "it's yours, now take it from here"—if we could figure out a way to do the true ownership, that's what I'm seeking. And I don't know how you do that.

Another IUP faculty member argued that there should be broad participation in planning including students, technology persons, and K–12 personnel:

> I'd change the constituency of the people who are in the planning phase. I'd make sure that there were administrators, I'd make sure that there were technology persons, I'd make sure that there were students, and I'd

> make sure that there were public school personnel who ostensibly will be using these materials for hiring or assessment.

A Rhode Island faculty member provided advice on how to obtain buy-in from potential resisters:

> Keep an open mind. Be flexible. Speak up if something isn't working. Have help groups or support groups. Meet separately with groups who don't want to use the system at all and show them how it can benefit down the line and now. Talk about some of the areas that sound like they're not going to work or could work more effectively—the inability to get in and actually write in to students' documents, the fact that we have to correct things twice, address those things when they come up. And I guess, most of all, be accessible to them.

It was emphasized that broad participation is the key if the electronic portfolio is going to be implemented program-wide. An EKU administrator pointed out:

> I think you also have to make sure that it is part of your whole program and not just, "Oh you do the portfolio in these classes and the rest of the time you don't have to worry about it." That's what we're going toward, trying to make sure it's part of our complete program at the elementary and middle, and to some degree the secondary, although we have less control of that. People have to see it as part of what they do also. It's not just somebody else's thing, it's everybody's.

CLARITY OF PURPOSE

One of the strongest recommendations was that adopters be able to articulate a clear purpose for the electronic portfolios for all stakeholders. The advice regarding clarity of purpose is a recurrent theme across sites and informants.

An IUP faculty member discussed the effect of a perceived change of purpose:

> I think you need to focus on what the purpose or purposes of these portfolios are going to be. And I don't think we did that. As we said repeatedly, we saw it as an electronic briefcase, a collection of your work and nothing more, when in reality we knew we wanted it to be above that. And it was going to involve artifacts from courses. So get your objectives out there, your purposes: are we going to have this as a view through the checklist vehicle? Good, that's one thing, but … what will the unit get out of it? In terms of the data collection? The accreditation information? What will the programs get out of it?

Open communication among stakeholders regarding purpose is a recurrent theme. A Rhode Island faculty member explained that the purpose should be clear and connected to the program's curriculum before beginning the electronic version of the portfolio:

> You have to develop a portfolio system that you would continue using if all the technology disappeared tomorrow and you had to do it on paper and pencil. We really saved ourselves a lot of pain—it wasn't intentional, but it worked out well for us—because we had done it on paper before we did it electronically. And that's not to say there hasn't been pain or that we're not changing it as we go along, but I think, if you are developing an e-folio system, it's really easy to get caught up in the "sexiness" of it, for lack of a better term: everybody's doing it, it's powerful ... but there's no reason to go and do it simply because it's technological.

The same faculty member articulated the need for faculty to develop a clear understanding of purpose:

> The first thing that you need to do—because if you don't do it at the beginning, you'll have to stop somewhere along the way to do it—is to sit down with everybody who's involved in using this portfolio—and I'm speaking of faculty, not students—and work out, put it down on paper concretely, why are you using portfolio assessment. What is the philosophy out of which this is coming? Now if it's because you have to do accreditation, and this is the best way to do it, I don't think that's problematic—that was a big guiding force for us—but we took the time to really talk about "why would we do this?"

Finally, a Rhode Island administrator explained the complexity and the balancing act involved in achieving clarity of purpose because the college has multiple and competing demands for both human and financial resources. The portfolios function is to further departmental goals, not to subsume them.

> I mean, I want to produce data that enables us to strengthen our programs, but I also want it to be streamlined and functioning in a way that allows us to do other things. We have scholarship to accomplish, we have grants to get, we have outreach to communities and schools, and we have teaching to do. We can't spend all our time nurturing a folio system, and we need to have a place for it, it needs to function well for us in that regard, so that we can do other things. And faculty have time to do other things, even within their classes.

PROVIDING SUFFICIENT ACCESS, TRAINING, AND SUPPORT

A major role of a leader is to provide access to technology, training, and support for faculty and students to use the electronic portfolio system. However, this is not as easy to manage as it might seem, because administrators must achieve a balance in providing resources for electronic portfolios with other college needs. In addition, training and support are ongoing tasks, not one-time events. A Rhode Island administrator articulated the difficulty:

> You need to look at the resources you have available to do this.... I mean, do you hire that language arts person, or do you bring in the person who's going to work with your databases and enable you to communicate between PeopleSoft [their university information system provider] and whatever folio system you use? Well, those are tough decisions and you'd better think about them up front.

A prerequisite for implementing an electronic portfolio program was sufficient access to technology, an adequate campus technology infrastructure, and continual support. A California Lutheran administrator explained:

> My advice would be to make sure that everyone has computer capabilities that are going to make the use of the Web folio as easy as possible for both faculty and students [so they] can upload them at the university easily.

A Rhode Island technical support person concurred:

> I think it's important to make sure you have the right technologies in place, and make sure they're working. You know, scanners, digital cameras, and digital video.

A California Lutheran administrator recommended providing sufficient support and training:

> And one of the things you need is lots and lots of training. And you have to keep the training up, not just for the first six months or year, but it has to be part of an ongoing set of meetings and activities where people get together and share experiences and get training from outsiders.

PLANNING, INCREMENTAL STEPS, AND PILOT PROGRAMS

All of the informants discussed electronic portfolio plans that started with smaller steps that provided the foundation for larger steps. An Iowa administrator explained the development process:

> And you can't just impose it; you have to start building it. And we did the pilot study. I think [you'd need to show] some success before you went in and did it, for a large program in particular. I think if you can show success with a smaller group first, it might be very helpful because then people can see the potential.

An IUP faculty member explained the need for planning and gradually implementing:

> First of all, it's just like anything else: plan it in advance. Set a time in the future to implement it; don't implement it on the run. And that would probably be the biggest key. And any project that requires change you do this: you spend time winning people over, you spend time training people, you spend time setting up your systems, and then you implement it. You don't implement it and then try to do everything on the run.

A California Lutheran support person recommended implementing in stages beginning with the early courses and continuing step by step through student teaching:

> Start them out with the simpler levels and then work them up to the student teaching and the field placement. The people out in the field doing their student teaching in the field placement are so overwhelmed as it is and that was the problem we had when we started. They were just overwhelmed the first, probably four years. Then when we started getting the people that were doing the foundations in then they would come up to methods and then go to student teaching and then into their masters courses and now our program is starting to use it. I think it worked a lot better after that first year. I would say ease [it] in rather than throwing everybody into it.

TIME REQUIRED FOR CHANGE

Consistent with the literature, the informants in this study stressed the need for time to implement electronic portfolio programs. The comments of a California Lutheran leader illustrated the sentiments of informants across colleges:

> I know an institution is not going to get there in a semester, or a year. Maybe two or three if they're real smart about their strategies and the buy-in from faculty, but the buy-in from faculty is real critical at that stage 3. And if you don't have that, they're just not going to move on. And even in our little journey with this, we knew that we would have to address why, what folios? And we did that in the beginning. And the third year into our grant, we thought, okay, we're past that. Oh no. You

> get this backlash from faculty again and we had to go back and revisit it again. I'm afraid I wasn't very good at that. I can see the vision, I can see what this can do, and for me to go back and talk with my colleagues about why we should be doing this, that they can't see it. I bit my tongue and we went through it again. And sure enough, there was buy-in.

Discussion

Our analysis of next steps and recommendations provides us with a virtual glimpse into the future. Although next steps inform us of the various directions in which the respective programs intend to go, the recommendations were intended to guide others' future adoption and implementation decisions. In analyzing themes across both, several key ideas emerge. First, findings of the study document the enormity of the change involved in implementing electronic portfolios on a large scale. As Fullan (2001) and Hall and Hord (2001) reinforce, change initiatives of this nature are complex sociocultural processes that take time, perhaps as long as 5 to 10 years. As might be expected, recommendations include clarifying the purposes for electronic portfolios, involving a broad base of participants in the planning process, and moving forward incrementally from initiation and implementation to institutionalization. It is interesting to note that recommendations for others support Hall and Hord's notion that most change efforts overly emphasize development at the expense of implementation. The recommendations given by informants in this study almost exclusively address implementation issues rather than logistics for development, seemingly sage advice.

The next steps discussed reflect the respective program's efforts to ensure sustainable change that meets the needs of the various stakeholders. From an administrative perspective, an important next step was to move forward with efforts to aggregate data, both for accreditation purposes and for program review and improvement. From the faculty and student perspective, important next steps were to streamline the process, making it more "do-able" and sustainable. Although there is much passion about the ideals of portfolios in teacher education, if the demands of the process are not reasonable and cannot be managed over time, then large-scale implementation of electronic portfolios will not likely be sustained.

Overall, even though this study provides us with a glimpse into future directions for the implementation of electronic portfolios, much research is still warranted. We need a range of studies that inform whether the large-scale implementation of electronic portfolios in teacher education is ultimately a good idea that should be pursued and sustained in the coming years.

Author Update

We began to study electronic portfolios (EPs) a few short years ago when EPs were gaining a foothold as a means of showcasing and assessing candidates' work in teacher preparation programs. We sought to analyze the factors that characterized programs identified as early adopters and mature users of this innovation. Informants across six sites identified leadership, support, and clarity of purpose for electronic portfolios as key factors influencing successful adoption of this technology tool. Next steps for sustaining EPs in programs included streamlining requirements and planning for data aggregation and program evaluation.

Today the technology has changed dramatically. Portfolio applications are now components of large-scale online systems that include capabilities for instructor feedback and discussion among students, candidate performance data aggregation and disaggregation, lesson planning tools, and integration with other database systems. Our subsequent research confirmed the increasing prevalence of such tools in accreditation efforts and further underscored the enduring aspects and challenges of implementation. We've found in studying recent NCATE Board of Examiner Reports that current issues raised include the need to ensure consistency and fairness in evaluation procedures and to aggregate and use data for meaningful program improvement.

In looking back at our earlier work, we believe that common themes remain in regard to the adoption process and the implementation of change. Consistent with the work of leading change theorists (Fullan, 2001; Hall & Hord, 2001; Rogers, 2003), our subsequent research has continued to emphasize the local context and culture that either supports or inhibits successful implementation and sustainability, including the time and effort involved and the benefits perceived by the various stakeholders.

The challenge that remains is to complete the learning and assessment puzzle by demonstrating how effective EP implementation helps candidates become better teachers and helps programs and accrediting bodies better assess candidates' performance. The journey continues.

Acknowledgments

The authors would like to thank participants from each of the six sites for graciously agreeing to share their insights and experiences with us. We especially would like to thank those who helped arrange and facilitate the respective site visits. Without their contributions this study would not have been possible.

References

Fullan, M. (2001). *The new meaning of educational change* (3rd ed.). New York, NY: Teachers College Press.

Hall, G. E., & Hord, S. M. (2001). *Implementing change: Patterns, principles, and potholes.* Needham Heights, MA: Allyn & Bacon.

Lincoln, Y. S., & Guba, E. G. (1985). *Naturalistic inquiry.* Beverly Hills, CA: Sage.

Shulman, L. (1998). Teacher portfolios: A theoretical activity. In N. Lyons (Ed.), *With portfolio in hand: Validating the new teacher professionalism* (pp. 23–37). New York, NY: Teachers College Press.

Strauss, A. (1987). *Qualitative analysis for social scientists.* New York, NY: Cambridge University Press.

Strudler, N., & Wetzel, K. (2005). The diffusion of electronic portfolios in teacher education: Issues of initiation and implementation. *Journal of Research on Technology in Education, 37*(4), 411–433.

CHAPTER

9

Teachers' Technological Pedagogical Content Knowledge and Learning Activity Types: Curriculum-Based Technology Integration Reframed

Judith Harris | College of William & Mary

Punya Mishra | Michigan State University

Matthew Koehler | Michigan State University

In this chapter we critically analyze extant approaches to technology integration in teaching, arguing that many current methods are technocentric, often omitting sufficient consideration of the dynamic and complex relationships among content, technology, pedagogy, and context. We recommend using the technology, pedagogy, and content knowledge (TPACK) framework as a way to think about effective technology integration, recognizing technology, pedagogy, content, and context as interdependent aspects of teachers' knowledge necessary to teach content-based curricula effectively with educational technologies. We offer TPACK-based "activity types," rooted in previous research about content-specific activity structures, as an alternative to existing professional development approaches and explain how this new way of thinking may authentically and successfully assist teachers' and teacher educators' technology integration efforts.

Introduction

Studies of K–12 teachers' instructional applications of educational technologies to date show many to be pedagogically unsophisticated; they are limited in breadth, variety, and depth and are not well integrated into curriculum-based teaching and learning (Groff & Mouza, 2008; Levin & Wadmany, 2008; Russell, O'Dwyer, Bebell, & Tao, 2007; Zhao, Pugh, Sheldon, & Byers, 2002). In a 20-year retrospective on U.S. educational technology policy, Culp, Honey, and Mandinach (2003) describe a mismatch between educational technology leaders' visions for technology integration and how most practitioners use digital tools. Researchers emphasize technology uses that support inquiry, collaboration, and reformed practice, whereas many teachers tend to focus on using presentation software, learner-friendly websites, and management tools to enhance existing practice. McCormick and Scrimshaw (2001) label these currently predominant uses for information and communication technologies as efficiency aids and extension devices, differentiating them from transformative devices (p. 31), which "transform the nature of a subject at the most fundamental level" (p. 47). These authors suggest that such technology-based curricular transformation happens only in those few content areas (e.g., music, literacy, and art) that are "largely defined by the media they use" (Harris, 2008, p. 254).

We argue that this discrepancy between a vision of transformative uses of educational technologies and the more prevalent efficiency and extension applications can be traced to the nature of how technology use in classrooms has been conceptualized and supported. Five general approaches dominate current and past technology integration efforts:

1. ***Software-focused initiatives.*** One of the earliest examples of software-focused technology integration approaches was in mathematical learning and general problem-solving skill development through students' use of the programming language Logo. Later software-based integration attempts made use of integrated learning system (ILS) software, which provides individualized instruction while tracking students' learning needs and progress.

2. ***Demonstrations of sample resources, lessons, and projects.*** Teachers often demand classroom-based and student-tested examples of appropriate technology use. Given this proclivity, it is not surprising that there is a wide range of sources (such as magazine articles, books, websites, and conference presentations) that recommend curriculum-based lessons, projects, and online resources that teachers have used successfully. Underlying this effort is the assumption that successful use of instructional plans and educational resources is easily transferable among different classrooms.

3. ***Technology-based educational reform efforts.*** These larger-scale, often grant-funded projects, such as Apple's Classrooms of Tomorrow (ACOT) 10-year initiative (Sandholtz, Ringstaff, & Dwyer, 1997), are usually organized around new visions for learning and teaching that are realized through novel uses of educational technologies. Projects are implemented primarily through systemic planning and intensive professional development efforts supported by the acquisition of hardware and software.

4. ***Structured/standardized professional development workshops or courses.*** Large-scale professional development initiatives such as Thinkfinity and PBS's TeacherLine are prestructured options that are adopted locally or by school district, region, or state. Some, like Thinkfinity, are structured as cascading professional development, where the parent organization trains district, regional, or state-level trainers, who in turn offer the prepackaged professional development to groups of teachers in their own jurisdictions. Others, like TeacherLine, license a wide variety of professional development courses to districts, regions, or states, so that teachers can pursue them in more individualized ways.

5. ***Technology-focused teacher education courses.*** Teacher education institutions—colleges/universities or districts/regions working either alone or collaboratively—offer educational technology courses to teachers, delivered online or face-to-face. These can serve as recertification courses taken on an unclassified student basis or as elements of graduate or undergraduate programs in education.

Though different from each other, these approaches tend to initiate and organize their efforts according to the educational technologies being used, rather than students' learning needs relative to curriculum-based content standards, even when their titles and descriptions address technology integration directly. These approaches are, in Papert's terms, "technocentric" (Papert, 1987) because they begin with technologies' affordances and constraints and the skills needed to operate them, then later attempt to discern how they can be integrated successfully into content-based learning at different levels. The comparatively weak and relatively sporadic instances of technology integration in most K–12 content areas suggest that such approaches are inadequate at best. Though educational technology leaders have been calling for content-based, pedagogically forward-thinking technology integration for more than a decade (e.g., Fisher, Dwyer, & Yocam, 1996; Means & Olson, 1997; Roblyer, Edwards, & Havriluk, 1997), professional development for teachers still emphasizes and is organized according to technologies' affordances and constraints (e.g., Friedhoff, 2008).

We argue that the greatest weakness of such technocentric approaches is that they have typically given short shrift to two key domains: content and pedagogy. The five approaches just outlined demonstrate implicit assumptions that the kinds of professional knowledge required of teachers for technology integration are the same, irrespective of whether one is teaching middle school science, high school social studies, or elementary language arts. This approach ignores the variation inherent in different forms of disciplinary knowledge and inquiry as well as the varied pedagogical strategies that are most appropriate for teaching this content. Different disciplines have differing organizational frameworks, established practices, ways of acknowledging evidence and proof, and approaches for developing knowledge (Koehler & Mishra, 2008). Moreover, knowledge of these disciplinary attributes is necessary but not sufficient without knowledge of the appropriate pedagogical strategies to use in each content area. Successful technology integration also recognizes the manner in which the myriad and ever changing contextual realities of the classroom and school influence what teachers do and what students learn (AACTE Committee on Innovation & Technology, 2008).

Technology integration approaches that do not reflect disciplinary knowledge differences, the corresponding processes for developing such knowledge, and the critical role of context ultimately are of limited utility and significance, as they ignore the full complexity of the dynamic realities of teaching effectively with technology. Understanding that introducing new educational technologies into the learning process changes more than the tools used—and that this has deep implications for the nature of content-area learning, as well as the pedagogical approaches among which teachers can select—is an important and often overlooked aspect of many technology integration approaches used to date.

In this chapter we introduce one approach, TPACK-based learning activity types, which can help teachers successfully integrate technology into their practice. This approach goes beyond technocentric strategies and emphasizes the importance of helping teachers develop and apply integrated and interdependent understandings of technology, pedagogy, content, and context. Before describing this approach in detail, we offer a brief description of the parameters of teacher knowledge and its interrelated components using the TPACK framework. (In this chapter, we use "technological pedagogical content knowledge," or TPCK, and "technology, pedagogy, and content knowledge," or TPACK, as synonyms).

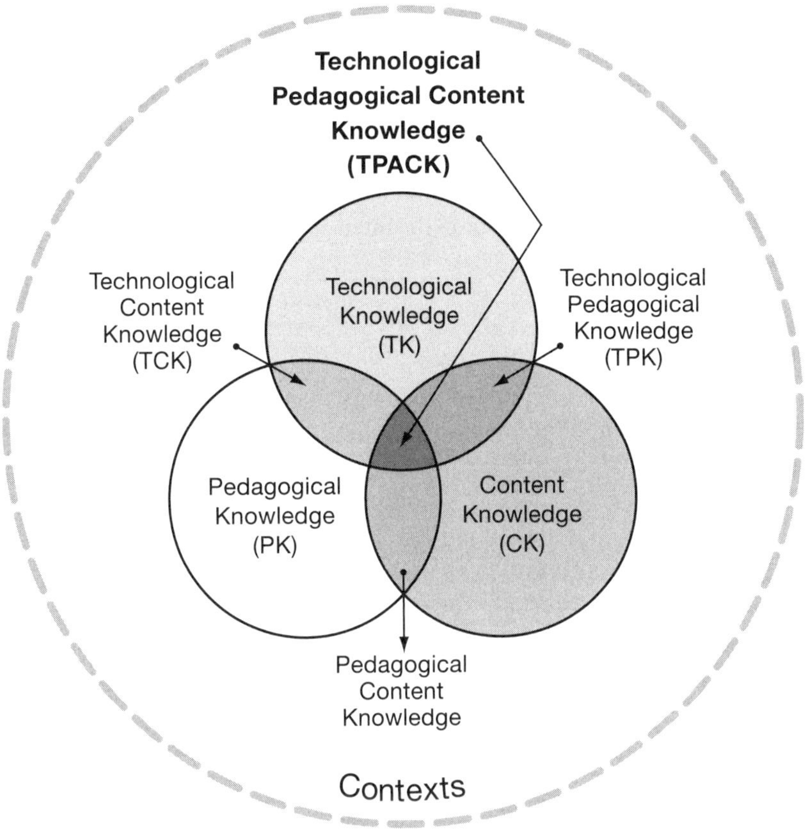

Figure 9.1 The TPACK Framework and Its Knowledge Components (Adapted from Koehler & Mishra, 2008)

Technological Pedagogical Content Knowledge (TPACK)

Considerable interest has surfaced recently in using the notion of technological pedagogical content knowledge (Koehler & Mishra, 2008; Mishra & Koehler, 2006) as a framework to understand teachers' knowledge required for effective technology integration. TPACK emphasizes the connections among technologies, curriculum content, and specific pedagogical approaches, demonstrating how teachers' understandings of technology, pedagogy, and content can interact with one another to produce effective discipline-based teaching with educational technologies. In this framework (see Figure 9.1), there are three interdependent components of teachers' knowledge—content knowledge (CK), pedagogical knowledge (PK), and technological knowledge (TK)—all framed within and influenced by contextual knowledge.

Equally important to this framework, and particularly relevant to the argument we put forth in this article, are the interactions among these bodies of knowledge, represented as pedagogical content knowledge (PCK), technological content knowledge (TCK), technological pedagogical knowledge (TPK), and technological pedagogical content knowledge (TPACK). In the following sections we will explore each of these types of knowledge, with particular emphasis on the intersections among technology, pedagogy, and content knowledge.

CONTENT KNOWLEDGE (CK)

Content knowledge is knowledge about the subject matter that is to be learned or taught, including, for example, middle school science, high school history, undergraduate art history, or graduate-level astrophysics. Knowledge and the nature of inquiry differ greatly among content areas, and it is critically important that teachers understand the disciplinary "habits of mind" appropriate to the subject matter that they teach. As Shulman (1986) noted, content includes knowledge of concepts, theories, ideas, organizational frameworks, methods of evidence and proof, as well as established practices and approaches toward developing such knowledge in a particular discipline. In the case of art appreciation, for example, such knowledge would include knowledge of art history, famous paintings, sculptures, and the influence of artists' historical and social contexts, as well as knowledge of aesthetic and psychological theories for understanding and evaluating art. The cost of teachers having an inadequate content-related knowledge base can be quite prohibitive; students can develop and retain epistemologically incorrect conceptions about and within the content area (Bransford, Brown, & Cocking, 1999; Pfundt & Duit, 2000).

PEDAGOGICAL KNOWLEDGE (PK)

Pedagogical knowledge is deep knowledge about the processes and practices of teaching and learning, encompassing educational purposes, goals, values, strategies, and more. This is a generic form of knowledge that applies to student learning, classroom management, instructional planning and implementation, and student assessment. It includes knowledge about techniques or methods used in the classroom, the nature of the learners' needs and preferences, and strategies for assessing student understanding. A teacher with deep pedagogical knowledge understands how students construct knowledge and acquire skills in differentiated ways, as well as how they develop habits of mind and dispositions toward learning. As such, pedagogical knowledge requires an understanding of cognitive, social, and developmental theories of learning and how they apply to students in the classroom.

TECHNOLOGICAL KNOWLEDGE (TK)

Technological knowledge is always in a state of flux—more so than content and pedagogical knowledge. This makes defining and acquiring it notoriously difficult. Keeping up to date with technological developments can easily become overwhelming to time-starved teachers. This also means that any definition of technology knowledge is in danger of becoming outdated by the time this text has been published. There are, however, ways of thinking about and working with technology that can apply to all technological tools, regardless of when they emerged. In that sense, our definition of TK is similar to the notion of Fluency of Information Technology ("FITness") as proposed by the Committee on Information Technology Literacy of the National Research Council (NRC, 1999). The committee argues that FITness goes beyond traditional notions of computer literacy to require that people understand information technology broadly enough to apply it productively at work and in their everyday lives. FITness therefore requires a deeper, more essential understanding and mastery of technology for information processing, communication, and problem solving than does the traditional definition of computer literacy. Also, this conceptualization of TK does not posit an "end state," but rather assumes TK to be developmental, evolving over a lifetime of generative interactions with multiple technologies.

PEDAGOGICAL CONTENT KNOWLEDGE (PCK)

Pedagogical content knowledge is the intersection and interaction of pedagogy and content knowledge. PCK is consistent with and similar to Shulman's (1986) conceptualization of teaching knowledge applicable to a specific content area. It covers essential knowledge of teaching and learning content-based curricula, as well as assessment and reporting of that learning. An awareness of students' prior knowledge, alternative teaching strategies in a particular discipline, common content-related misconceptions, how to forge links and connections among different content-based ideas, and the flexibility that comes from exploring alternative ways of looking at the same idea or problem, and more, are all expressions of pedagogical content knowledge and are essential to effective teaching.

TECHNOLOGICAL PEDAGOGICAL KNOWLEDGE (TPK)

Technological pedagogical knowledge is an understanding of how teaching and learning change when particular technologies are used. This includes knowing the pedagogical affordances and constraints of a range of technological tools and resources as they relate to disciplinarily and developmentally appropriate pedagogical designs and strategies. Developing TPK requires building an understanding of the potential benefits and limitations of particular technologies as they can be applied within particular types of learning activities, as well as the educational contexts within which these technologically supported activities function best.

An important aspect of TPK is the creative flexibility with available tools necessary in planning to use them for specific pedagogical purposes. Consider, for example, the whiteboard as an educational tool. Although this technology has been in use for a long time, its very nature in some ways presupposes the kinds of functions it can serve. Because it is usually placed in the front of the classroom and is therefore usually under the control of the teacher, its location and use impose a particular physical order on the classroom, determining the placement of tables, chairs, and therefore students, thus framing the nature of student–teacher interaction. Yet it would be incorrect to say that there is only one way that whiteboards can be used. One has only to compare the use of a whiteboard in a brainstorming session in a design studio to see a rather different technological application. In this context, the whiteboard is not controlled by a single individual. Rather, it can be used by anybody on the collaborating team, and in this situation, it becomes the point around which discussion and the negotiation and construction of meaning occurs.

The flexible use of tools becomes particularly important because most popular software programs are not designed for educational purposes. Software such as the Microsoft Office Suite (Word, PowerPoint, Excel, Entourage, and MSN Messenger) is designed for use in business environments. Web-based technologies such as blogs and podcasts are designed for purposes of entertainment, communication, and social networking. Teachers, therefore, must have the knowledge and skills that allow them to appropriate technologies for pedagogical purposes, so that they can use Excel, for example, to help children organize and analyze data, and they can create podcasts as ways to share constructed knowledge with others. Thus, TPK must include a forward-looking, creative, and open-minded seeking of technological application, not for its own sake, but for the sake of advancing student learning and understanding.

A large proportion of technology-based learning activities that have been developed in the past to illustrate technology integration, through their lack of emphasis on content and pedagogy, illustrate an incomplete and comparatively superficial form of TPK. Examples include recommendations for use of generic strategies—such as keypals, telefieldtrips (Rogers, Andres, Jack, & Clausen, 1990), blogging/journaling, preparing PowerPoint presentations, building websites, and podcasting—without incorporating acknowledged PCK and PK. Such generic (and technocentric) strategies are described typically in content- and context-neutral terms, assuming that each would work just as well within any content area, at any grade level, and in any classroom.

TECHNOLOGICAL CONTENT KNOWLEDGE (TCK)

Technological content knowledge (TCK) includes an understanding of the manner in which technology and content influence and constrain one another. In planning for instruction, content and technology are often considered separately. It is assumed that developing content is what content experts do (i.e., historians develop history and physicists develop physics), whereas technologists develop technologies (e.g., hypertexts or overhead projectors) and technology integration strategies. When we think of subject matter that students study in school, we often do not think of curriculum content's relationships to the digital and nondigital technologies that learners and teachers use. Historically, however, technology and knowledge have been deeply connected. New understandings in medicine, history, archeology, and physics have emerged, in part, from the development of new technologies that afford the representation and manipulation of information and ideas in novel and fruitful ways. Using new technologies (or existing technologies in new ways) can prompt fundamental changes in the nature of the disciplines themselves. Roentgen's discovery of X-rays, for example, changed both diagnostic processes and the nature of knowledge in medicine. The carbon-14 dating technique similarly revolutionized the field of archeology. Consider also how the advent of the digital computer changed the nature of physics and mathematics work, placing a greater emphasis on the role of simulation in understanding phenomena.

Effective teaching requires developing an understanding of the manner in which subject matter—specifically, the types of content-based representations that can be constructed within and across disciplines—can be changed by the use of different technologies. Teachers must understand which technologies are best suited for addressing which types of subject matter, and how content dictates or shapes specific educational technological uses, and vice versa. We identify three ways in which technology and content have related to one another.

First, the advent of new technology has often changed fundamentally what we consider to be disciplinary content. In addition to the examples given earlier, consider how the discovery of radiation changed the way we understand the evolution of life, whereas the invention of hypertext transfer (HTTP) and other Internet protocols dramatically changed the ways in which we work and communicate. Content (be it physics or engineering or sociology) shapes new technologies and offers new uses for existing technologies, while at the same time the affordances and constraints of technologies shape how this content is represented, manipulated, and applied.

Second, technology is not neutral with regard to its effects on cognition. Different technologies (or media) engender different mindsets or ways of thinking (Koehler, Yadav, Phillips, & Cavazos-Kottke, 2005; Mishra, Spiro, & Feltovich, 1996). Every new technology—from the telephone to the camera to the digital computer—has had its effects on human cognition. For example, the advent of moveable type and printing in the 15th century was followed by a series of dramatic changes in all aspects of social, cultural, political, and scientific life in Europe and, eventually, most of the rest of the world. Many of the effects of the invention and diffusion of print can be traced to certain specific properties of print media. Print created texts that were mobile, immutable, presentable, and readable, and these properties led to fundamental changes in human cognition (Latour, 1990). They helped to ensure that discussions could be carried beyond the conversational arena that predominated in the oral cultures of the time. These print objects allowed ideas to be transported and shared without change, so that they could be encountered in consistent ways that mutable, oral retellings would typically disallow. A similar change—though this time toward increased flexibility and connectivity—can be seen in the emergence of web-based texts that are nonlinear, unbounded, and dynamic. This is especially apparent in the so-called "Web 2.0" technologies that foster communal and shared document generation.

Finally, technological changes offer us new metaphors and languages for thinking about human cognition and our places in the world. Viewing the heart as a pump or the brain as an information-processing machine is just one of the ways technologies have provided new perspectives for understanding phenomena. These representational and metaphorical connections are not superficial. Considering the brain as akin to a clay tablet, for example, offers a very different view of cognition and learning than considering it similar to an information-processing machine. Having these metaphors and analogies as part of a general cultural consciousness influences how technologies are appropriated for teaching and learning.

TECHNOLOGICAL PEDAGOGICAL CONTENT KNOWLEDGE (TPACK)

Underlying truly effective and highly skilled teaching with technology, we argue, is technological pedagogical content knowledge. TPACK is different from knowledge of its individual component concepts and their intersections. It arises instead from multiple interactions among content, pedagogical, technological, and contextual knowledge. TPACK encompasses understanding and communicating representations of concepts using technologies; pedagogical techniques that apply technologies appropriately to teach content in differentiated ways according to students' learning needs; knowledge of what makes concepts difficult or easy to learn and how technology can help redress conceptual challenges; knowledge of students' prior content-related understanding and epistemological assumptions, along with related technological expertise or lack thereof; and knowledge of how technologies can be used to build on existing understanding to help students develop new epistemologies or strengthen old ones. TPACK is a form of professional knowledge that technologically and pedagogically adept, curriculum-oriented teachers use when they teach.

Many aspects of these ideas are not new. As Shulman (1986) and others have argued, teachers' knowledge for effective practice requires the transformation of content into pedagogical forms. What has been overlooked in most cases, we suggest, are the critical roles that technology can play. For example, Shulman writes that developing PCK requires teachers to find "the most useful forms of representation of [the subject area's] ideas, the most powerful analogies, illustrations, examples, explanations, and demonstrations—in a word, the ways of representing and formulating the subject that make it comprehensible to others" (p. 9).

It is interesting to note here that each of the components described by Shulman—representations, analogies, examples, explanations, and demonstrations—are constrained, constructed, and defined in critical ways by the affordances and constraints of the digital and nondigital technologies used to formulate and represent curriculum-based content. In one sense, there is no such thing as pure content, pure pedagogy, or pure technology. It is important for teachers to understand the complex manner in which all three of these domains—and the contexts in which they are continually formed—coexist with, co-constrain, and co-create each other.

Each instructional situation in which teachers find themselves is unique; it is the result of an interweaving of these interdependent factors. Accordingly, there is no single technological solution that will function equally well for every teacher, every course, or every pedagogical approach. Rather, a solution's success lies in a teacher's ability to flexibly navigate the spaces delimited by content, pedagogy, and technology, and the complex interactions among these elements as they play out in specific instructional situations and contexts. Ignoring the complexity inherent in each knowledge component—or the complexities of the relationships among the components—can lead to oversimplified solutions or even failure. Teachers need to develop fluency and cognitive flexibility not just in each of these key domains—content, technology, and pedagogy—but also in the manners in which these domains interrelate, so that they can effect maximally successful, differentiated, contextually sensitive learning.

DEVELOPING THE INTERACTING COMPONENTS OF TPACK

How are teachers to acquire an operational understanding of the complex relationships among content, pedagogy, technology, and context? As noted earlier, typical approaches to technology-related professional development are based on assumptions that it may be enough to just expose teachers to particular educational technologies and possible curriculum-based uses of those tools and resources. Approaches that teach only skills (technology or otherwise) are insufficient. Learning about technology is different from learning what to do with it instructionally. Teaching technology skills (the T in the model described earlier) in isolation does little to help teachers develop knowledge about how to use technology to teach more effectively (TPK), its relationship to disciplinary content (TCK), or how to help students meet particular curriculum content standards while using technologies appropriately (TPACK) in their learning.

Using the TPACK framework to frame the development of teachers' knowledge does not necessitate a rigid or algorithmic adherence to a single approach to technology integration. For example, one teacher interested in integrating technology in history may consider use of primary sources available on the Internet, whereas another may choose to have students develop hypertexts that reveal multiple cause-effect relationships among related historical events. One mathematics teacher may choose to provide data sets that students represent with graphs and charts created with spreadsheet software, whereas another may choose to help her students to discover data patterns represented by the changing slope of a sine wave as it is constructed and altered dynamically with a graphing calculator. Thus, the development and demonstration of teachers' TPACK knowledge requires flexibility and fluency—not just with curriculum-based content, but also with pedagogy, technology, and context—remembering that each influences the other in pervasive ways.

In speaking of Shulman's notions of PCK, Beyer, Feinberg, Pagano, and Whitson (1989) suggested that PCK "implicitly denies the legitimacy, even as a matter of conceptual convenience, of the forced disjuncture between thought and action and content and method" (p. 9). We would argue that this denial of the split between thought and action, and content and method is true of TPACK as well. TPACK is most helpful when not described in isolation from techniques for developing it. It is not, however, a professional development model. TPACK is a framework for teacher knowledge, and as such, it may be helpful to those planning professional development for teachers by illuminating what teachers need to know about technology, pedagogy, and content and their interrelationships. The TPACK framework does not specify how this should be accomplished, recognizing that there are many possible approaches to knowledge development of this type. Koehler and Mishra (2005) have explored learning-by-design approaches to the development of TPACK. Here, we suggest a different approach to TPACK-based professional development for teachers that foregrounds pedagogical content knowledge as it shapes and is shaped by the particular affordances and constraints of using different digital and nondigital educational technologies to assist students' curriculum-based learning.

Using Learning Activity Types to Develop and Apply TPACK

To help teachers to develop and use TPACK in ways that attend to the particular demands of different subject matter domains, we suggest that an important first step is creating awareness of the range of possible learning activity types (Harris, 2008; Harris & Hofer, 2006) within a particular content area, matching them to multiple ways that both digital and nondigital technologies can be used to support each type of learning activity. After determining the content and process goals for a particular lesson, project, or unit, teachers can then select from among the full range of activity types in that particular content area, combining the types selected in ways that are congruent with students' standards-based, differentiated learning needs and preferences. This approach is based on an empirical assumption that maximally appropriate and effective instruction with technology is best planned considering students' content-related learning needs and preferences primarily, selecting and applying technologies only in service of that curriculum-based learning.

The acknowledged focus in this approach to planning instruction is on content-based (and content-specific) pedagogy, which is facilitated by judiciously selected and implemented technologies. This emphasis is in accordance with the situated, event-structured, and episodic nature of teachers' knowledge (Putnam & Borko, 2000). Moreover, given that most teachers distinguish learning activities primarily by curriculum content (Stodolsky, 1988), and curriculum content is rooted in academic disciplines (Shulman, 1986) that are epistemologically (if not ontologically) distinct, a pedagogically focused approach to assisting the development of teachers' TPACK-in-action in the classroom should emphasize the differences among learning activities in different content areas rather than their similarities. In this way, it becomes easier for teachers to match particular activities to specific content-based learning goals and standards, and, more important, to interpret and implement these activities in ways that are congruent with the disciplinary roots of the discipline-based content that students are learning.

ORIGINS OF CONTENT-BASED ACTIVITY TYPES

Activity types are based on research catalyzed by teacher educators' realizations of the critical importance of Shulman's (1986) notions of pedagogical content knowledge. They are a "friendlier" interpretation of the "activity structures" revealed in social semiotic discourse analyses of classroom interactions and later studied in science and mathematics classrooms (e.g., Lemke, 1987; Windschitl, 2004). Activity structures are composed of "activity segments," which were first examined and explicated by ecological psychologists. Activity segments are the individual parts of a lesson, each of which has a particular focus, format, setting, participants, materials, duration, pacing, cognitive level, goals, and level of student involvement. Activity structures are combinations of activity segments that are recognizable to and used by teachers when planning instruction (e.g., "KWL activities") (Stodolsky, 1988). For example, the first commonly cited activity structure in educational literature—Mehan's (1979) I-R-E (teacher initiation, student reply, teacher evaluation) sequence—emerged from the study of classroom-based discourse.

In another example, Windschitl (2004) identifies several activity structures when recommending pedagogical practice for science labs, defining the term as follows:

> The term "activity structure" is borrowed from the sociocultural theorists, meaning a set of classroom activities and interactions that have characteristic roles for participants, rules, patterns of behavior, and

> recognizable material and discursive practices associated with them. "Taking attendance," "having a discussion," and "doing an experiment" could all be considered activity structures. While the term "activities" refers to specific phenomena occurring in classrooms, the structures underlying these are more general and applicable across multiple contexts. (p. 25)

Polman (1998) sees activity structures functioning on both classroom and school levels—and beyond. To him, predominant activity structures are cultural tools that perpetuate and standardize communication patterns—and therefore interaction norms and expectations—primarily according to teachers' memories of dominant discourse patterns from their own school-related childhood experiences. Some activity structures, therefore, can represent a mismatch between teachers' and students' differing socioculturally based expectations for teacher–student and student–student interaction (e.g., preferences for competitive or collaborative schoolwork) and therefore should be selected in as student-centered a way as possible. When a paradigmatically new teaching approach is attempted, Polman argues, because there isn't an "obvious set of well-established cultural tools to structure … interaction" (p. 4), teachers' resulting confusion and resistance can undermine educational reform efforts. We believe a similar phenomenon can occur when a new technology is introduced. The resulting confusion and resistance can similarly undermine the process and goals of the learning activity. For this reason, we advocate conscious identification, explication, and exploration of new (or revised) technologically enhanced activity structures, which, with experience, we have learned to refer to as "activity types" to make their nature and instructional uses more transparent to teachers.

Lemke (1987) applied the notion of recurring discourse structures to the social semiotics of science education more broadly, noting that every action in the classroom has both interactional and thematic meaning. That meaning unfolds, according to Lemke, within two independent discourse structures: activity structures and thematic structures. Activity structures are "recurring functional sequences of actions" (p. 219), and thematic structures are familiar ways of speaking about a topic, such as the curriculum-based focus of a unit or lesson (Windschitl, 2004). Lemke's underlying assertion is that meaning cannot be separated from action; the structure of curriculum content, therefore, cannot be separated from the structure of content-related learning activities. Given the similar underlying assumptions of the interdependence of TPACK's conceptual components described earlier, we argue that tool and resource use—both digital and nondigital—can similarly not be separated from content/theme and activity structure. Therefore, TPACK-related activity types for teachers' use should be conceptualized and presented in terms of their specific disciplinary discourses, and in conjunction with their technological affordances. Given the content-based nature of activity structures (Stodolsky, 1988) and teachers' experience teaching in specific content areas, using

TPACK-based activity types represents a promising—and decidedly nontechnocentric—approach to professional development in technology integration.

CULTIVATING USE OF ACTIVITY TYPES

Several educational researchers have examined the intentional cultivation and use of activity structures in professional development for teachers. Kolodner and Gray (2002), for example, proposed a system of "ritualized" learning activity structures to assist learning and teaching in project-based science work. The authors recommended ritualizing activity structures at both strategic and tactical levels—that is, in sequencing both the steps for participating in a particular type of learning activity and the order of activities that are comprised in a project or unit. Their activity structures are specific to the science-related skills that each helps students to develop. For example, there are three different types of presentations included: presentations of ideas, of experimental results, and of experiences with multiple solutions to similar problems. Kolodner and Gray discovered that—contrary to expectations that naming too many different activity structures would overwhelm students and teachers—such fine-grained differentiation actually assisted both learners and instructors in knowing what to expect from and how to participate in each activity type, plus how the activity is connected to the development of content-specific processes and goals.

Polman's (1998) two-year classroom-based study sought to document a project-based alternative to the traditional I-R-E activity structure. He discovered and named a B-N-I-E structure used in a middle school science class, in which students "bid" by suggesting topics that they would like to research, then "negotiated" the details of the projects based on those possible topics, then "instantiated" their understanding with work on the project according to their understanding of the instructor's guidelines, then received and considered formative "evaluation" from the teacher on their work. The evaluation results then formed the basis for a new recursion of the B-N-I-E sequence as the students revised and continued their learning.

Polman's (1998) research continued as he then tested the B-N-I-E activity structure in a different discipline—history. He found that the structure could be modified to accommodate another curriculum area, but the adaptation must involve choices "along the dimensions of act (what) and agency (how)" (p. 22) because the natures of inquiry and expression in different disciplines differ in essential ways—for example, between a lab report and an historical narrative. Polman's work with the same activity structure in two disparate disciplines demonstrates the discipline-specific (not transdisciplinary) nature of activity structures and types.

How are activity structures/types connected to larger school-based social, professional, and organizational structures and networks, if they are indeed linked? During an in-depth study of science education practices in Japan, Linn, Lewis, Tsuchida, and

Songer (2000) compared the presence and use of science activity structures in multiple classrooms. To their surprise, they found the activity structures to be consistently present and similarly described by both students and teachers. The Japanese participants framed the structures in terms of what students do during each science-related learning experience. The researchers hypothesized that the highly collaborative nature of Japanese teacher interactions may have yielded the similarities in descriptions and discussions. Yet, contrary to popular U.S. perceptions, "Japanese teachers ultimately choose the instructional approaches they will use in the classroom," but "shared research lessons may offer opportunities for teachers to collectively build and refine not just instructional techniques, but also norms about what is good instruction" (p. 11). This points to an essential feature of successful use of activity structures/types as instructional planning/design tools: As Linn et al. recommend, they are best used flexibly and in the context of active teacher discourse communities to "enable deep, coherent instruction" (p. 4).

MATCHING ACTIVITY TYPES, CONTENT, AND TECHNOLOGIES

Technologies' affordances create opportunities for both enhancing existing learning activity types and creating new ones. Effective teaching requires knowledge of both the activity structures/types that are appropriate for teaching specific content and the manners in which particular technologies can be utilized as part of the lesson, project, or unit design. What happens when a new learning activity type is used without conscious attention to all aspects of the TPACK framework? In the following section, we examine WebQuests as one example of a comparatively new activity structure made possible (and by some accounts, "gone viral") by the advent of the web.

WebQuests are inquiry-oriented activities in which some or all of the information with which learners engage comes from sources on the Internet. They represent an extremely popular activity structure and have been used in classrooms across the world. However, facilitating learning effectively with WebQuests is not a trivial task. In response to a widespread misapplication of this activity structure, Dodge (2001) published and promoted "five rules for writing a great WebQuest." As he described,

> A quick search of the web for the word WebQuest will turn up thousands of examples. As with any human enterprise, the quality ranges widely.... Some of the lessons that label themselves WebQuests do not represent the model well at all and are merely worksheets with URLs. (p. 7)

Dodge and March originally intended the WebQuest to be an inquiry-based activity that requires students' use of information found online at analysis, synthesis, and evaluation levels (Dodge, 1995), applicable to any content area and most grade levels. With posted evaluation standards now available and encouraged for teachers' use (Dodge, Bellofatto, Bohl, Casey, & Krill, 2001), WebQuests' creators are hopeful that a greater proportion of newly created WebQuests will reflect the purposes for, and types of, learning originally conceptualized. Yet we wonder whether this content-neutral activity type is, by virtue of its technological (web-based) emphasis, prone to instructional application that is mismatched both pedagogically and in terms of disciplinary content with its original intent and design. The same could be suggested for the other technology-based learning activity types mentioned earlier: keypals, telefieldtrips, blogging/journaling, educational podcasting, and more. If teaching and learning are conceptualized and characterized in action by teachers primarily according to content matter (Stodolsky, 1988), then the design of professional development for teachers—including the ways that learning activity types are delineated and used—should be similarly organized within content areas while still considering the concomitant relationships among content, technology, pedagogy, and context.

SAMPLE ACTIVITY TYPES

Using content foci as cognitive organizers for professional learning, teachers can learn to recognize, differentiate, discuss, select among, combine, and apply TPACK-based activity types in curriculum standards-based instructional planning. By planning with activity types, teachers can function as designers in time-efficient ways that accommodate the crowded and pressured nature of their daily schedules.

As an example, consider a taxonomy of TPACK-related learning activity types developed for the social studies. Harris and Hofer (2006, 2009) identified 42 distinct learning activity types from structural analyses of social studies learning activities used in classrooms and reported in curriculum, research, pedagogical journals, and/or social studies methods texts. The activity types are divided into 13 knowledge-building and 29 knowledge-expression structures. Knowledge-expression activity types were further divided into activities that emphasize either *convergent* (6 types) or *divergent* (23 types) thinking processes.

In this chapter we connect these content-driven pedagogical strategies with specific and compatible technologies. The key idea is that not every technology is appropriate for use with each activity type. Rather, particular applications of specific technologies, based on their affordances, should be selected carefully to match the activity type(s) under consideration. There are three genres of learning activity types in the social studies that can be supported by varied uses of technology.

Table 9.1 Knowledge-Building Activity Types

Activity	Activity Description	Compatible Technologies
Read Text	Students extract information from textbooks, historical documents, census data, etc.	Books, web browsers, CD-ROM, document viewers
View Presentation	Students gain information from teachers, guest speakers, and their peers	Presentation software, note taking tools, audio/video recorders, white-boards, concept mapping software
View Images	Students examine both still and moving (video, animated) images	Image/animation/video editing and display software
Listen to Audio	Students listen to recordings of speeches, music, radio broadcasts, oral histories, and lectures	Websites, MP3 players, podcasts, radio, tape players, CD players
Group Discussion	In small to large groups, students engage in dialogue with their peers	Discussion forums, blogs, wikis, chat rooms
Field Trip	Students travel to physical or virtual sites connected with the curriculum	Video, virtual reality systems, online museums, galleries, and exhibitions
Simulation	Students engage in paper-based or digital experiences that mirror the complexity and open-ended nature of the real world	Virtual reality websites, simulation software, animations
Debate	Students discuss opposing viewpoints with their peers	Discussion forums, e-mail, chat
Research	Using a variety of sources, students gather, analyze, and synthesize information	Traditional and online books, encyclo-pedias, and journals; Wikipedia
Conduct an Interview	Face to face, on the telephone, or via e-mail, students question someone on a chosen topic	Telephone, VoIP (e.g., Skype), e-mail, chat rooms
Artifact-Based Inquiry	Students explore a topic using physical or virtual artifacts	Artifact kits, online museums and exhibitions, video games
Data-Based Inquiry	Using print-based and digital data available online, students pursue original lines of inquiry	Websites, online databases, WebQuests
Historical Chain	Students sequence print and digital documents in chronological order	Websites, primary sources (paper-based and virtual), timeline software
Historical Weaving	Students piece together print and digital documents to develop a story	Story construction software, concept mapping software, word processors, storyboard tools
Historical Prism	Students explore print-based and digital documents to understand multiple perspectives on a topic	Websites, primary sources (paper-based and virtual), online newspapers, journals

Note: Based on Harris & Hofer, 2006, 2009.

Table 9.2 Convergent Knowledge Expression Activity Types

Activity	Activity Description	Compatible Technologies
Answer Questions	Students respond to questions posed by the teacher, peers, or the textbook	Discussion boards, wikis, white-boards, quiz and polling software, textbooks
Create a Timelinc	Students develop a visual representa-tion of sequential events	Data mapping software, timeline soft-ware, concept mapping software
Create a Map	Students label existing maps or produce their own	Cartographic software, Google Maps, drawing software
Complete Charts/ Tables	Students fill in teacher-created charts and tables or create their own	Excel or other data processing soft-ware, concept mapping software
Complete a Review Activity	Students engage in some format of question and answer to review course content	Courseware, quiz and polling soft-ware, wikis
Take a Test	Students demonstrate their knowl-edge through a traditional form of assessment	Quiz software, survey software

Note: *Based on Harris & Hofer, 2006, 2009.*

Typically completed first in a social studies project, unit, or series of connected lessons, knowledge-building activity types are those in which students build content-related understanding through information-based processes. The names and brief descriptions of each of the 13 knowledge-building social studies activity types, along with a list of compatible technologies, appear in Table 9.1.

Most often scheduled to follow knowledge-building activities, Harris and Hofer describe knowledge expression activity types for the social studies as those that help students deepen their understanding of content-related concepts using various types of communication. Convergent knowledge expression activities ask students to create, respond to, or complete structured representations of prior knowledge building. Table 9.2 summarizes the names and definitions of each of the six identified convergent knowledge expression activity types, and the technologies that are used most appropriately for each.

Finally, divergent knowledge expression activity types in social studies are described as those that help students to extend their content-related understanding via alternative forms of communication. Table 9.3 describes these 29 written, visual, conceptual, product-oriented, and participatory knowledge expression activity types, along with specific technologies that are compatible with each.

Table 9.3 Divergent Knowledge Expression Activity Types

Activity	Activity Description	Compatible Technologies
Written Knowledge Expression		
Write an Essay	Students compose a structured written response to a prompt	Word processing, wikis, blogs, concept mapping software
Write a Report	Students author a paper from a teacher- or student-derived topic	Word processing, wikis, blogs, concept mapping software
Generate a Historical Narrative	Using historical documents and secondary source information, students develop their own story of the past	Primary sources, timeline software, concept mapping software, word processors
Craft a Poem	Students create poetry connected with course content/ideas	Word processing software, wikis, blogs
Create a Diary	Students write from a first-hand perspective about an event from the past	Word processing, concept mapping, primary and secondary sources (paper based and virtual)
Visual Knowledge Expression		
Create an Illustrated Map	Students use pictures, symbols, and graphics to highlight key features in creating an illustrated map	Cartographic software, graphics editing software, clip art, stock art, Google Maps
Create a Picture/ Mural	Students create a physical or virtual mural	Multimedia editing and graphics tools
Draw a Cartoon	Students create a drawing or caricature of a content-based concept	Drawing/painting software, handheld drawing tools
Conceptual Knowledge Expression		
Develop a Knowledge Web	Using teacher- or student-created webs, students organize information in a visual/spatial manner	Concept mapping software, wikis, brainstorming aids, interactive whiteboards
Generate Questions	Students develop questions related to content/concepts	Word processing, wikis, Google Docs
Develop a Metaphor	Students devise a metaphorical representation of a content-based topic/idea	Image banks, graphics editors, multimedia authoring tools
Product-Oriented Knowledge Expression		
Produce an Artifact	Students create a 3D or virtual artifact	CAD/CAM software, virtual reality creation software
Build a Model	Students develop a mental or physical representation of a course concept/ process	Modeling, simulation construction, graphics software, multimedia production tools
Design an Exhibit	Students synthesize and describe key elements of a topic in a physical or virtual exhibit	Presentation software, word processing, web authoring tools, graphics tools

Table 9.3 *Continued*

Activity	Activity Description	Compatible Technologies
Product-Oriented Knowledge Expression, *continued*		
Create a Newspaper/ News Magazine	Students synthesize and present information in the form of a print-based or electronic periodical	Desktop publishing software, word processing, wikis
Create a Game	Students develop a game, in paper or digital form, to help themselves and other students learn content	Word processors, imaging tools, web authoring software, specialized game-making software
Create a Film	Using some combination of still images, motion video, music and narration, students produce their own movie	Multimedia recording and editing tools and software
Participatory Knowledge Expression		
Do a Presentation	In oral or multimedia format, students share their understanding with others	Presentation software, multimedia authoring tools, video and audio editing suites
Engage in Historical Role Play	Students portray historical figures	Presentation software, multimedia capture/editing software
Do a Performance	Students develop a live or recorded performance (oral, music, drama, etc.)	Word processing, storyboarding software, video/audio editing tools
Engage in Civic Action	Students write to government representatives or engage in some other form of civic action	Word processing, website design, blogs, wikis, e-mail

Note: Based on Harris & Hofer, 2006; 2009.

Note that each of these 42 social studies activity types, as they have been described briefly here, do not privilege one particular type or class of educational technology, nor do they recommend a particular pedagogical approach, in keeping with the situated and flexible aspects of the TPACK framework described earlier in this article. Instead, we acknowledge that different combinations of pedagogical strategies and technologies, each with unique affordances and constraints, are appropriate for different discipline-based curricula, differentiated student learning needs and preferences, and different contextual realities.

Our goal in identifying and sharing activity types, and the manner in which specific technologies are used more (or less) appropriately with each, is to help teachers become aware of the full range of possible curriculum-based learning activity options and the different ways that digital and nondigital tools support each. This can help teachers (and teacher educators) efficiently select among, customize, and combine activity types that are well matched to both students' differentiated learning needs and preferences and classroom contextual realities, such as computer access and class time available for learning activity work. Using this loosely structured design approach, teachers keep students' needs, preferences, and relevant past experience in front-and-center focus as they plan classroom-based learning experiences, with curriculum standards and possible activity-type (and technology) selections in close visual peripheries, so that all are considered concurrently, albeit with differing emphases at different times and under different conditions (Harris, 2008).

It is important to note that using these lists of activity types and technological aids should not be seen as the total process of instructional planning. Effective planning for students' learning is not merely an activity-by-activity endeavor, because curriculum-based units, projects, and sequences are much more than the sums of their respective parts, and their effective use requires related but distinct types of pedagogical, content, and technological expertise. Describing how use of activity types is integrated into instructional planning overall, and what the accompanying mechanisms of that holistic planning process are, is unfortunately beyond the scope of this article. Interested readers can track forthcoming publications that address the use of TPACK-based activity types in instructional planning by visiting the Learning Activity Types Wiki periodically at http://activitytypes.wmwikis.net.

Conclusion

Because teachers' TPACK is not limited to a particular approach to teaching, learning, or even technology integration, it is important that TPACK-based professional development for teachers be flexible and inclusive enough to accommodate the full range of teaching philosophies, styles, and approaches. One way to ensure that flexibility is to share the full range of curriculum-based activity types within each discipline area, encouraging teachers to select among them based on perceived appropriateness and advantage with reference to students' learning needs and preferences, and to engage in this selection/combination process each time they plan a new lesson, project, or unit.

Given that the first taxonomy of content-specific TPACK-based activity types has been tested comparatively recently, and that it refers to just one curriculum content area, it is clear that much more work in this line of inquiry needs to be done. Activity type taxonomies for other K–12 curriculum content areas will have been developed and posted by the time this article is in print for elementary literacy, mathematics, science, secondary English, and world language learning, in addition to the social studies activity types described here (activity-type taxonomies for these content areas, along with surveys to capture vetting feedback, are available at http://activitytypes.wmwikis.net). These taxonomies should be tested and refined according to what teachers and teacher educators discover and recommend when using them. Also, teachers and researchers should compare the efficacy of students' learning that was planned using content-based activity types with instruction planned in more content-neutral, technologically focused ways. They should similarly explore and compare the efficacy of other TPACK-based professional development models, such as the learning-by-design approach mentioned earlier, and the creation of additional models is encouraged.

The continual evolution of technology, pedagogy, and content often brings new learning activity types to light. This means that activity-type taxonomies are not static entities, but rather continually evolving as we develop new technologies, new ways of representing content, and new ways of helping different students learn it. Given the ever-evolving nature of educational research and practice, and of TPACK's defining elements, it is clear that what we face is both a tall order and an appealing opportunity: to continue to invent, revise, expand, update, test, and otherwise explore the ways in which we understand and help teachers to develop TPACK. Because of the emergent and interdependent nature of this particular type of professional, applied knowledge, this can be best accomplished as a collaborative endeavor among content experts, educational technology developers, educational researchers, and pedagogical practitioners.
We invite our readers to join us in this worthy endeavor.

Author Update

In the years since Mishra and Koehler's conceptualization of technological pedagogical content knowledge (TPACK) was first published, this theoretical framework has diffused at nearly viral speeds among educational technology leaders and professional development providers in both school districts and universities. The framework's authors have consistently reminded their readers, however, that their depiction of the complex interdependencies among curriculum content, pedagogy, technologies, and educational contexts is not the first of its kind. We suspect that the rapid spread of this particular rendering is due, to a considerable extent, to the timing of its appearance in educational technology literature.

TPACK appeared at the same time as pressure to demonstrate students' measurable, content-based learning outcomes was intensifying; as technology and professional development budgets were being cut; as awareness of a widening digital divide was growing; and after 20–25 years of educational technology experimentation in elementary, middle, and high schools had not produced the predicted revolutions in learning and teaching. In short, the deep complexities revealed by the TPACK framework explained why technology integration efforts, by and large, had not transformed most classrooms and were so challenging to undertake. In doing so, we were reminded of the primacy of content, pedagogy, and context in effective technology integration, as this article explores.

During the first three years of its spread within and across educational communities, most TPACK work was focused on the framework itself. Though that theoretical work continues, TPACK researchers' attention has turned to the development and assessment of teachers' TPACK. This chapter presented one of approximately six different TPACK development approaches that have been shared to date. During the next five years of TPACK's use, we expect to see additional assessments created and tested. We hope that these tools and evaluation approaches will be used to test and refine the TPACK development strategies that are emerging concurrently.

References

AACTE Committee on Innovation & Technology (Ed.). (2008). *Handbook of technological pedagogical content knowledge for educators.* New York, NY: Routledge.

Beyer, L. E., Feinberg, W., Pagano, J. A., & Whitson, J. A. (1989). *Preparing teachers as professionals: The role of educational studies and other liberal disciplines.* New York, NY: Teachers College Press.

Bransford, J. D., Brown, A. L., & Cocking, R. R. (Eds.). (1999). *How people learn: Brain, mind, experience, and school.* Washington, DC: National Academies Press.

Culp, K. M., Honey, M., & Mandinach, E. (2003). *A retrospective on twenty years of education technology policy.* Washington, DC: U.S. Department of Education, Office of Educational Technology. Retrieved February 20, 2007, from www.nationaledtechplan.org/participate/20years.pdf

Dodge, B. (1995). *Some thoughts about WebQuests.* Retrieved February 20, 2007, from http://webquest.sdsu.edu/about_webquests.html

Dodge, B. (2001). FOCUS: Five rules for writing great WebQuests. *Learning & Leading with Technology, 28*(8), 6–9, 58. Retrieved February 20, 2007, from www.iste.org/AM/Template.cfm?Section=May16&Template=/MembersOnly.cfm&ContentID=7702

Dodge, B., Bellofatto, L., Bohl, N., Casey, M., & Krill M. (2001). *A rubric for evaluating WebQuests.* Retrieved February 20, 2007, from http://webquest.sdsu.edu/webquestrubric.html

Fisher, C., Dwyer, D. C., & Yocam, K. (Eds.). (1996). *Education and technology: Reflections on computing in classrooms.* San Francisco, CA: Jossey-Bass.

Friedhoff, J. R. (2008). Reflecting on the affordances and constraints of technologies and their impact on pedagogical goals. *Journal of Computing in Teacher Education, 24,* 117–122.

Groff, J., & Mouza, C. (2008). A framework for addressing challenges to classroom technology use. *AACE Journal, 16*(1), 21–46.

Harris, J. B. (2008). TPACK in inservice education: Assisting experienced teachers' planned improvisations. In AACTE Committee on Innovation & Technology (Eds.), *Handbook of technological pedagogical content knowledge for educators* (pp. 251–271). New York, NY: Routledge.

Harris, J., & Hofer, M. (2006, July). *Planned improvisations: Technology-supported learning activity design in social studies.* Session presented at the National Educational Computing Conference 2006, San Diego, CA. Retrieved November 19, 2008, from http://center.uoregon.edu/ISTE/NECC2006/program/search_results_details.php?sessionid=13514149

Harris, J., & Hofer, M. (2008, June). *Truly technologically integrated planning for teaching and learning.* Session presented at the National Educational Computing Conference 2008, San Antonio, TX. Retrieved July 27, 2008, from http://center.uoregon.edu/ISTE/NECC2008/program/search_results_details.php?sessionid=42063550&selection_id=42863643&rownumber=6&max=6&gopage=

Harris, J., & Hofer, M. (2009). Instructional planning activity types as vehicles for curriculum-based TPACK development. In C. Maddux (Ed.), *Research highlights in technology and teacher education 2009.* Chesapeake, VA: Association for the Advancement of Computing in Education.

Koehler, M. J., & Mishra, P. (2005). What happens when teachers design educational technology? The development of technological pedagogical content knowledge. *Journal of Educational Computing Research, 32*(2), 131–152.

Koehler, M. J., & Mishra, P. (2008). Introducing TPACK. In AACTE Committee on Innovation & Technology (Eds.), *Handbook of technological pedagogical content knowledge for educators* (pp. 3–29). New York: Routledge.

Koehler, M. J., Yadav, A., Phillips, M. M., & Cavazos-Kottke, S. (2005). What is video good for? Examining how media and story genre interact. *Journal of Educational Multimedia and Hypermedia, 14*(3), 249–272.

Kolodner, J. L., & Gray, J. T. (2002, April). *Understanding the affordances of ritualized activity for project-based classrooms.* Paper presented at the International Conference of the Learning Sciences, Seattle, WA. Retrieved February 14, 2009, from www.cc.gatech.edu/projects/lbd/pdfs/activitystructures.pdf

Latour, B. (1990). Drawing things together. In M. Lynch & S. Woolgar (Eds.), *Representations in scientific practice* (pp. 19–68). Cambridge, MA: MIT Press.

Lemke, J. L. (1987). Social semiotics and science education. *The American Journal of Semiotics, 5*(2), 217–232.

Levin, T., & Wadmany, R. (2008). Teachers' views on factors affecting effective integration of information technology in the classroom: Developmental scenery. *Journal of Technology and Teacher Education, 16,* 233–263.

Linn, M., Lewis, C., Tsuchida, I., & Songer, N. (2000). Beyond fourth-grade science: Why do U.S. and Japanese students diverge? *Educational Researcher, 29*(3), 4–14.

McCormick, R., & Scrimshaw, P. (2001). Information and communications technology, knowledge, and pedagogy. *Education, Communication and Information, 1*(1), 37–57.

Means, B., & Olson, K. (1997). *Technology and education reform.* Office of Educational Research and Improvement, Contract No. RP91-172010. Washington, DC: U.S. Department of Education. Retrieved February 3, 2003, from www.ed.gov/pubs/SER/Technology/title.html

Mehan, H. (1979). *Learning lessons: Social organization in the classroom.* Cambridge, MA: Harvard University Press.

Mishra, P., & Koehler, M. J. (2006). Technological pedagogical content knowledge: A framework for integrating technology in teacher knowledge. *Teachers College Record, 108*(6), 1017–1054.

Mishra, P., Spiro, R. J., & Feltovich, P. (1996). Technology, representation & cognition. In H. von Oostendorp (Ed.), *Cognitive aspects of electronic text processing* (pp. 287–306). Norwood, NJ: Ablex.

National Research Council (NRC). (1999). *Being fluent with information technology literacy.* Computer science and telecommunications board commission on physical sciences, mathematics, and applications. Washington, DC: National Academies Press.

Papert, S. (1987). *A critique of technocentrism in thinking about the school of the future.* Retrieved February 20, 2007, from www.papert.org/articles/ACritiqueofTechnocentrism.html

Pfundt, H., & Duit, R. (2000). *Bibliography: Students' alternative frameworks and science education* (5th ed.). Kiel, Germany: University of Kiel.

Polman, J. L. (1998, April). *Activity structures for project-based teaching and learning: Design and adaptation of cultural tools.* Paper presented at the annual meeting of the American Educational Research Association, San Diego, CA. Retrieved February 14, 2009, from www.eric.ed.gov/ERICDocs/data/ericdocs2sql/content_storage_01/0000019b/80/17/0e/26.pdf

Putnam, R. T., & Borko, H. (2000). What do new views of knowledge and thinking have to say about research on teacher learning? *Educational Researcher, 29*(1), 4–15.

Roblyer, M. D., Edwards, J., & Havriluk, M. A. (1997). *Integrating educational technology into teaching.* Upper Saddle River, NJ: Merrill.

Rogers, A., Andres, Y., Jacks, M., & Clausen, T. (1990). Keys to successful telecomputing. *The Computing Teacher, 17*(8), 25–28.

Russell, M., O'Dwyer, L. M., Bebell, D., & Tao, W. (2007). How teachers' uses of technology vary by tenure and longevity. *Journal of Educational Computing Research, 37,* 393–417.

Sandholtz, J. H., Ringstaff, C., & Dwyer, D. C. (1997). *Teaching with technology: Creating student-centered classrooms.* New York, NY: Teachers College Press.

Shulman, L. (1986). Those who understand: Knowledge growth in teaching. *Educational Researcher, 15*(2), 4–14.

Stodolsky, S. S. (1988). *The subject matters: Classroom activity in math and social studies.* Chicago, IL: University of Chicago Press.

Windschitl, M. (2004). *What types of knowledge do teachers use to engage learners in "doing science?"* Paper commissioned by the National Academy of Sciences. Washington, DC: Board of Science Education. Retrieved February 20, 2007, from www7.nationalacademies.org/bose/MWindschitl_comissioned_paper_6_03_04_HSLabs_Mtg.pdf

Zhao, Y., Pugh, K., Sheldon, S., & Byers, J. L. (2002). Conditions for classroom technology innovations. *Teachers College Record, 104*(3), 482–515.

CHAPTER

10

Extending Content-Focused Professional Development through Online Communities of Practice

Cynthia B. Vavasseur | Nicholls State University

S. Kim MacGregor | Louisiana State University

This mixed method case study provides insights about how the professional development of middle school teachers is facilitated through their participation in content-focused online communities of practice. A key finding from this research reveals that the online community provided teachers with enhanced opportunities to share ideas, to discuss issues, and to make new connections with colleagues as well as with their principal. In addition, teachers gained curriculum-based knowledge, developed enhanced self-efficacy with respect to implementing technology, and collaborated on the development of interdisciplinary curriculum units.

Purpose of the Study

Teachers are faced with pressures to implement instructional reform and accountability measures, both of which require new knowledge and skills. Reports from national commissions on the status of education highlight the need for promoting ongoing teacher growth (National Commission on Teaching and America's Future [NCTAF], 2003). Professional development typically offered as a detached workshop activity that is not connected to a teacher's pedagogy or to student achievement has not produced desired outcomes (Glazer & Hannafin, 2006). A long-term commitment is required to support the development of teachers' content knowledge and the improvement of their technical skills (NCTAF, 2003).

With increasing attention on the middle school curriculum and teacher effectiveness, there is a pressing need for reforming professional development at this level (Killion, 1999). Although many schools provide planning time during the day for teams of teachers, a shift toward creating communities of active teacher–learners is recommended. The professional development approach that was the target of this study incorporated aspects of just-in-time learning, content-focused inquiry groups, and participation in an online community of practice. The purposes of the present study were to gain insights about the following:

- In what ways did this experience influence teachers' sense of efficacy and their ability to plan for and implement technology in their curricular areas?
- What was the focus of the interactions among teachers while they participated in the online community of practice?
- How did teachers perceive the participation of their school leaders in the online community?

Theoretical Perspectives

This research is informed by literature related to professional development focused on technology integration, communities of practice, and teacher efficacy. According to the guidelines of No Child Left Behind, a minimum of 25% of all funds spent on educational technology must be allocated for high-quality professional development. In addition, the International Society for Technology in Education (ISTE) has developed standards for technology integration that have now been adapted or referenced by 90% of state departments in the United States (2006, www.iste.org/nets/bystate/). NETS, or the National Educational Technology Standards, identify the fundamental concepts concerning technology that should be mastered by teachers, students, and administrators (ISTE, 2000, 2002, 2007). NETS•A, or the National Educational Technology Standards for Administrators, much like the standards for students and teachers, identifies technological competencies that should be mastered by school administrators (ISTE, 2002). NETS•A were built on the previous

Technology Standards for School Administrators, or TSSA, document (ISTE, 2002). In addition, TPCK, or technological pedagogical content knowledge, is a framework that also identifies essential knowledge required by teachers regarding technology integration (Mishra & Koehler, 2006). Going deeper than simply defining competencies, TPCK focuses on three forms of knowledge: content knowledge, pedagogical knowledge, and technological knowledge. All forms must work together for a teacher to successfully master the integration of technology (Mishra & Koehler, 2006).

Technology integration, and therefore effective professional development for technology integration, has now become an additional mandate. Many schools and school systems offer workshop-type sessions focused on the use of a particular software package or system as opposed to ongoing professional development focused on technology integration. The National Implementation Research Network (2007) states the importance of recognizing new mandates placed on schools and school systems and discusses how professional development should go beyond simple paper implementation in a school. The professional development program in this research strove to put in place new workshops, with supervision from principals and researchers, providing process implementation of a professional development experience.

Past school reform efforts have created schools and teachers who want to improve practices, but are not supported in doing so (Darling-Hammond, 1998). The problem of school improvement, therefore, is not one of motivation, but a problem of expertise that can only be improved through serious, systemic, and sustained investment in increasing the knowledge base of educators (Darling-Hammond, 1998.) Current approaches aimed at increasing this knowledge base include just-in-time learning, peer mentoring, content-focused inquiry groups, online professional development, and communities of practice (Hughes, Kerr, & Ooms, 2005; Liew & Huang, 2000; Parr, 1999). Just-in-time professional development involves teachers participating in professional development within their classrooms and within their schools. Often, when the focus of professional development is technology, the availability of a technology specialist is required to provide teachers with help when it is needed (Hofer, Chamberlin, & Scot, 2004). Peer mentoring is a collaborative approach to professional development with teacher leaders who are assuming the role of mentor. In addition, peer mentoring requires teachers to have time to collaborate within a school day. Many believe that this type of collaboration, used in conjunction with interdisciplinary teaming, is the key to the professional development of middle-grades teachers (Flowers, Mertens, & Mulhall, 2003). Teaming allows teachers with common daily planning times to collaborate and grow professionally. In content-focused inquiry groups (Hughes, Kerr, & Ooms, 2005), the participants engage in collaborative inquiry whereby they exchange ideas about alternative practices and beliefs about their content area and grade level. The inquiry group is situated in the school context, and participants select a focus on which they develop ideas and share the results of implementation.

Online delivery of professional development offers many benefits, including convenience, immediate application, professional growth, and economic advantages (Tinker, 2003). Although the benefits of online professional development are numerous, many teachers remain uncomfortable with technology-based training (Schlager, Fusco, & Schank, 1999). Although online instruction poses challenges, online communities of practice allow teachers to communicate with each other across physical space and time (Dias, 1999). Communities of practice is a term that describes a group of people in a professional environment who come together to share experience and expertise (Wenger & Snyder, 2000). Within these communities, there is no clear boundary between developing skills and developing new identities as leaders in a field. Both can occur as the community interacts (Barab & Duffy, 2000). In short, participants in a community of practice learn together by focusing on problems that are directly related to their work (Wenger & Snyder, 2000).

The literature related to communities of practice suggests that adult learners work more effectively when placed in a social, collaborative environment (Wenger & Snyder, 2000). Furthermore, successful communities rely on participants learning about something meaningful (Brown, 1997). Through a community of practice, teachers can become less isolated and more inclined to discuss new ideas, can solve problems that arise concerning technology integration, and can form a support system to foster new ideas.

> Teachers are in many ways the most isolated of professionals—teaching is still by and large a solo pursuit. Renewed teaching relies on generating new ideas and on having opportunities to examine one's own teaching. A supportive community of practice can help to sustain the slow, step-wise process that eventually leads to a fundamental transformation in teaching philosophy and practice. (Spitzer, Wedding, & DiMauro, 1994, p. 1)

Teacher collaboration added to a traditional technology training program not only allows teachers to acquire and construct knowledge (Dias, 1999), but also leads to improving student knowledge and skill (Hawkes, 1999).

One study (Lieberman & Grolnick, 1996) found that teacher collaboration in educational reform networks, or collaborative communities, produced five themes in relation to the organization and collaboration among teachers: purpose and direction, building collaboration, consensus and commitment, activities and relationships as important building blocks, leadership, and dealing with funding problems. A key element of building collaboration is the creation of a network where the tone is welcoming and relaxed. Furthermore, engaging teachers in activities that facilitate both individual and group learning and reflection encourages teachers to assume leadership roles and to value one another's expertise. In initial conversations, teachers often use their time to share their feelings about school life (Lieberman & Grolnick, 1996; Routman, 2002). However, over time, collaborative communities, such as educational reform networks, result in teachers discussing complex educational issues that often do not have a simple solution (Lieberman & Grolnick, 1996; Little, 1993).

Successful collaborative communities such as these may provide a useful tool for teachers in relation to increasing teacher self-efficacy. Teacher self-efficacy is a critical issue often not addressed in designing and developing effective professional development. Self-efficacy is defined as a person's beliefs about his or her capabilities to perform at a given level of achievement, or a person's influence over other people (Bandura, 1994). Self-efficacy can affect a person's life choices, motivation in an activity, success in an activity, and resilience to adversity (Bandura, 1994; Tschannen-Moran, Woolfolk Hoy, & Hoy, 1998). A teacher's sense of efficacy can also affect his or her involvement in a professional development experience, as well as his or her later classroom implementation of the material. Teaching efficacy can be affected in positive ways by participation in experiences that foster the development of a professional learning community (Tschannen-Moran et al., 1998). In such a community, a teacher can be exposed to others' successes with a given task, as well as gain the support needed to change self-efficacy beliefs. A teacher's sense of efficacy can be influenced through collective efficacy (Glazer & Hannafin, 2006; Tschannen-Moran et al., 1998) and leadership (Tschannen-Moran et al., 1998). Collective efficacy is the extent to which efficacy is shared across teachers in a school building and can be established through collaborative, supportive experience among teachers within a school: "Schools where teachers work together to find ways to address the learning motivation and behavior problems of their students are likely to enhance teachers' feelings of efficacy" (Tschannen-Moran et al., 1998, p. 217).

A positive leadership presence can also influence a teacher's sense of efficacy. Research has shown that when a principal displays strong leadership, teachers' collective sense of efficacy is greater (Fuller & Izu, 1986). A well-established body of research on the principal's role in school leadership suggests that to promote teacher learning and to prevent attrition, principals should build interpersonal relationships among teachers (Blase & Blase, 2000; Bolman & Deal, 2002; Fleming, 1999; Fullan, 2002; McLaughlin, 1991; Morrissey, 2000) and emphasize the importance of continued teacher learning (Darling-Hammond, 2003; Elmore, 2002; Fullan, 2004). In short, successful principals strive to foster healthy school climates by promoting collaboration and by fostering teachers' professional learning (Drago-Severson, 2005). However, given the busy schedule and daily responsibilities of a K–12 principal, leading reform often proves challenging (Chan & Pool, 2002; Furman & Zibrida, 1990). This research is designed to provide insights about a model of professional development that is situated in a community of practice, which includes both teachers and their principals who interact in both face-to-face and online contexts.

Methodology

This study was designed as a mixed-method comparative case study, allowing the researchers to focus on contemporary events, while acknowledging the lack of control of behavioral events within the research setting (Yin, 2003). Quantitative and qualitative approaches to data collection and analysis were implemented alternatively over a period of four months to provide triangulation and a more complete picture of the process and outcomes.

PARTICIPANTS

Two middle schools located in the same school district in the mid-South were selected through homogeneous purposeful sampling. The schools were similar demographically (Table 10.1) and were chosen because of their ongoing commitment to professional development.

Table 10.1 School Demographics

	School A	School B
Student information		
Number of students	427	336
Percent of regular education students	88%	85%
Percent of students with disabilities	12%	16%
Percent of students on free or reduced lunch	22%	45%
Attendance rate	95.1%	95.1%
Dropout rate	0.0%	0.4%
Teacher information		
Number of teachers in Grades 6–8	24	16
Mean years of experience	15.2	12.1
Mean years at current school	7.8	5.4
Mean number of students per class in Grades 6–8	21	24
Number of white teachers/African American teachers	20/4	14/2
Number of male/female teachers	1/23	5/11
Number of teachers with a bachelor's degree	16	10
Number of teachers with graduate degrees	8	6
School information		
School performance score	111.9	102.8

Participants from each school included principals and sixth, seventh, and eighth grade teachers of core subjects such as English, language arts, math, science, and social studies, as well as resource teachers. All teachers and their respective principal participated in the online community, as well as all data collection methods. Teachers at the two schools lacked the competency to successfully integrate technology into their teaching practices. Only 9% of teachers at the participating schools had participated in the state's 52-hour professional development program in technology integration.

A school's performance score is based on students' achievement on state-developed criterion-referenced content mastery tests and the Iowa Test of Basic Skills, student attendance, and student dropout rates. Scores of 111.9 and 102.8 give both schools the distinction of three stars. Schools with a School Performance Score between 100 and 119.9 receive three stars. The state average is 87.6, and the highest distinction is five stars for a school receiving a School Performance Score of 140 or above.

CONTEXT OF THE PROFESSIONAL DEVELOPMENT PROGRAM

Although professional development in the participating schools was an ongoing component of teacher teaming time, this research focused on the implementation of a module designed to facilitate the integration of technology. The content of the training sessions emerged from a needs assessment conducted with the schools' teachers and principals. An initial meeting with principals revealed concerns about their teachers' ability to implement a newly mandated state curriculum that required appropriate integration of technology. Teachers responded to a brief survey to provide input about their immediate needs with regard to implementing technology within the context of the new curriculum. From their responses it was determined that the focus of the professional development would be on using technology as a tool for productivity, research, and communication. These topics were embedded into the larger issue of curricular and instructional reform. In conjunction with these topics, teachers were provided with opportunities to learn the extent to which their activities fulfilled the National Educational Technology Standards (NETS) for students and teachers (ISTE, 2000, 2007).

Face-to-face sessions were conducted twice per week during the teachers' team planning time throughout the course of the professional development experience. In conjunction with the face-to-face training, teachers and principals participated in online communities of practice designed to facilitate teacher collaboration and principal support. It was determined that math and science teachers would be paired for membership in an online community, and English teachers would be paired with social studies teachers for another online community. Using the Blackboard Courseware Management System, two online communities were developed at each school, resulting in a total of four communities. The Communication section of Blackboard was utilized, and a Group Page was set up for each of the content-focused teams at each school. The Group Page contained a discussion board, e-mail capabilities, and external links associated with each of the professional development topics. In the online community, teachers engaged in weekly discussions about topics pertaining to the face-to-face training. Specific prompts, drawn from the needs assessment with the principal and teachers, were provided on a periodic basis by one of the researchers to stimulate and focus the online discussion. Hawkes (2001) noted that nondirected discourse may not be conducive to reflective online dialogue. The prompts included questions and scenarios designed to elicit teachers' beliefs about teaching and learning, the status of their knowledge about various topics, descriptions of their experiences in implementing new approaches to instruction, and how these approaches addressed the NETS (ISTE, 2007). For example, one prompt asked teachers to identify ideas for creating interdisciplinary activities using technology. In another prompt, a scenario was provided in which students were working on a project requiring Internet research, but were found to be checking sports scores. The teachers were asked to relate their concerns about what the students were doing in this scenario and how they would handle the situation.

DATA COLLECTION

Quantitative data were derived from two sources. The first source was a teacher efficacy survey administered to all teachers. The purpose of the efficacy survey was for teachers to provide a self-report at the beginning and end of the professional development program. The second source of quantitative data was derived from teacher performance on the culminating project, a technology-enhanced unit plan. The teacher efficacy survey was adapted from six instruments (Box, 1999; Christensen, 1998; Knezek & Christensen, 1997; Norris & Box, 2005; Schwarzer & Jerusalem, 1995). This 32-item, Likert-scale survey was designed to determine the level of teacher expertise in using technology, the perceived value of technology in the instructional process, teacher efficacy in using technology, and general teaching efficacy. The quality of the technology-enhanced unit plan was assessed on six criteria: (1) connections to the curriculum and its standards, (2) clearly defined objectives, (3) alignment of learning activities with objectives, (4) appropriate integration of technology, (5) alignment with technology standards, and (6) assessment procedures. A rubric designed by the state technology center was used to establish levels of quality and consisted of a rating scale from zero to three for each of the six criteria.

Qualitative data were derived from two sources: focus group interviews with all teachers, and the online threaded discussions. Focus group interviews were conducted at the end of the professional development experience with each content-focused team of teachers. The interviews were audiotaped and transcribed for subsequent analysis. The purpose of the focus groups was to gain an understanding of newly achieved teaching knowledge and competencies, of teachers' perceptions about the participation of their principal, and of the benefits and challenges associated with the online community. An analysis of the threaded discussions was conducted to develop an understanding of the nature of the interactions among teachers and between teachers and their principal in the online community.

Quantitative data were analyzed using statistical procedures. The analyses of the focus group interviews and threaded discussions were conducted through constant comparative analysis (Glaser & Strauss, 1967). Using this method, the content of the threaded discussions and the interview transcripts was segmented and coded according to significant themes and patterns. Two researchers coded the data from the interview transcripts and the threaded discussions and achieved consensus in the classification of themes to segments of text. Interrater reliability was established through consensus.

Results

The following sections are organized to address the research questions using data from both quantitative and qualitative sources.

IMPACT ON TEACHER COMPETENCE AND EFFICACY

Four forms of data were analyzed to address the impact of the experience on teachers: teacher reflections, the teacher efficacy survey, teacher focus group interviews, and the unit plans created by each interdisciplinary content-focused team of teachers.

TEACHER COMPETENCIES

Teachers at both schools identified several areas where their proficiency with technology was gained. Experiences revealed in interviews and the threaded discussions indicated that, while the teachers were developing new skills and knowledge, they were also implementing new instructional approaches in their classrooms. Examples are provided in Table 10.2.

Teachers worked in content-focused teams of two to four to develop technology-enhanced unit plans that were compatible with the goals and objectives of the newly mandated curriculum. The plans were submitted to the state's educational technology center, where they were evaluated by an educational technology specialist. Table 10.3 displays the detailed results of the evaluation of the unit plans for each content-focused community team and school. Analyses of the unit plans revealed appropriate instructional applications of the basic productivity, research, and communication tools that were the focus of this professional development experience. However, a maximum score of 18 was possible, suggesting that there was room for teachers to develop further expertise in this task.

To compare the total scores earned on the unit plans developed by the teacher teams in the two schools, an independent means t-test was conducted and revealed a significant difference between means ($t(10) = -2.272$, $p = .046$). There was a significant difference between the overall quality of the unit plans in favor of School B. In addition, subscores were examined, and it was determined that although both schools achieved similar scores for the content and evaluation components, School B had significantly higher scores for the technology integration component ($t(22) = -3.39$, $p = .003$).

TEACHING EFFICACY

In a pilot study, the researcher designed teacher efficacy survey was administered to 74 teachers from nonparticipating schools. A factor analysis was conducted to reduce the number of variables measured to a few factors by combining variables that correlated to one another (Gall, Borg, & Gall, 1996). Principal component analysis was used to extract the factors from the data set, resulting in the emergence of nine factors. The eigenvalues from this analysis showed that the first four factors accounted for 53.9% of the total variance. Following the pilot study, the survey was revised and administered to participants at the beginning and end of the professional development experience (Table 10.4).

Table 10.2 Technology Competencies Gained

Using technology as a productivity tool	Teachers using technology to make a useful product; students using technology to display knowledge	I did the timelines twice. Once with Rosa Parks and once with American history. They (the students) really did well ... I just walked them through it. We used Excel in graphing survey results from class newspaper reports.
Using technology as a research tool	Teachers using technology to gain information; students safely using the Internet to conduct research	Like the WebQuest, you look at one and see all of the work that goes into it and then think, "I can't do that." I've done that when looking at them. I've used them before and thought, oh, I could never make one of those, and we did! And it was not that difficult! Granted, you made it a bit easier because you gave us a template, but I'll always have that template, and now I could stray if I needed to. The template just gave me the jump start to what I needed to do.
Using technology as a communication tool	Teachers using the online community to collaborate and share ideas with other teachers and their principal	Sharing new ideas on Blackboard (the online community). Using Trackstar and WebQuest got me interested in other ways I can use technology. Ms. Smith got into the conversation and told me of a grant I could write to get about thirty computers. I don't think I would have had that opportunity without Blackboard because I don't get to really interact with the teachers at other grade levels that much, and it was nice to, you know, she offered to help me out and give me more information, so it really got things going for me.

A difference score was computed to represent the growth score from the pre- to post-assessment on each factor from the efficacy survey. A MANOVA was computed to test the difference between the two schools for the four dependent growth scores. The Wilks' lambda was significant ($F(4, 23) = 3.3, p = .026$), revealing a significant difference between the two schools in teachers' growth in teaching efficacy. Teachers at School A demonstrated a more positive growth in teaching efficacy than teachers at School B on the collective factors. In looking at the change scores for each factor, it is interesting to note, however, that the teachers at both schools showed an increase from pre- to post-assessment on their perception of the value of computers in teaching.

Table 10.3 Unit Plan Evaluation Scores

	Science/Math Unit Plans						English/Social Studies Unit Plans					
Sub-Area Assessed	School A			School B			School A			School B		
Content												
Curriculum Standards	2	2	2	2	2	2	1	1	2	1	2	2
Objectives	2	2	1	2	2	2	1	1	2	1	1	1
Learning Activities	2	2	2	2	2	2	2	2	2	2	2	2
Content Mean	1.89			2.00			1.55			1.55		
Technology Integration												
Integration into Plan	1	1	1	2	2	1	2	1	1	2	2	1
Technology Standards	1	1	1	2	2	2	2	1	1	2	2	1
Technology Integration Mean	1.00			1.83			1.33			1.67		
Evaluation												
Assessment	2	2	2	2	2	2	2	2	2	2	2	2
Total Group Mean	9.67			11.67			9.33			10.0		

TEACHER INTERACTIONS IN THE ONLINE COMMUNITY

Four online communities, two at each school, were ongoing during the course of this study. Each teacher was a member of one content-focused community; however, the principals participated in both of the content-focused communities at their schools. Table 10.5 provides details about the number of participants and their levels of participation for the online communities in each school.

Individual teachers posted between 2 and 16 times at School A and 2 and 12 times at School B. The mean number of postings in the two content-focused communities by Principal A was 11.5, and Principal B was 15.5.

Table 10.4 Mean Scores on Teaching Efficacy Survey

Factor	Pre-test School A	Post-test School A	Pre-test School B	Post-test School B
Expertise in using technology	4.11	4.38	4.69	4.02
Perception of technology value	4.74	4.83	3.95	4.59
Technology efficacy	3.91	3.87	4.06	3.86
General teaching efficacy	4.27	4.43	4.50	4.12

Note: 1 = Strongly Disagree to 5 = Strongly Agree

Table 10.5 Composition of and Participation in Online Community Groups

	School A	School B
Mean number of postings for teachers	7.6	6.3
Range of postings for teachers	2–16	2–12
Mean number of postings by principal	11.5	15.5
Number of online community groups	2	2
Number of teachers in each group (ELA/SS-M/S)	13–10	9–6
Number of females (ELA/SS-M/S)	13–9	8–5
Number of males (ELA/SS-M/S)	0–1	1–1

The threaded discussions from each of the online communities were analyzed to uncover the nature of the interactions. A cross-case analysis was conducted to identify themes consistent across the four online communities. An a priori framework for assigning categories to the content of the messages in the online discussions was not utilized. However, the themes emerging from the analysis of the message content supported several categories identified by Hawkes (2001) including technology use, technology integration, curriculum implementation, student assessment, and resource sharing. These categories are embedded and interwoven throughout the three prevailing themes identified in our analysis: teachers' perceptions of their personal computing efficacy, content-focused dialogue, and concerns about students' use and misuse of technology. Collaborative reflection (Schon, 1987, 1991) is evident throughout the conversations in each of the online communities.

TEACHER TECHNOLOGY EFFICACY

Teachers openly discussed their limitations concerning the integration of technology.

> I am not very proficient with this technology stuff. However, I do recognize the importance of it in the classroom. I sometimes feel like I need a 504 plan. The students are more proficient, but it's all good. I am learning, and I am actually better this year than last. I'm loving it.

Other teachers felt comfortable enough to share similar thoughts: "I feel that sometimes the kids know more than I do about searching on the Internet, which scares me!" These words of insecurity often were met with other teachers' reassuring words and humor. In these ways teachers provided moral support and encouragement to one another in their use of new technologies. "That's so great that you've gotten your students involved in online journaling; it's addictive. I'll bet your students enjoy writing ten thousand times more when it's on laptops in your classroom." Another teacher provided encouragement for working through mistakes, "You can teach an old work horse new tricks. I knew you could do this. See, I was right. Hang in there. We profit from our mistakes. You and I make plenty, but we keep on trucking."

Similarly, teachers also used humor to support one another. Many teachers, on seeing a serious conversation about fear of technology, would add comments such as, "Well, it probably won't blow up anything new," and "By the end of the year, we will be technologically dangerous, if we aren't already." Many times such comments stirred more humorous comments, such as "She's not a dork, she's my hero," creating an atmosphere of ease and comfort. Overall, encouraging messages among teachers provided a collegial atmosphere, emphasizing the benefits of teacher collaboration. "This is easily done if everyone works together. Which we are."

It is interesting to note that the results from the teaching efficacy survey revealed that the teachers at both schools showed growth in relation to valuing computers in their teaching practice. It is likely that the sharing of experiences and support gained through their participation in the online community contributed to this outcome. Bandura (1997) postulated sources of self-efficacy including vicarious experience and social persuasion. Through their participation in the online community of practice, the teachers had the opportunity to gather ideas about how others implemented and managed their instructional computing experiences. Personal persuasion from peers provided encouragement and specific examples of solutions to problems. It is believed that these types of vicarious experience and social persuasion have a positive impact on teachers' beliefs about their teaching efficacy (Tschannen-Moran et al., 1998).

CONTENT-FOCUSED DIALOGUE

Within the online communities, teachers not only debated the utility of technology implementation, but provided alternative ideas concerning the instructional use of technology. For example, ways of using technology to enhance students' opportunities to engage in higher order thinking were discussed. One teacher noted: "I think it is important to allow students to evaluate the importance of information found using technology. This is one of those 'real life' skills that will allow students to think critically." Other teachers shared how technology use has changed the ways in which their students learn: "Technology involvement has become essential.... We can do interviews online with people we'd never meet, research surveys and polls done by large numbers and turn surveys into graphs with the push of a button. Life is sweet."

Teachers also asked for and provided resources to help one another. For example, one teacher posted the following: "I saw that you mentioned Alfred Hitchcock. I don't know if you are still working with that, but I am a huge fan and I have several DVD's if you want to use them in class." Other teachers posted open requests for assistance: "I have been thinking about my National Board lesson. May I have all your information about poetry?" Most requests for resources were simple, such as: "If you have any great ideas for vocabulary graphic organizers or lessons on grammar, please share!!" Other requests for resources sparked detailed discussions about new technology applications. One group of teachers had recently begun incorporating blogging, or online journaling, into their English classes. On hearing about this, other teachers asked for more information on the subject:

> I remember you telling me about this the other day. Is there a tutorial on Blogger.com that gives detailed instructions on how to tie your account to students? I played on Blogger the other day ... fun, fun! I need to play some more to become more familiar with the site.... Thank you for all you've done for me—I appreciate you greatly!

Teachers who had been using this type of application were quick to respond to comments and questions:

> You will also need to exercise caution when the students blog. Before you begin blogging with your class, you need to set up your account. Also, you want the students' accounts tied to your e-mail address. Then if anyone tries to change their password or create a bogus profile you receive an e-mail about the requested changes.

Another group of teachers engaged in a conversation concerning materials and the writing of local grants to gain new technology materials.

> I was curious about writing a grant for some laptops for seventh grade (I had heard through the grapevine that the eighth grade team wrote a grant for them). Does the grant program still exist, and if so, do you know where I can find out more info?

Again, teachers who had received monies were quick to respond: "Our grant is an 8G grant.... I will help you any way I can in the writing process."

In order for teachers to accomplish newly formulated tasks, it is necessary for the individuals to understand the structure of the task as well as to have the resources to accomplish it (Nespor, 1987). In this case, the teachers were required to implement a new curriculum in conjunction with the application of instructional technologies. Participation in the dialogue focused on the task at hand and collegial offerings of ideas provided these teachers with the opportunity to internalize and engage in processing relevant strategies.

USE AND MISUSE OF TECHNOLOGY

A major theme emerging from the online discussion was the concern teachers had about their students' use and misuse of the Internet. A lively discussion ensued about the various safety issues that arose while students were researching given topics on the Internet. The teachers shared their fears and concerns. One teacher noted: "I have many concerns about Internet safety. I find that the students have a little bit of knowledge, and they think they are computer gurus. They are not aware of the dangers of the Internet." Another voiced: "I am VERY [*sic*] concerned about what the kids can get into while they are working on the Internet. There is so much trash out there! Plus, I want to make sure that my students are engaged." Another commented: "Internet safety is a very serious concern for teachers, parents, and administrators. Students are very vulnerable on the Internet and have too much knowledge about accessing inappropriate sites." These comments reveal the range of teachers' concerns, from issues of student safety to the appropriate use of class time and resources.

As more concerns were posted, teachers moved toward explicit discussion of how students who misuse the Internet should be handled. While discussing what to do if a student was looking at a non-school-related site, a number of teachers offered suggestions for preventing the misuse of the Internet by students: "Close monitoring is the only way to keep our students on task with the computers. If they know you are constantly monitoring them, they will be less likely to go onto sites they should not be on." Other teachers discussed their "zero-tolerance" policies on the misuse of the Internet: "I would take the computer and not allow those students to work on them for the rest of the assignment." Such comments fostered debates, with many teachers agreeing with such strict policies: "The students would lose computer privileges for the assigned task and be required to complete the task in the library (public or school). Zero tolerance in order to stress the seriousness of disregard for Internet safeguard precautions." Other teachers disagreed with such strict regulations: "I would share with the students how much I like that website as well, but that we have to save that for later. Students would then be redirected to the appropriate website." Despite the debate, one teacher summarized the concerns over prior experiences with students' use of the Internet:

> The main safety concern I have with the Internet is that students may give out personal information online or agree to meet someone they have met online. The only way to guard against this, especially since they use the Internet at home, is to discuss the dangers of either of those things.

It was clear that these teachers used the online community as a forum to identify problems and to share potential solutions.

TEACHERS' PERCEPTIONS OF PRINCIPAL PARTICIPATION

During the focus group interviews, teachers described their reactions to their principal's participation in the online community. Most teachers believed that their principal's involvement was pivotal to their success in the experience: "She would have had to be involved; otherwise, you think she doesn't care." Beyond this, two key themes emerged: pressure and support. The perception of how these themes characterized each of the principals was somewhat different. There was evidence of how the climate of the two schools was influenced by the principals and how this climate was echoed in the online participation of the teachers. Preexisting conditions, beliefs, and values that make up a school culture (Matthews & Crow, 2003) are likely to influence the level of openness expressed through this medium.

Pressure applied by School A's principal during this experience was consistently seen as positive: "We know that she is interested in what is going on in our class. She is pushing us to continue our education, and pushing us to be better teachers, holding us to a level of expectations." Teachers were less consistent with their reactions to the pressures applied by School B's principal. She often was viewed as aggressive, and some teachers perceived her participation as "watching" their online conversations. One teacher articulated this concern: "Her being on Blackboard made me feel like she was watching me. That is why I didn't like to participate because I felt like if I put a comment there, it might come back at me later." Other teachers, however, were indifferent to the pressure, stating that their principal was simply trying to encourage their participation in the experience.

Both principals were viewed as role models who genuinely were putting forth effort to support their teachers in the learning process. An analysis of the principals' participation revealed that their postings reflected an interest in their teachers' perspectives, ideas, and concerns. Principal A posted specific ideas relevant to the teachers' conversation and her personal reactions to specific issues, whereas Principal B posted more general "pat on the back" kind of messages with occasional opinion-oriented messages. Although the nature of the pressure and support put forth by each principal was perceived differently, the teachers at both schools believed that the online conversation was productive. Interestingly, in School A, where teachers viewed the pressure as motivational and received continued praise from their principals, teacher responses on the teaching efficacy survey indicated that they also developed a stronger sense of efficacy about their capacity to be successful. In contrast, the teachers at School B produced more highly rated unit plans, which might have been a result of their desire to receive continued praise from their principal.

RECOMMENDATIONS FOR ENHANCING THE ONLINE COMMUNITY

Professional development, focused on the integration of technology, can be a successful collaborative experience when delivered using face-to-face and online mediums. Key aspects that led to the success of this program were:

- ***The use of a needs assessment:*** Teachers and principals had a voice in the focus of each professional development module.
- ***Principal introduction to the experience:*** Principals in this experience gave attention to the opening of the experience through face-to-face and virtual announcements. These introductions welcomed teachers and conveyed the principals' enthusiasm about the online community and their participation as a collegial member of each content-focused team.
- ***Facilitation of the online community:*** Thought-provoking weekly discussion board prompts were provided, technical support was available, and relevant resources for each topic were given. An online facilitator prompted teachers when needed and provided clarification on difficult topics when appropriate.
- ***Effective online communication:*** In the online community, principals and teachers engaged in reflective conversations concerning efficacy and the tasks to be completed.

Following the experience, teachers voiced the desire for a change in the schedule of the program. Many teachers wanted the experience to include less frequent face-to-face sessions spanning a longer period of time. Teachers also suggested changes for the composition of the online community. Although the community was effective within a school, teachers and principals in this study voiced the need for an online community that encompassed more teachers within the school district. Teachers from both schools believed that their online interactions with their school colleagues were effective; however, it was suggested that interaction would be more productive if teachers teaching similar grades and subjects throughout the district were involved in the online community. Public web-based professional development sites such as Tapped In (SRI International, 1995–2007; http://tappedin.org) could be utilized to extend the community beyond the walls of a local school or school system. Large-scale professional development websites provide features such as chat rooms, event rooms, mentoring programs, and online help, thus allowing teachers to gain benefits from an ever-increasing range of resources.

LIMITATIONS OF THE STUDY

Limitations of this study center on the limited period of time for which the online community was observed. It would be interesting to explore how the online community would evolve over an extended period of time. In addition, it is uncertain as to whether the members of the community will be able to sustain their participation over time. Also, one of the researchers provided the prompts for stimulating the discussion in the online community. Different prompts may lead to further insight into the conversations among teachers in the online community.

Discussion

This research demonstrated that an online community of practice, added to existing face-to-face technology professional development, can be used to increase communication and collaboration among teachers. Assessment of the interactions within these communities revealed that the teachers were engaged in collaborative reflection (Schon, 1987, 1991). The teachers identified problems that were contextualized in their daily practice and shared potential solutions to those problems. Higher levels (Hawkes & Romiszowski, 2001) of reflection were evident, including explanations of events within the context of their practice and references to ethical issues and personal beliefs with respect to those issues. It allowed principals to motivate and support teachers while establishing a presence in the professional development experience. Implementing online communities of practice facilitates the extension of communication beyond weekly team planning sessions, thus enabling opportunities for ongoing dialogue. This study supports previous findings that have demonstrated the importance of the principal's instructional leadership in the implementation of professional development (Liew & Huang, 2000; Little, 1993; McLaughlin, 1991; Morrissey, 2000; Parr, 1999). These findings also agree with those of Farrell (2001) that suggest that successful professional development emphasizes the importance of principals grouping teachers by teams, focuses on content instead of software, emphasizes being flexible and listening to the needs of teachers, and models classroom examples.

Interestingly, over the course of the professional development module, the teachers at both schools developed more favorable views of the value of computers in teaching. However, this experience had a differential effect on teacher competence in planning for and using technology and on teaching efficacy. There was a significant difference between the two schools in the quality of the teacher-produced unit plans. Higher quality unit plans were produced in the school where the principal applied more pressure, while also posting more messages of praise. The teachers at this school were clear about their understanding of the principal's expectations and their role in helping to achieve the goal of implementing the technology-infused curriculum. In contrast, the teachers in the other school demonstrated an increase in their teaching efficacy with using technology to enhance instruction. It has been suggested that two specific ways to influence teacher efficacy are through collective efficacy effects (Glazer & Hannafin, 2006) and leadership (Tschannen-Moran et al., 1998). Moreover, improved teaching efficacy could relate to reduced stress among teachers, as well as improved relations among teachers and administrators (Tschannen-Moran et al., 1998). The current research mirrors such findings and found that teachers who demonstrated significant growth in overall efficacy also had a more favorable perception of their principal's participation.

The online community in this study provided an opportunity for teachers to increase communication with their fellow teachers and principals. Within this community, teachers who normally do not communicate with one another were able to engage in reflective practice and provide support for each other in adopting innovation. Insights gained from this and future research could be used to design collaborative, supportive online communities to make technology professional development more meaningful for teachers.

Author Update

We are only beginning to understand the utility of virtual communities for providing a vehicle whereby teachers can be engaged in the processes essential for knowledge sharing and building. Research reveals that participation in these communities provides opportunities for sharing ideas and helping their colleagues, and at the same time allows for the development of a culture of camaraderie. Given that teachers often conduct professional responsibilities in a state of relative isolation, these technologies hold great promise for creating cultures that support ongoing professional development.

In the current era of accountability, there is an imperative to find ways to improve the effectiveness of schools. It is known that situated professional development and constructive interactions between teachers as well as between teachers and the school principal contribute to the collective efficacy of a school. The role of the principal as a leader, manager, and change agent is recognized as essential for creating effective schools. Online social communities provide an environment whereby teachers and busy principals can interact with each other and focus on issues of immediacy and relevance, thereby constructing knowledge among the group. The development of newer, more cost-effective, easier-to-use social networking technologies enhances the feasibility of creating and implementing virtual communities for knowledge sharing and building.

Although our research provided a glimpse into how a virtual community composed of teacher and principal participation facilitates the professional development of teachers, there is a need for ongoing investigation into this promising approach. Future research should determine how teachers might best use social communities and for what purposes, and how new knowledge is constructed and applied to practice. More specifically, research is needed to identify the features and attributes that best facilitate participation and to deepen our understanding of knowledge-sharing behaviors within these virtual social environments.

References

Bandura, A. (1994). Self-efficacy. In V. S. Ramachaudran (Ed.), *Encyclopedia of human behavior* (Vol. 4, pp. 71–81). New York, NY: Academic Press.

Bandura, A. (1997). *Self-efficacy in changing societies.* New York, NY: Cambridge University Press.

Barab, S. A., & Duffy, T. M. (2000). From practice fields to communities of practice. In D. H. Jonassen & S. M. Land (Eds.), *Theoretical foundations of learning environments* (pp. 25–55). Mahwah, NJ: Erlbaum.

Blase, J., & Blase, J. (2000). Effective instructional leadership. *Journal of Educational Administration, 38*(2), 130–141.

Bolman, L., & Deal, T. (2002). Leading with soul and spirit. *The School Administrator, 59*(2), 21–26.

Box, K. (1999). *Technology integration phases.* Sponsored by the Texas Center for Educational Technology, Denton, TX. Retrieved July 20, 2005 from www.tcet.unt.edu/research/online/phases.htm

Brown, A. (1997). Transforming schools into communities of thinking and learning about serious matters. *American Psychologist, 52*(4), 399–413.

Chan, T., & Pool, H. (2002, April). *Principals' priorities versus their realities: Reducing the gap.* Paper presented at the Annual Meeting of the American Educational Research Association, New Orleans, LA. (ERIC Document Reproduction Service No. ED 465230)

Christensen, R. (1998). *Effect of technology integration education on the attitudes of teachers and their students.* Doctoral dissertation. University of North Texas, Denton.

Darling-Hammond, L. (1998). Teachers and teaching: Testing policy hypotheses from a national commission report. *Educational Researcher, 27*(1), 5–15.

Darling-Hammond, L. (2003). Enhancing teaching. In W. Owens & L. S. Kaplan (Eds.), *Best practices, best thinking and emerging issues in leadership* (pp. 75–87). Thousand Oaks, CA: Corwin.

Dias, P. (1999). *Web-based learning communities.* Paper presented at the Annual Meeting of the Conferencia Internacional Challenges, Braga, Portugal.

Drago-Severson, E. (2005, April). *New opportunities for principal leadership: Shaping school cultures for sustaining teacher development.* Paper presented at the annual meeting of the American Educational Research Association, Montreal, Canada.

Elmore, R. (2002). The limits of "change." *Harvard Education Newsletter,* 2002. Retrieved from: www.edletter.org/past/issues/2002-jf/limitsofchage.shtml

Farrell, G. (2001). Learning to grow trees: Tenacity, leadership and school reform. In J. Murphy & A. Datnow (Eds.), *Leadership lessons from comprehensive school reform.* Thousand Oaks: Corwin. Retrieved February 27, 2006, from www.vtaide.com/png/ERIC/Techno-Development.htm

Fleming, G. (1999). Principals and teachers: Continuous learners. *Issues ... about change, 7*(2), 1–9.

Flowers, N., Mertens, S., & Mulhall, P. (2003). Lessons learned from more than a decade of middle grades research. *Middle School Journal, 35*(2), 55–59.

Fullan, M. (2002). The change leader. *Educational Leadership, 59*(8), 16–21.

Fullan, M. (2004). *Leadership and sustainability: System thinkers in action.* Thousand Oaks, CA: Corwin.

Fuller, B., & Izu, J. (1986). Explaining school cohesion: What shapes the organizational beliefs of teachers? *American Journal of Education, 94,* 501–535.

Furman, R., & Zibrida, R. (1990). *The hurried principal.* McMurray, PA: Furman Educational Resources.

Gall, M. D., Borg, W. R., & Gall, J. P. (1996). *Educational research: An introduction.* White Plains, NY: Longman.

Glaser, B. G., & Strauss, A. L. (1967). *Discovery of grounded theory: Strategies for qualitative research.* Chicago, IL: Aldine.

Glazer, E., & Hannafin, M. (2006). The collaborative apprenticeship model: Situated professional development within school settings. *Teaching and Teacher Education, 22*(2), 179–193.

Hawkes, M. (1999). Exploring network-based communication in teacher professional development. *Educational Technology, 39*(4), 45–52.

Hawkes, M. (2001). Variables of interest in exploring the reflective outcomes of network-based communication. *Journal of Research on Computing in Education, 33*(3), 299–315.

Hawkes, M., & Romiszowski, A. (2001). Examining the reflective outcomes of asynchronous computer-mediated communication on inservice teacher development. *Journal of Technology and Teacher Education, 9*(2), 283–306.

Hofer, M., Chamberlin, B., & Scot, T. (2004). Fulfilling the need for a technology integration specialist. *T.H.E. Journal, 32*(3), 34–38.

Hughes, J., Kerr, S., & Ooms, A. (2005). Content-focused technology inquiry groups: Cases of teacher learning and technology integration. *Journal of Educational Computing Research, 32*(4) 367–379.

International Society for Technology in Education (ISTE). (2000). *National Educational Technology Standards for Teachers.* Eugene, OR: Author.

International Society for Technology in Education (ISTE). (2002). *National Educational Technology Standards for Administrators.* Eugene, OR: Author.

International Society for Technology in Education (ISTE). (2007). *National Educational Technology Standards for Students.* Eugene, OR: Author.

Killion, J. (1999). *What works in the middle: Results-based staff development.* Oxford, OH: National Staff Development Council.

Knezek, G., & Christensen, R. (1997). *The teachers' attitude toward computers questionnaire version 5.1.* Denton: University of North Texas and the Texas Center for Educational Technology.

Lieberman, A., & Grolnick, M. (1996). Networks and reform in American education. *Teachers College Record, 98*(1), 7–45.

Liew, S., & Huang, H.-M. (2000). Enhancing interactivity in web-based instruction: A review of the literature. *Educational Technology, 40*(3), 41–45.

Little, J. W. (1993). Teachers' professional development in a climate of educational reform. *Educational Evaluation and Policy Analysis, 15*(2), 129–151.

Matthews, L. J. & Crow, G. M. (2003). *Being and becoming a principal: Role conceptions for contemporary principals and assistant principals.* Needham Heights, MA: Pearson Education.

McLaughlin, M. W. (1991). Enabling professional development: What have we learned? In A. Lieberman & L. Miller (Eds.), *Staff development for education in the 90s: New demands, new realities, new perspectives* (pp. 61–82). New York, NY: Teachers College Press.

Mishra, P., & Koehler, M. J. (2006). Technological pedagogical content knowledge: A framework for teacher knowledge. *Teachers College Record, 108*(6), 1017–1054.

Morrissey, M. (2000). *Professional learning communities: An ongoing exploration.* Austin, TX: Southwest Educational Development Laboratory. Retrieved November 2, 2005, from www.sedl.org/pubs/change45/plc-ongoing.pdf

National Commission on Teaching and America's Future (NCTAF). (2003). *No dream denied: A pledge to America's children.* Washington, DC: Author.

National Implementation Research Network (2007). *Implementation research: A synthesis of the literature.* Retrieved July 3, 2007 from http://nirm.fmhi.usf.edu/resources/publications/ Monograph/

Nespor, J. (1987). The role of beliefs in the practice of teaching. *Journal of Curriculum Studies 19*(4), 317–328.

Norris, C. & Box, K. (2005). *Teachers and technology: A snap-shot survey.* Denton: Texas Center for Educational Technology. Retrieved July 19, 2005, from www.tcet.unt.edu/research/online/snapshot.htm

Parr, J. (1999). Extending educational computing: A case of extensive teacher development and support. *Journal of Research on Computing in Education, 31*(3), 280–292.

Routman, R. (2002). Teacher talk. *Educational Leadership, 59*(6), 32–35.

Schlager, M., Fusco, J., & Schank, P. (1999). Cornerstones for an online community of education professionals. *IEEE Technology & Society Magazine, 17*(4), 15–23.

Schon, D. A. (1987). *Educating the reflective practitioner.* San Francisco, CA: Jossey-Bass.

Schon, D. A. (1991). *The reflective turn: Case studies in and on educational practice.* New York, NY: Teachers College Press.

Schwarzer, R., & Jerusalem, M. (1995). Generalized self-efficacy scale. In J. Weinman, S. Wright, & M. Johnston (Eds.), *Measures in health psychology: A user's portfolio. Causal and control beliefs* (pp. 35–37). Windsor, UK: NFER-NELSON.

Spitzer, W., Wedding, K., & DiMauro, V. (1994). LabNet: An intentional electronic community for professional development. *Computers in Education, 24*(3), 247–255.

SRI International (1995–2007). *Tapped in: A community of educational professionals.* Available: http://tappedin.org

Tinker, B. (2003). *NetCourses for staff development.* Santa Monica, CA: Milken Family Foundation. Retrieved June 19, 2003, from www.mff.org/edtech/article.taf?_function=detail&Content_uid1=107

Tschannen-Moran, M., Woolfolk Hoy, A., & Hoy, W. K. (1998). Teacher efficacy: Its meaning and measure. *Review of Educational Research, 68,* 202–248.

Wenger, E. C., & Snyder, W. M. (2000). Communities of practice: The organizational frontier. *Harvard Business Review, 78*(1), 139–145.

Yin, R. (2003). *Case study research: Design and methods* (3rd ed.). Thousand Oaks, CA: Sage.

Index

Page numbers followed by f (for example, 71f) indicate figures.
Page numbers followed by t (for example, 199t) indicate tables.

U

V

W